Onslaught against Innocence

Onslaught against Innocence

Cain, Abel, and the Yahwist

ANDRÉ LACOCQUE

CASCADE *Books* · Eugene, Oregon

ONSLAUGHT AGAINST INNOCENCE
Cain, Abel, and the Yahwist

Cascade Books
A Division of Wipf and Stock Publishers
199 W. 8 th Ave., Suite 3
Eugene, OR 97401

www.wipfandstock.com

ISBN 13: 978-1-55635-789-3

Cataloging-in-Publication data:

LaCocque, André.

    Onslaught against innocence : Cain, Abel, and the Yahwist / André LaCocque.

    x + 178 p.; 23 cm. Includes bibliographical references and index.

    ISBN 13: 978-1-55635-789-3

    1. Cain (Biblical figure). 2. Abel (Biblical figure). 3. Genesis IV—Criticism,
interpretation, etc. 4. Fratricide—Biblical teaching. I. Title.

BS580.C3 L33 2008

Manufactured in the U.S.A.

To Michel and Pierre-Emmanuel,

exemplary sons and brothers

". . . all the righteous blood shed on earth, starting with the innocent Abel."

—1 John 3:12

"I know well what awful harm I am about to inflict, but my passionate rage overbears my thinking, rage that brings to humans their greatest harm."

—Euripides *Medea* 446–50

"If we imagine self-transcendence not as unification with the other through love but as the destruction of the other, then we approach the domain of evil."

—Kahn, *Out of Eden*, 50

Contents

Abbreviations

Ancient and Medieval

Ant.	Josephus, *Antiquities of the Jews*
b.	Babylonian Talmud (*Babli*)
Ber.	*Berakot*
Cherub.	Philo, *De cherubim* (On the Cherubim)
Deut. Rab.	*Deuteronomy Rabbah*
Gen. Rab.	*Genesis Rabbah*
J	the Yahwist
Lev. Rab.	*Leviticus Rabbah*
LXX	Septuagint
m.	Mishnah
Mek.	*Mekilta*
MT	Masoretic Text
Num. Rab.	*Numbers Rabbah*
P	the Priestly writers
Pesiq. Rab.	*Pesiqta Rabbati*
Post.	Philo, *De posteritate Caini* (On the Posterity of Cain)
PRE	*Pirqe de Rabbi Eliezer*
Q.G.	Philo, *Quaestiones et solutiones in Genesin* (Questions and Answers on Genesis)
R.	Rabbi
Sacr.	Philo, *De sacrificiis Abelis et Caini* (On the Sacrifices of Abel and Cain)
Sanh.	*Sanhedrin*
Tanḥ.	*Tanhuma*
Tg. Ps.-J.	*Targum Pseudo-Jonathan*

Modern

ABD	*The Anchor Bible Dictionary.* 6 vols. Edited by David Noel Freedman. New York: Doubleday, 1992

ANET	*Ancient Near Eastern Texts Relating to the Old Testament.* 3rd ed. Edited by James B. Pritchard. Princeton: Princeton University Press, 1969
GKC	Wilhelm Gesenius, *Hebrew Grammar.* Enlarged and edited by E. Kautzsch. Translated and revised by A. E. Cowley. 2nd ed. Oxford: Clarendon, 1910
JBL	*Journal of Biblical Literature*
SE	Sigmund Freud, Standard Edition
VT	*Vetus Testamentum*
VTSup	Supplements to Vetus Testamentum
ZAW	*Zeitschrift für die alttestamentliche Wissenschaft*

CHAPTER ONE

Introduction

The Object of This Book

THIS BOOK IS A companion volume to *The Trial of Innocence: Adam, Eve, and the Yahwist*.[1] It prolongs my essay on the dialectic anthropology according to J in Gen 2:4—4:1. Each book stands on its own, however, and can be read independently.

Here again, because the story of Cain and Abel is so well and so universally known, as is the tale of Adam and Eve, there can hardly be a first "reading" of it. Even our first encounter with the text is already a "rereading." There is nothing to lament about for, as Gary Saul Morson states, the rereading "makes the reader a character in the work."[2] And, following the lead of Paul Ricoeur, it takes the reader to a "second naiveté." Chances are, as a matter of fact, that a rereading will not remain at the level of superficiality.

In the preceding myth on Adam and Eve, J (the so-called Yahwist literary source responsible for much of the narrative part in the chapters 2–11 of Genesis, amidst a larger work) masterfully showed that the human is always torn between the innocence of Eden and its denial, between what J now calls "doing well" and "not doing well"; in short, he is involved in a *dialectical trial of her innocence*. Each word—dialectical, trial, and innocence—is important here, since the cliché of "the Fall" is inadequate to characterize the events of Genesis 3. If one insists, nonetheless, on this worn out notion, it would be in the sense of an always recurring but avoidable fall of the human into existential guilt, a constant defeat of a human's capability to innocence. Nothing is determined, however, nothing

---

1. Cascade Books, 2006.
2. Morson, "Contingency and the Literature of Process," 256.

is transmitted seminally from generation to generation, for the world's redemption is always recurring and constant, thanks to those whom a Jewish tradition calls the *Lamed Vav*, the "thirty-six" righteous ones. Or is it perhaps the one unique just one—whose choice of innocence in our jungle-like society rescues it from being pure hell and constitutes as much a miracle as life itself?

Engaging another aspect of human dialectical existence, J in the story of Cain and Abel imagines a personification of innocence after Eden. Abel is such an incarnation, but, significantly, it is a transient and ghostly incarnation. Innocence is doomed to be short-lived. Its existence is to be quickly felt as unbearable and to be eliminated by the "powers that be," which Cain represents. Is it because innocence is a foreign body in humanity's organism? Not so, for the innocent Abel is the brother, perhaps the twin brother, of Cain. In the Adam and Eve myth, J had presented the original relation between male and female using the metaphor of a bifacial androgyny.[3] Now, another bifacial reality is conjured up: *I* and the *Other*, *I* and *Thou*, two siblings, same and different. Born of the same father and of the same mother, worshippers of the same God, with different and complementary occupations, the tiller and the shepherd, the sedentary and the nomad, the ground and the horizon, the plough and the lyre, Cain and Abel are—or should be—"one flesh." But, if humanity cannot survive without the plough,[4] tragically it believes that it can live without the lyre. In the eyes of the one whose name is Cain, that is, etymologically "Possession," innocence is not only as inconsistent as a dawn vapor on the surface of a field (Abel means "Breath"), but soon becomes offensive to his lifestyle. Then, from a trial of innocence (Genesis 3), history tumbles into an onslaught against innocence.

J's logic in having the Cain and Abel myth follow on the heels of the Adam and Eve myth is convincing. It is particularly evidenced in the first sentence of the second story: the birth of children continues the process of creation described in the first story. Literary criticism shows that, in all probability, the earlier tradition reported a mere genealogy right after the extradition of the primal couple from Eden. The genealogy is still apparent in 4:1–2 and 17–26.

---

3. See LaCocque, *The Trial of Innocence*, 114–27.

4. The pickax is one of the greatest gifts of the gods to humanity according to Mesopotamian mythology.

In this taxonomy of generations there are, as we shall explicate later, ominous details. But, in and of itself, a genealogy right there after the evocation of the horror of death upon the humans, is nothing short of a cry of victory. The created human innocence is on trial; it has not been relinquished wholesale to death. Life is triumphant. Eve's exclamation at the first ever birth of a child is immensely elating and enormously important. The translation of Gen 4:1 should not be reductive. Eve says that she has created a man with Yhwh. (She uses the verb *qanah* here instead of *bara'*, which is appropriate on at least two grounds: only God in the Bible is the subject of the verb *bara'*; and *qanah* is in alliteration with the name Cain.) Such a momentous text begs for more elaboration.[5]

J has inserted into the initial genealogy the story of two brothers' relationship. Its purpose is to pursue and prolong the anthropology started in Genesis 2–3. In those episodes, J showed that the transgression of the divine will has made dysfunctional the relationship with spouse and world. In the new development on Cain and Abel, the reader is introduced into the human family life. "Family life," says Eigen, "is a kind of primal swamp, a seedbed of possibilities. . . . Life teems in tangled ways."[6] But, as Immanuel Kant says, the evil in man starts "as soon as he is among men"[7]—even when the proximate is a brother, as J says.

Thus the dysfunction initiated by Adam and Eve's rebellion permeates ring after ring of human existence, until it reaches the whole of humanity and the world. The historical progression after Genesis 2–3 risks, in fact, being a regression to the chaos that preceded creation. Everything would be lost for good—as it almost will with the Flood—were it not for the advent of Abraham in Genesis 12. Then history transforms itself—in part—into a *Heilsgechichte* (a "history of salvation").

The following study is a literary-critical analysis of the myth of Cain and Abel. I read the narrative as an integrated didactic tale. Accordingly, I shall here consider the story in Genesis 4 as a literary unit. Besides,

---

5. This co-creation with God, Catherine Keller calls *creatio cooperationis* or *creatio ex profundis*; see her *Face of the Deep*, 117. I have myself stressed this point in my *The Trial of Innocence*.

6. Eigen, *Rage*, 54.

7. Kant, *Religion within the Limits of Reason Alone* (B 128–29, A 120–21, [85]); see below, 111 n. 100.

both the tight structure of the narrative and its uncanny density seem to confirm the textual integrity of the narrative, as Umberto Cassuto's study indicates.[8] Its verbal structure is well balanced:

> a/ Genealogy: "Adam knew his wife" (1–2)
>   b/ Cain and Abel: their entreaty of Yhwh (3–5)
>   c/ Dialogue: Yhwh and Cain (6–7)
>   d/ Dialogue (aborted): Cain and Abel (8)
>   c'/ Dialogue: Yhwh and Cain (9–15)
>   b'/ Cain: exits from the presence of Yhwh (16)
> a'/ Genealogy: "Adam knew his wife" (17–26)

As for the problem of the origins of the narrative, I suggest starting our inquiry with the end of the composition (just as it would be appropriate in treating the Gospels in the New Testament, for instance). Genesis 4:23–24 registers one of Cain's descendants' poetic sayings, the so-called Song of Lamech. It is probably one of the oldest songs recorded in the Hebrew Bible (along with the core of Exodus 15; Num 21:17–18, 27–30; and Judges 5).

Now the wording of the Lamech poem is most interesting. It poetically sets in parallel the terms "man" (*'iš*) and "child" (*yeled*), the latter coming surprisingly instead of the expected "human being" (*ben-'adam*).[9] But it is to be noted that *yeled* would refer in this context either to Cain or to Adam, which is certainly not what Lamech had in mind. Second, the text of Gen 4:1 strikingly uses the word "man" instead of the expected "child," as we shall further expound. Thus, in one case (4:1) "man" has displaced "child," and in the other place (4:23d) "child" has displaced "man."

Clearly, within the Cain and Abel story, Lamech's song at the end counterbalances Eve's exclamation at the beginning and creates a nice contrasting *inclusio* with it. Eve's creation is of a man, *'iš*; Lamech's destruction is of an *'iš*. With Cain's birth at the beginning of the tale, a great expectation has been expressed, the expectation of Eden's restoration. At the end, Eden has never been so remote. Violence has prevailed. Inexorably, the author conducts the story to its fatal dénouement. Cain's or Lamech's world is doomed. Human violence will be paid off with violence.

---

8. Cassuto, *Genesis*, 1:178–248. See also van Wolde, "The Story of Cain and Abel." About the structure of the literary unit, let us note that the words "Abel" and "brother" appear seven times each; the same is true as regards the word *'adamah* (soil, ground).

9. See Gevirtz, "Lamech's Song to His Wives."

So, if Lamech's song is very ancient, then J's later composition in Gen 4:1 reversed the message imbedded in the ancient song's terms—all the more in that Lamech mentions Cain and his potential sevenfold vengeance. Since Gen 4:1–2a may be considered as the beginning of the genealogy that continues in 4:17–22, now interrupted by the story of Cain murdering his brother, I believe that J has found an inspiration for his narrative in Lamech's old bardic saying and in a preexisting genealogy of Cain.

The Yahwist as Author

The author of the Cain and Abel myth is the greatest storyteller in the Hebrew Bible.[10] The characters he created in Genesis 2–3, Adam and Eve, or in Genesis 4, Cain and Abel, have become universally known for some two and a half millennia. They have inspired thousands of books, paintings, sculptures, and films. The stories are so vivid and profound that the serious reader feels she will never get to the bottom of them. All has not been said about Adam and Eve, Cain and Abel, and never will. It is like the hoary Oedipus myth that has become in our times the cornerstone of psychoanalysis. John Steinbeck wrote about Gen 4:1–16, "these sixteen verses are a history of mankind in any age or culture or race."[11]

The storyteller is unknown. Scholars call him "J," that is, the Yahwist (in German "Jahwist"). He is so identified because he prefers to use the Name *Yhwh*[12] for God rather than the more general appellation *Elohim*, commonly translated in English as "God." These are the "ABCs" of scholarship concerning J. But here the question arises: Why did he continue to use the "tetragrammaton" beyond his story of the creation and the "trial of innocence"? He is now reporting, so to speak, the first-ever murder in history, and he has shown in Gen 3:1b–7 that he did not feel under

10. By "myth" I mean, with Moye, "an independent, closed, symbolically rich narrative about some archetypal character whose story, which takes place in the primeval time of the beginning, represents some universal aspect of the origins or nature of humanity in its relation to the sacred or the divine" ("In the Beginning: Myth and History in Genesis and Exodus"). See also Ellis's definition emphasizing the presentation "in symbolic story-form [of] some transcendental reality or truth intuitively grasped." J did "depaganize" ancient myths and "retheologized" them as myths "for his own theological purposes" (Ellis, *The Yahwist*, 142).

11. Steinbeck, *East of Eden*, 304.

12. For the meaning of the Name, explicated in Exod 3:14, see LaCocque and Ricoeur, *Thinking Biblically*, 307–61.

any compulsion to use "Yhwh" in all circumstances.[13] In this scene of the dialogue between Eve and the serpent, J's designation of God is Elohim (more generally translated as "God," "the divine"). The avoidance of all promiscuity between Yhwh and a rebellious animality is evident. Now, the literary kinship between Genesis 4 and Genesis 3 could have implied a pure correspondence of Cain with the serpent. Both, for instance, raise impudent questions, like "Did God really say . . . ?" or "Am I my brother's keeper?" Both remain brazenly unmoved by the divine intervention. Both are also cursed and their malediction has something to do with the ground and its dust.

So, J could have set Cain's character in parallel with the serpent's, and, consequently, shifted here from his use of "Yhwh" to "Elohim." This did not happen. The pendant of Genesis 3's serpent is not Cain, but "the sin that is crouching at the door" of his heart. Cain will not be presented as a demon; throughout the story his humanity is honored. God speaks to him and with him.[14] God puts a protective shield upon him. And the man Cain is not reduced to a vagrant zombie. He eventually settles and builds the first city.

J's use of "Yhwh" to designate God is fully justified. The "covenantal God" is as concerned with Cain as he is with Abel (to whom, incidentally, he does not speak!). True, Cain is a "man of little faith" (Matt 14:31), but he remains human and, as such, he is not deterministically controlled. Anything remains possible.

J's God is from the beginning in a dialogical and intimate relationship with humanity (see here esp. 4:26). Yhwh is a narrative character, like Adam and Eve, like Cain and Abel. Yhwh soils his hands with mud to shape the first humanity; he strolls in the evening breeze in the Garden of Eden; he inquires about the disappearance of Adam, hidden behind a tree, "Where are you?", or about Abel asking Cain, "Where is your brother Abel?" These concretizations are called divine anthropomorphisms, and they are not without theological problems, or even at times raising mis-

---

13. Nietzsche, comparing (superficially, I must say) the Greek myth of Prometheus and the "Semitic" myth of Adam and Eve, said that the first crime was committed by a man [we may think also of Cain] and the first sin by a woman; *The Birth of Tragedy*, par. 9, in Kaufmann, *The Portable Nietzsche*.

14. True, it is a call to Cain's accountability and therefore a provocative address. But it is not, on God's part, an aloof demand, leaving God untouched. For what Cain must be for the one who is his other, God is for him. See Bakhtin, "Author and Hero in Aesthetic Activity," 56: "What I must be for the other, God is for me."

understandings, as we shall show in the body of the present work. A God so immanent may be so close to people as to become suspect of provoking human crimes himself or, at least, disobedience. In which case, Adam is seen as flouted by God, and Cain as a victim of divine capriciousness. Clearly not every traditionist in ancient Israel was ready to run that interpretive risk. Therefore, other biblical writers used names, nouns, and circumlocutions, more fitting God's transcendence—with the reverse risk of severing the ties between Creator and creatures.

J was a daring thinker and a great poet. Like Homer, for instance, J left no autobiographical clue describing him as singer of tales. No external evidence points to his personality, only literary characteristics, one of which is that he pushed the human traits of the divine to their limits. As we said, God walks; he looks around; he closes the door of Noah's ark; and he comes down from heaven to see what is going on in the plain of Shinar with the builders of Babel. And J himself was also walking with his audience. He did not consider it beneath his poetic ingenuity to "come down" to where his readers were, beings of flesh and blood, moved by impure desires, inclined to rebellion against God, to envy, jealousy, fratricidal impulses—in short, struggling with what Freud called the "id."[15]

J was a singer of tales who keenly observed human nature. The picture he drew of the humans is so true, so penetrating that his purposeful austere economy of words speaks volumes. A few strokes of his brush and here is the Garden of Eden. A few more strokes and the obscene murder of a brother is recounted. We are not told what Cain said to Abel in the field before killing him—although he spoke, that much we know. We do not know how he killed him, how he disposed of his brother's body, how he explained Abel's disappearance to his parents (in contrast to Joseph's brothers reporting his "death" to Jacob), how his parents reacted to the news, or how all of them—slayer and mourners—approached the new (to them) phenomenon of death. The only thing J cares to share with us is the core of the event: Cain killed Abel. The rest is up to the reader to imagine.

---

15. Scheler finely notes that envy is preempted by a mentally "illusory *appropriation of the good*," so that the other person "appears . . . as a 'force' which takes it away from us"; *Ressentiment*, 147 n. 6. Fromm classifies Cain's fury with what he calls "reactive violence," provoked by envy. But the murder of Abel, I think, reflects more Cain's *impotence*. His move is an onslaught against life itself. Fromm says that the impotent one "*takes revenge on life for negating itself to him*"; Fromm, *The Heart of Man*, 31 (his emphasis).

The reader must tell the story with the minstrel. Her interpretation is respected: not imposed by J, it becomes an integral part of the tale itself.

The author's sobriety is an open invitation to the reader to come at the story as a creative collaboration, but the interpreter sometimes goes astray. In fact, some scholars have abusively minimized what was already so condensed in the tale. Distorting the pithiness of J's exposition, they have blotted out Abel the innocent as superfluous.[16] Then the story is not about an onslaught against innocence, but an exclusive and difficult exchange between God and a murderous man named Cain.[17]

Date of Composition

After more than a century of scholarly consensus in attributing J's work to the time of the Davidic monarchy (ca. 950 BCE), the problem of dating this material has been recently raised anew. Such a stance is today rightly questioned, as I did myself in my study on the myth of Adam and Eve.[18] In agreement with other modern critics' conclusions, I also arrive at a late (exilic or postexilic) dating. As is well known, the striking characters of the poet's narrative do not reappear in the Hebrew Bible in spite of their intrinsic appeal, already a sign of the probable late composition of J. In the body of this essay, furthermore, I shall throw into relief the exile of Cain "east of Eden" (4:16), that is, toward Mesopotamia.[19]

The curious absence of the Conquest tradition in the Yahwist's saga provides a further clue. As a matter of fact, it seems evident that this epic—written allegedly under king David's battles on multiple fronts and in the wake of the king's military prowess—bypasses the alleged he-

16. See below, in chapter 4, the section on "The Psychology of Cain."

17. Such ignorance of the victim makes one think of Ellison's *The Invisible Man*.

18. See LaCocque, *The Trial of Innocence*. In the controversy between Rendtorff and Van Seters on the composition of Genesis (and particularly of Genesis 1–11), I side with Van Seters. See Rendtorff, *Das überlieferungsgeschichtliche Problem des Pentateuch*; and Van Seters, *Abraham in History and Tradition*; and his response to Rendtorff in "The Yahwist as Theologian? A Response." Now, in a recent article, Christoph Levin argues that J's narratives, including the primeval history (Genesis 2–11), were "only at a later stage . . . linked to form the continuous narrative we have today." It may be, he says, that P constitutes the basic document into which "non-Priestly narratives have been inserted at a later point." "The Yahwist: The Earliest Editor in the Pentateuch," 209–10.

19. Moye strongly emphasizes the "main" Pentateuchal theme of "exile and return" (sixth century BCE). About J's narratives, he writes, "In each of these narrative sequences [i.e., Gen 12:1–9, 10, 11–16; 12:17—13:4], there is a distinct pattern based on the motif of exile and return"; "In the Beginning," 595.

roic origins of the land occupation and its territorial claims. Now, the post-exilic Israelite literature shows little interest in the deuteronomistic Conquest traditions reported for example in the book of Joshua. This is arguably due to the irrelevance of triumphalism at a time when Israel (or what was left of it) had been so utterly crushed by the Babylonian empire. J's disregard for the Conquest of Canaan (*kibbuš kena'an*) corresponds, as well, with his universalistic ideology.[20]

True, some respected scholars are convinced that J wrote an account of the Conquest that was lost or deleted by the final redactors of the Pentateuch. But then the question is why any traditionist would deliberately destroy such a crucial elaboration on a "glorious" series of events. It does not make much sense. Preferable is the opinion of Hans Walter Wolff, who speaks of "a striking decline of interest in the conquest."[21] It is not that J ignored the theme of the Conquest (see Gen 27:39–40; Numbers 14; 21), but, most probably based on his convictions, he refrained to harp on the topic. The traditionists otherwise included so many duplicate narratives that this point militates against the exclusion of a whole chapter that the Yahwist would have written on the Conquest allegedly to avoid redundancy.

If David J. A. Clines is right that Genesis 1–11 "is heard in exile as a story of God and Israel" with "a word of hope to the exiles,"[22] it is clear that the exile in Babylon was sternly understood as being on the pattern of Cain's wandering but marked with a divine sign that guaranteed his survival and even his eventual settlement in a city built for this purpose.[23]

The vexing problem whether the characters are J's creation belongs to the inquiry about when J wrote his stories. It is hard to arrive at an unequivocal answer. He certainly used preexisting sources as we already intimated above, but his creativity is evident at every step. Gerhard von Rad also thinks that J found disparate narrative traditions already extant, which he sewed together. At a minimum, the Yahwist's literary contribution is their coordination. As they now stand, these traditions "serve only one purpose, which is to show how all the harm in the world comes from

20. See Gen 3:20; 8:21–22; 12:3. Let us note that J's universalism corresponds with the same broad vision of a Deutero-Isaiah, for instance. Both are roughly contemporary. See also Psalm 82 (esp. v. 8).

21. Wolff, "The Kerygma of the Yahwist," 133.

22. Clines, "Theme in Genesis 1–11," 308.

23. Regarding Gen 4:15, Speiser refers to Exod 13:16; 28:38; Deut 6:8; 11:18; and Ezek 9:4, 6; *Genesis*, 31.

sin."[24] In the story of Cain and Abel, using as it does an ancient genealogy (of Cain and of Seth), J displays one of his innate gifts: his ability to weave together traditional threads into one cloth, and with a purpose different from the original.

One of the author's aims is to display a worldview according to which Israel's God is at work in human history from the very beginning. Before there was a entity called Israel, there was an interconnection of God and humanity at large. The first chapters of Genesis are dedicated to that theological principle. True, J's use of the Name Yhwh instead of the more general and universal Elohim to designate God needed to be compensated on this score by the composer's universalism. It is also the motivation behind J's closing the Cain and Abel story with the grandiose declaration, "then people started to call on the name of Yhwh" [not just Elohim] (4:26).

This evidently implies a certain conception, not only of the world in general, but of Israel in particular. National isolationism is defeated by J's worldview. The Yahwist's understanding of "chosen people" is not static but dynamic. One is not chosen, one becomes chosen (by choosing God). Seth, Noah, Abraham, Isaac, Jacob, and Moses do not belong to a constituted chosen people, but they certainly constitute themselves as the chosen people.[25] So does Abel in the J story we are dealing with here. We can be assured that not everyone in historical Israel was pleased with this J's conception. This is especially true if he wrote during or after the Babylonian exile.[26] As we shall see in the course of this study, J's narrative is at times polemical.

Authorial Omniscience

The story of Cain and Abel is just that—a story. The bard felt free to imagine not only the action of the tale but also the dialogues (or their absence, see 4:8) of the characters, including God. Such freedom on the

---

24. Von Rad, *The Problem of the Hexateuch and Other Essays*, 65.

25. It is within this framework that it becomes understandable why the call to Abraham in Ur of Chaldea beacons to all nations of the earth that they may also constitute themselves as the chosen (by God) people (see Gen 12:2–3). More needs to be said on this important topic in J's view; see chapter 3 below, "The Theological Dimension."

26. The interrelation of narrative and genealogy in Genesis 4 points into the same direction; see Moye, "In the Beginning." On the genealogical element of the story, see below, chapter 5.

part of J explains his choice either to explain certain things or to leave them unexplained. For example, we know neither why God had no regard for Cain's offering nor how Cain learned about it. The only thing we are made privy to is what it implied for both Cain and Abel. As stated earlier, this narrative gap has led some scholars to conclude that the deity acts capriciously—even sadistically—toward Cain. For what reason, they do not say. Pure divine arbitrariness? Then, J's admirable sobriety is turned against him for not being more explicit.

Now, it is clear that J builds his narrative against a preexisting background of certain faith principles that he takes for granted. An example is provided with the motif of Cain and Abel worshipping God by means of a sacrifice. J felt no compulsion to justify the anachronism of the brothers offering a (thanksgiving?) sacrifice to the deity before the ordinance of the Law much later (at least according to the fictional chronology of J's story set in the antediluvian era). The same is true of ethical principles presented as fundamental: murder and adultery, for instance, are sins against the deity (see Gen 34:7; 39:9; 2 Sam 12, esp. 12:13[rape]).[27] In a similar way, I would say, J felt no necessity to explain that God is free to agree more with some offerings than with others.[28] J assumed that his audience would *not* conclude that the deity was acting capriciously but would rather question either the kind of sacrifice disregarded by God or the integrity of the of the one offering it. No ancient commentator, Jewish or Christian, missed that point. From the time of the incipient biblical traditions down to the present post-modern period, there has been a faithful confidence that God is *not* capricious—a term that fits pagan gods; not even Job believed that he is. God is unfathomable, yes; erratic, no. It belongs to a false conception of God to apply a logic according to which if God does not shield the innocent from being slaughtered, he has the power to do so but does not (perhaps by whim).[29]

Moreover, a common feature in ancient Near Eastern stories is the avoidance of psychological analyses. Facts only are reported in their "bareness." It is not that such an almost systematic understatement would be without evoking in the reader a psychological feeling, however. From the non-sentimental report-like dialogue with Cain initiated by God, we

27. One should note this "unexpressed assumption of the existence of a moral law operative from the beginning of time"; Sarna, *Understanding Genesis*, 31.

28. See J in Exod 33:19 (see Rom 9:6–33; 1 Cor 1:17–31); Gen 25:23; 1 Sam 16:7.

29. In the section on "Violence" below, I raise the problem of theodicy.

appropriately conclude that Cain looks like someone unaffected by his own crime: "Am I my brother's keeper?"[30] When he expresses some distress shortly after that, it is not because of his monstrous act, but because of his chastisement: "My punishment is too heavy." His turning to the very judge of his crime for clemency and protection sets a paradoxical diptych with the blood of his brother crying out for justice to God. There is indeed no one else to turn to.[31]

There are precious few windows into Cain's soul. It is not even certain how we should interpret them. It would be hard to construe his complaint as repentance (as the *Genesis Rabbah* does). He is condemned to wander endlessly; but what his thoughts and his feelings are is not stated. A thousand and one novels may be written on the model of *East of Eden* to fill the gap, but they will all be speculative. Erich Auerbach has eloquently emphasized this phenomenon.[32] It fits well the Hebrew short story, which is characterized by a minimum number of personages and the bare facts affecting them.

What is true of the human characters in the story is also true of God. There is here no authorial attempt at "psychologizing" God, and thus J's theology is tightly restrained. True, God acts and speaks, but what motivates him is told only in the most basic way. We can, nonetheless, readily ascertain with the "cloud of witnesses" that he is moved by love and justice; but is there also, perhaps, a dark side of God? J may have been too shy on this score. An exceptionally gifted minstrel such as him no doubt could have reconstructed God's feelings narratively. And at times he does, like when Yhwh vents some uneasiness and asks, "Where are you?" in Gen 3:9, or again when interrogating Cain, "What have you done?" in 4:10. The divine soliloquies (Gen 3:22; 8:21 for instance) belong to this category of texts. J's omniscience indeed goes occasionally so far as to

30. The psychoanalyst Willard Gaylin says, "[W]hat one does, one's behavior, is a better definition of the self than one's inner feelings"; *Hatred*, 134. Paul W. Kahn says, "Because power and powerlessness can coexist in the same person, one can be evil and yet see oneself as a victim. Suffering from the terror of powerlessness, the subject asserts a power to master death"; *Out of Eden*, 17.

31. Freud said, "[For the aggressive instinct] injury or annihilation of the object is a matter of indifference"; "Instincts and their Vicissitudes," 139. Let us note that there is a strange irony in the oxymoron of the dead foe finding his voice at this point. Elias Canetti in his study of crowds rightly states, "When [the enemies] have all been cut down, [they are] silenced forever. The stillest crowd is the crowd of the enemy dead"; *Crowds and Power*, 38.

32. Auerbach, *Mimesis*, 3–23. See chapter 4 below, "The Psychological Dimension."

know the intimate thinking of God: in Genesis 2 already, God reflects to himself, "It is not good that man be alone" (2:18).

Reading Genesis 4 without immoderate skepticism will require our provisional suspension of suspicion and our readiness to be disoriented by the text so as to be perhaps reoriented by it. A theological reflection on the "dark side" of God will have to be shelved for a while as it is preempted by some issues to be dealt with first.

A Matter of Temporality

J has created a new paradigmatic narrative, this time about Cain and Abel. Born to Adam and Eve, they guarantee the survival of the human race.[33] On the model of the Adam and Eve story, J again uses his amazing skill of understatement and economy of means. Brevity is characteristic of J's style. His narrative displays a "tremendous concentration."[34] He uses parataxis (the man knew Eve his wife / she was pregnant / she gave birth to Cain / . . . she was again pregnant with his brother Abel / Abel was a shepherd / Cain was a ground tiller / etc.). As Auerbach states (about the same paratactic construction in Gen 1:3):

> The sublime in this sentence from Genesis is not contained in a magnificent display of rolling periods nor in the splendor of abundant figures of speech but in the impressive brevity which is in such contrast to the immense content and which for that very reason has a note of obscurity which fills the listener with a shuddering awe. It is precisely the absence of causal connectives, the naked statement of what happens—the statement which replaces deduction and comprehension by an amazed beholding that does not even seek to comprehend—which gives the sentence its grandeur.[35]

The story works by allusion and implication. Paul Grawe states, "Implication is the basis of artistic meaning just as exact statement is the basis of discursive meaning."[36] But then J comes with a deceptively simple

33. Voegelin states that "the paradigmatic narrative is, in the historical form, the equivalent of the myth in the cosmological form"; *Israel and Revelation*, 124. H. Richard Niebuhr speaks of "an image by means of which all the occasions of personal and common life become intelligible," so that "furnishes the practical reason with a starting point for the interpretation of past, present, and future history"; *The Meaning of Revelation*, 97.

34. Auerbach, *Mimesis*, 41–42, 192.

35. Ibid., 110.

36. Grawe, *Comedy in Space, Time, and in Imagination*, 20.

narrative, thus perpetuating the camouflage over the extreme complexity of the preceding tale on Adam and Eve in the Garden of Eden. The profoundest doctrines are told in "childish" narratives, like a grandfather telling a story to his grandchild, or like a Hasidic tale. No anthropologist will ever go "deeper" than J in Genesis 2–3 and 4.

As Adam and Eve represent the whole of humanity throughout history, so too are Cain and Abel specimens of humankind. As Genesis 2 and 3 are not to be read only diachronically but also synchronically (Genesis 3 does *not* supersede Genesis 2), so Cain and Abel can be said to be the *figurae* of the human condition. Each human being is both Abel and Cain, that is, the incarnate poem of innocence and its slaughter.[37] True, the narrative of Cain and Abel is about the onslaught against innocence, yet it unwinds against the background of the trial of innocence, as described by J in Genesis 2–3.[38]

J's dialectical dual identity confronts everyone. The human being is this and also that. Not in equal terms, however, but always with the primacy of one of the two, while innocence is primary. Sin is "at the door" of original innocence, ready to change "Abel" into "Cain." In short, we are not born guilty but innocent. It takes Cain's move of "not doing well" to open the door to the *rabiṣum*, the demon in the background of the animalistic description of sin in 4:7.[39] Our guilt is thus a failure of responsibility.

Abel can become Cain, and Cain can become Abel. There is between the doppelgängers an identity that is original. At the beginning of the tale, when the two brothers are grownups—let alone when they were born—they are interchangeable. Abel is Cain's brother, and both mimetically work the same act of worship, as in a mirror. Although Cain is the elder and Abel the younger—a motif imbued with importance in the tale, as we shall see—there is initially nothing to set them mutually apart, but perhaps their discrete occupations.

---

37. It is how the story of Cain and Abel is paradigmatic. The massacres of Columbine and Virginia Tech, for instance, are in narrative continuity with the fratricide recounted in Genesis 4. This *continuum* is in reference to a common life experience. It is this paradigmatic dimension that critical reflection must put in relief and thus "liberate the narrative from any character of occupation for child's nurses," as Robert Musil says; *Tagebücher*, 778).

38. In the twelfth century "Mystère d'Adam," for instance, the story of Adam and Eve is carried over to Abel's murder. The division of the biblical text in chapters and verses is, of course, a late development.

39. See below "A Crux Interpretum."

Yet, when it comes to the balance between the two, once their personal existential choice is posited, their equality remains only in the sociological realm. We must note, with Auerbach (speaking of Simon Peter in the scene of denial) the (relatively) "low social station" of the *dramatis personae* introduced by the Yahwist. Cain and Abel are "average." One is a tiller of the ground, the other is a shepherd. No chivalry or heroic deeds are expected from them. Calling them "heroes" would not make much sense; but each of them, like Peter in the Gospel of Mark, is "the image of man in the highest and deepest and most tragic sense." Auerbach insists on such stories' incompatibility with "the sublime style of classical antique literature." He writes,

> For the great and sublime events in the Homeric poems take place far more exclusively and unmistakably among the members of a ruling class; and these are far more untouched in their heroic elevation than are the Old Testament figures . . . [F]rom the very first, in the Old Testament stories, the sublime, tragic, and problematic take shape precisely in the domestic and commonplace: scenes such as those between Cain and Abel, between Noah and his sons . . . are inconceivable in Homeric style.[40]

The myth of Cain and Abel is playing on two levels of understanding: a political-social-cultural level of interpretation,[41] and a psychological-anthropological one. In addition, from the point of view of its temporality, the story requires that we read it along the changing nature of the diachronic line while respecting its concomitant synchronism.

Diachronically, we are presented with a neat succession of events along an evolutionary development that appears logical: the two brothers offer a sacrifice to God; one is welcome, the other is not; Cain becomes angry and kills his brother Abel. At this point, the limelight focuses entirely upon Cain and there is a divine statement that eventually leaves Cain speechless, a feature probably to be interpreted as indicating Cain's pouting and continued rage.[42]

---

40. Auerbach, *Mimesis*, 22.

41. As a matter of fact, myths often derive from their socio-cultural environment albeit the events represented proceed from diverse historical complexes that are yoked together into a fictional unity. See pages 26ff. below.

42. On anger as a prelude to murder, see also Gen 34:7; Wis 10:3. Philo (*Q.G.* 1:77) says that, among the diverse chastisements meted out on Cain, one was "upon the tongue and the organs of speech, for being silent about things that should be said and for saying things that should be kept silent"; quoted by Kugel, *The Bible As It Was*, 95).

Synchronically, however, there is no "before" and no "after" in a folk-tale.[43] Cain's offering comes from someone who "does not do well" (v. 7). His fratricide is demonstration, not of a "temporary insanity"—in which, for instance, Hamlet found an easy excuse for killing Polonius—but of his murderous drive. Cain *can* "master it," but he does not.[44]

Commentators have sometimes pointed to the fact that, when Cain killed his brother, there was not yet any law prohibiting murder. The crime of murder is not explicitly forbidden until Gen 9:6 (**P**, the Priestly literary source). Then it is the first time that legislation is explicit about the shedding of human blood. True, but as I have already pointed out, before regarding the brothers' offerings without their move being regulated by law, the reader must distinguish between the ostensible temporality of the tale and its actual setting in life (that is, in the sixth century BCE). Moreover, we shall note the difference of conception between **J**'s reference to God as the only judge and punisher in Genesis 4, and **P** attributing capital punishment to human beings: "by the human shall his [the murderer's] blood be shed" (Gen 9:6). **P**, however, is crystal-clear on the rationale for prohibiting murder: human beings are in the image of God, a feature that constitutes the very foundation of their humanity.

Incidentally, Cain is not slaughtered (by God or "by the human"), but he is punished (by exile). Otherwise, there would be a tacit condoning of the crime. The culprit's punishment (according to either **J** or **P**) is

43. Westermann writes, "One should not apply criteria belonging to historical thought patterns to the presentation of the primeval events"; *Genesis 1–11,* 311. Diachronically, for example, Cain's only contemporaries are his parents and his brother. But he fears "anyone" after his crime, and he is able to find a wife, to build a city, etc. When banished, he goes to dwell in the city of Nod (= Wandering). Fretheim rightly sees in this the "collaps[ing of] the distance between the 'then' of the story and the 'now' of the reader (for instance, 2:24)"; *God and World in the Old Testament,* 77).

44. First John 3:12 says, "his [Cain's] own deeds were evil and his brother's righteous" (see Heb 11:4 and 12:24). In the present work, I take exception to Westermann's rejection of the interpretation of both late Judaism and the New Testament according to which Cain's offering came from an evil man. This ancient interpretation is indeed textually debatable, but its intuition is correct. If we approach the text from the point of view of modern literary criticism and read it synchronically as well as diachronically, we gain a new appreciation for the traditional understanding. This ancient confirmation is one more argument in favor of my interpretation here. Cf. *Hamlet,* act 3, sc. 3, ll. 37–38, where King Claudius calls his own "offense": "the primal eldest curse . . . A brother's murder!" In act 5, sc. 1, Cain's murder is called "the first foul murder." True, Cain is no Hamlet! But King Claudius's character may be modeled on Cain. (Will there be advocates for Claudius among the post-modern theorists?)

strikingly not revenge. It is for fairness sake; it responds to Abel's blood clamoring for justice.

Abel's blood has a voice transcending time, not a taboo power of its own as it would in many religious worldviews. God is the one who now and evermore heeds the voice. There is no trace here of ancestors' alleged power over the living. In fact, the spilled blood of Abel crying for justice, a need for vindication not extinguished by his demise, does echo another shout, although an oxymoronic silent one. For Cain's is "an act of murder screaming for help, a murder screaming for recognition" to borrow the words of Michael Eigen.[45]

God's address to murderous Cain shows that both screams are heeded here and now. As re-readers of the tale, we know that the latter ends on a different, hopeful note: "people began to call on the Name of Yhwh." But the divine discourse to the "fallen" human precedes this appeal to God. In the relationship, God always comes first. He wraps the human, front and back, like the moving pillar of cloud in the desert of Israel's wandering (Exod 14:19).

45. Eigen, *Rage*, 109.

CHAPTER TWO

The Anthropological Dimension

Cain Is an Agriculturist and Abel Is a Shepherd

J STATES THAT CAIN offered the fruit of his fare to God. Abel did the same with the product of his shepherding. From the very beginning of his narrative composition, J has displayed a striking preoccupation with the human *work*. Does it mean originally the opposite of rest and enjoyment? J's first answer comes with the myth of Adam and Eve, and it is a resounding No. In the Garden of Eden, the human enjoyable activity was work (see Gen 2:15). But, while the origin of work is devoid of pain and anxiety, it is transformed after the human transgression (see Gen 3:16–19). Then human work becomes problematic and complicated. In the originally unified "tilling and keeping," there occurs a splitting of labor: Cain is a tiller and Abel is a flock tender, and work is further fragmented with the descendants of Cain (Gen 4:17–23). Not surprisingly, each aspect of human work—here epitomized by Cain and Abel's occupations—entails in an idiosyncratic way a particularly religious hue, so to speak. To the diversification of labor corresponds a diversification of the religious and such a bond between the economic and the religious is far-reaching. Regarding Cain the agriculturist and Abel the shepherd, it is precisely the very difference in their discrete offerings that subjectively raises suspicion in one of them.

Religion is founded on awe and angst in various proportions according to the subjects and their circumstances. But, the diversified religious situations make Cain uncomfortable. His angst even leads him to murder. The clash between the brothers is the first war of religion. We will have to assess the contrast between Cain and Abel not only as anthropologically rooted but also as religiously significant.[1]

---

1. See chapter 3 below.

The Brothers' Sacrifices from a Phenomenological Viewpoint

What kind of sacrifices did the two brothers offer? Peace offerings? Sin offerings? Communion meals? The narrator does not specify. It is true that at some point in time, the word *minḥah* is used exclusively for cereal offerings (see Lev 2:1–3, 14–16 [P]), but elsewhere, as in our text here, *minḥah* includes animals (see also 1 Sam 2:17; 26:19). More generally speaking, anthropologists tell us that sacrifice, like war, is a way for humanity to force the gods to reveal whom they favor (the sacrificers'/warriors' survival proclaims that they are preferred by the gods). In our tale, God's response was apparently clear: Abel was chosen—and hence Cain was not. When we set this competition within its proper framework of immortality-seeking, it appears that Cain is taking exception to God's decision by dramatically showing that the preferred Abel can die.[2] A corpse loses its entire claim to favors!

Inasmuch as sacrifice reveals the soul of the sacrificer, there is within God's disregard for Cain's offering and his reception of Abel's an uncanny "reading" of the hearts of the one and the other.[3] It must be emphasized that the favor/disfavor of God is not *based* here upon the kind of material offered—for instance favoring the pastoralist at the expense of the agriculturist—but upon God's essential freedom (see Exod 33:19) and upon the personalities of the story's characters. Verse 7 clearly indicates that there is no question of the nature of things offered.[4] All this is surely explicated by the text mentioning that the favor of God went to "*Abel* and his tribute" (in this order).

Another idea is advanced by some scholars to the effect that Cain's sacrifice was shunned because it came from a cursed soil (*'adamah*).[5] This

2. On the notion of immortality-seeking, see below chapter 5, the section "J and the Origin of Culture and Civilization."

3. The Midrash says, "The sacrifices are worth what the sacrificers are."

4. Davidson tersely says, "This implies that what was wrong with Cain was not the type of sacrifice he brought, but the spirit in which he brought it"; *Genesis 1–11*, 52. See the somewhat different approach of Westermann (*Genesis 1–11*, 297): "this has nothing to do with the matter of the sacrifice, but with the meaning and function of the sacrifice in the immediate context of their work." Cain "was guilty even *before* he killed; his murderous deed only brought to a climax that which was already there"; Wiesel, "Cain and Abel," in *Messengers of God*, 58. It is, however, to be noted with Sarna that the text of 4:3–4 soberly makes a difference between Cain's offering "from the fruit of the ground" and Abel's "the choicest of the firstlings of his flock"; *Understanding Genesis*, 29. See my development on this point below.

5. See Herion, "Why God Rejected Cain's Offering"; and Spina, "The 'Ground' for

must be rejected on three grounds. Cain's offering is not refused but only less favored.[6] The vegetable sacrifices in the Bible are never problematic. And the soil is cursed *for Cain* only *after* the fratricide. In fact, Cain himself becomes cursed *from* the ground; and the soil that had already lost much of its fertility (3:17), now refuses to the slayer in a second degree what remains of its fecundity.

The non-rejection of Cain's sacrifice is self-evident from a close reading of v. 5. God had "no regard" means something different from hate and rejection.[7] The phrase is part of an expression contrasting preference and "second choice."

Regarding Cain's offering of the fruits of the soil, it is to be noted that the Hebrew repulsion for the ambient fertility rites did not extend to a sheer rejection of vegetable sacrifices. For that matter, a close material kinship always existed between Canaanite and Hebrew sacrifices.[8] Further, righteous Noah is called a man of the soil (*'iš ha-'adamah*; Gen 9:20).[9] The issue in Genesis 4 is one of ethics, not of sacrificial ingredient.[10]

On this basis, nonetheless, there exists a possibility that such a comparative ethical value be *reflected* in the quality of sacrifices offered. In a statement that falls in parallel with Nahum Sarna's opinion, Richard S.

Cain's Rejection (Gen 4).

6. See Kass, *The Beginning of Wisdom*, 137, who quotes Robert Sacks, "The Lion and the Ass: A Commentary on the Book of Genesis [Chapters 1–10])," 69: "Cain's sacrifice was not rejected but merely not accepted. . . . From Cain's reaction it appears as though he understood God's disregarding his sacrifice as a simple rejection, but this is not necessarily the case."

7. In Mal 1:3, for instance, God declares his hatred of Esau.

8. See de Vaux, *Ancient Israel*, 2:438.

9. Esau also, it is true (Gen 25:27). The great Jewish interpreters in the Middle Ages translated Gen 4:11, "you are cursed more than the ground [has been according to Gen 3:17]." Hence, Cain had to wander far away to find more fertile ground.

10. Interestingly enough, Malbim (R. Meir Leibush ben Yehiel Michael, nineteenth century) reads Gen 4:7 as meaning, "[Isn't it true that] whether you improve or not improve your offering *śe'eth*, see Ezek 17:8], sin lies at the door [anyway]?" (*Otsar Pirushim*). Indeed, the text of Gen 4:7 comes with an ambiguous but revealing term *śe'eth*, which means either the restoration of Cain's face (*panim*)—"lost" because he mistook the offerings to God as competitive—or the forgiveness of his sins. In the former sense, see Mal 1:8; Ps 82:2; see Gen 19:21; 32:20; in the latter, see Gen 18:24, 26; 50:17; Ps 32:5 (the *Tg. Ps.-Jon.* has: "the forgiveness of your evil deed"). Castellino is adamant that the term designated by *śe'eth* "can only be *panim* (or *paneka*)" ("Genesis IV 7," 443; he refers to Job 9:27; Jer 3:12). The same is true of Hamilton (*The Book of Genesis, Chapters 1–17*, 227), who reads *śe'eth* as having a "nominative force" and is "an abbreviation of *śe'eth panim*. Cain then would go with his head lifted up.

Hess, for example, says, "By giving the first-born and the best of the animal (i.e., the fat), Abel would be understood as having given everything to God."[11]

More fundamentally, however, George W. Coats says that the tale "depicts the fate of all subsequent creation, not in terms of tribes and unions, but in terms of individuals."[12] Rather than reading into the narrative a rivalry between farmers and shepherds, one should be sensitive to J's main point in this matter, namely, that original humanity belonged to one group and was living in an integrated world. So, tillers and shepherds are fundamentally brothers with one language and one mind (see Gen 11:1). When they offer a sacrifice, they come with their own discrete produce, and there is no objective ground for discriminating between the ingredients offered. As Cain and Abel represent two aspects of the human occupation, so their sacrifices represent two aspects of the human offering, *so long as the two brothers are true to their original innocence.*

Obviously, in Genesis 4, one of them is not. But if, therefore, the issue is basically ethical, it comes as no surprise that the individual options be reflected in the discrete offerings of the two brothers. It thus behooves us to concentrate on the issue of the sacrifices and examine afresh the purpose of J here.

To do this, a good start is to mention that Cain sacrificed *miqqeṣ yamim* (4:3). This phrase is often incorrectly translated as: "at the end of days" (the NRSV translates, "In the course of time"). Some conclude from this that Cain procrastinated. But then one must add that Abel waited even longer! In fact, the expression points to the end of an era, of a season. It means that a new period is about to commence. The new beginning is marked by a human initiative toward Yhwh. Cain offers a sacrifice; he takes a break from plowing the ground; and Abel, emulating his brother, also stops herding. Time, as it were, has come to a standstill, a sort of midnight point, tottering between "yesterday" and "tomorrow." *Horror vacui*: the vacuum aspires to being filled.

But Cain is "glued" to the ground, and what he offers is at no distance from it. He remains throughout the "servant/slave" (*'ebed*, see 4:2) of the soil and does not succeed in distancing himself from the dust from where he comes. There is in Cain's sacrifice no discrimination among the

---

11. Hess, "Abel," 10.
12. Coats, *Genesis*, 66.

vegetables offered. Anything will do because anything is unselectively a sample of the global 'Adamah.

Thus, the problem with Cain's sacrifice is that his "participation" leaves no room for "dissociation." As with a written text's interpretive process that must allow an intermediary space between the "author" and the "audience," sacrificing is a triadic proposition involving the performer, the recipient, and the vehicle. They correspond to author, reader, and discourse. Text and sacrifice demand a treble distancing: from the author/sacrificer (the text says more than the writer meant to say/the symbol must be allowed to transcend itself); from the situation of the discourse/offering (which may not be allowed to blot out past and future—hence God's question to Cain, "why are you so down now?"); and from the immediate intended recipient (there is the God imagined by Cain; and there is the God who subsequently displays a will and an expectation that take Cain by surprise).[13]

Again, it must be emphasized that the matter is not one of the ingredients of the sacrifices. It is one of human dispositions. With the same ingredients, the human roles could have been reversed: Cain being priestly and Abel being enslaved to his flock. Then Cain would have selected the best of what earth can offer, and Abel would have killed an animal gingerly picked up at random from the herd.

God, according to the Torah, wants the best. At the root of sacrifice is discrimination, which itself is judgment, evaluation, distance. Its opposite is non-differentiation, indifference, confusion, blindness. True, what is discriminated as worthy to be offered (back) to God is only a *pars pro toto* (the part signifying the whole), a metonymy of sorts—but it must be the best part, because only the best can be representative of the whole.

With the dialectic movement of *participation* and *distancing* we have singled out the main principle of sacrificing (and of reading). A second principle, essentially depending upon the first, is *substitution*. For the veritable sacrifice, that is, the offering to God of the best, should be the slaughter of "your son, your only son, Isaac, the one you love" (Gen 22:2). What Genesis 22 says is that we are all survivors by substitution like Isaac. In the story of Cain and Abel, the substitution for Abel's life is in the blood of a choicest firstling lamb; the substitution for Cain's is in vegetables.[14]

13. Distancing and "outsideness" are key concepts in Bakhtin's work. See *Art and Answerability*, 25, 78; idem, *The Dialogic Imagination*, 20, 23, 357.

14. Note that Milgrom sees in the cereal offering a poor person's sacrifice; *Leviticus* (2004), 175.

Speaking of the defense mechanism of the ego going through a process of decentralization by treating a part of the body as an "it" (when in pain, for instance),[15] David Bakan sees the sacrifice as duplicating this very process: "That which is 'me' is made into something which is 'not-me' and in which that 'not-me' is sacrificed in order that 'I' might continue to live."[16] Within this perspective, the lamb offered by Abel is clearly more appropriate than Cain's vegetables. If, indeed, what is sacrificed is a substitute for the sacrificer, the victim is symbolically the slaughterer's self.

Abel's sacrifice is discriminatory: he brings up the fat parts of the firstlings of his flock. A double discrimination then: literally the best of the best. Abel could never be said to be the slave (*'ebed*) of the herd like Cain is the slave of the soil. Here occurs the indispensable standing back from the object. Cain and his sacrifice were locked in a circle; Abel breaks the circle and he alone of the two becomes a priest, a mediator, in the intermediary space between God and creation. While the grubby Cain offers a sacrifice coming from a clot of clay, Abel himself is not physically the slaughtered lamb on the altar; he stands between God and the victim. The chasm that separates the brothers is gaping.

Gerhard von Rad has qualified as divisive the building of two altars by the brothers.[17] But, as we shall see below when noting the atavistic north–south rivalry, from a social-political point of view, it was inconceivable to have Cain-Israel and Abel-Judah use one and the same altar. In fact, J bore in mind the altars built by the secessionist northerners in Dan and Bethel and, consequently, he emphasized the discrete offerings of the two brothers. As one is agreeable and the other is not, it was improper to allow any promiscuity between the two. And regarding the very principle of offering sacrifices to God, both vegetable and animal,[18] it must be remembered that J is a late document; it takes sacrifices for granted. Some commentators do not take this chronological reality sufficiently into consideration.[19]

15. Decentralization makes one think of the psychoanalytic "externalization" or "hysterical technique," according to Ronald D. Faibairn.

16. Bakan, *Disease, Pain, and Sacrifice*, 79. This definition of sacrifice is applicable to the apotropaic types of sacrifices, which include most probably Cain's and Abel's sacrifices.

17. Von Rad, *Genesis*, ad loc.

18. And, therefore, not to be mixed.

19. A case in point is Kass's, *The Beginning of Wisdom*. The sacrifice is, in the ancient Near East, a normal and self-evident phenomenon; it need not be officially instituted. As

The sacrifice "lifts up" the creation to heaven. It is an act of reaching, of transcendence. The parallel with the notion of *kashrut* is evident, the issue being then whether the repast is liturgical/sacred or common/mundane, whether it is significant or insignificant. Due to the nature of Cain's sacrifice's lack of distinctiveness and distinction, it is reduced to *terefah*, as it were, that is, to insignificance.

In view of the preceding, we may understand the expression "at the end of a period of time" in a way that better fits the context of the myth, namely, "at the end of a season." As an agriculturist, Cain is bound to cyclical time. Mikhail Bakhtin says,

> The agricultural life of men and the life of nature (of the earth) are measured by one and the same scale, by the same events; they have the same intervals, inseparable from each other, present as one (indivisible) act of labor and consciousness. Human life and nature are perceived in the same categories.[20]

In fact, Cain is a man of nature, even "man-as-nature." In the words of Bakhtin, "Man-as-nature is experienced in an intuitively convincing manner only in the other, not in himself." Hence Cain's fixation on Abel as successful, for Abel stands at a distance from nature. Abel "confronts the outside world as object and . . . is incapable of being contained in it."[21] Anything that Cain offers is undifferentiated in itself: it represents nature and nature pervades everything. Abel's offering is selective: it does not represent nature but distances itself from nature. It affirms Abel's subjectivity and, by the same token, God's subjectivity.

A textual benchmark is found in the bothers' relationship. Cain wants Abel to relinquish his difference and become *same*. He wants a merger, not a communion. For the latter "consists in the intensification of one's own *outsideness* with respect to others, one's own *distinctness* from

---

I said earlier, the "lateness" of the J story is underscored by the fact that Cain and Abel are never again mentioned in the Hebrew Bible. The same situation obtains as regards Adam and Eve. Cain and Abel will again be referred to in the very late document 4 Macc 18:11 (ca. 19–54 CE).

20. Bakhtin, "Forms of Time and the Chronotope in the Novel," in *The Dialogic Imagination*, 208. Bakhtin expresses a negative judgment on this type of temporality as "time's forward impulse is limited by the cycle"; ibid., 209–10.

21. Bakhtin, *Art and Answerability*, 40.

others: it consists in fully exploiting the privilege of one's own unique place outside other human beings."[22]

For Cain, an "end of a period" means the end of a season. His sacrifice is seasonal, it is cyclical. Not so for Abel. His "chronotope" (Bakhtin) is different: his time is not circular, and his space is not unchanging. Strikingly, Cain's offering is soulless—in the biblical sense that understands the soul as in the blood (see Lev 17:11; Deut 12:23), while Abel offers a living animal. This difference is not what makes one sacrifice agreeable and the other not, but the discrete ingredients are reflections of the distinct worlds in which the two brothers are actually living (see Matt 12:35). In the sight of God, one is preferred to the other, for—again to cite Bakhtin—one of the two worlds is "finalized" while the other one is "unfinalized," that is, open on "the unpredictability of the dialogue . . . [of a] world in which anything might 'suddenly' happen."[23]

Remarkably, in response to Cain's despondency, God tells him to *do* well. Cain's remedy is not in finding better ingredients to offer—although this also may happen if he *does* well—but in a dynamic ethical choice (see Deut 30:15, 19). He may not allow "the end of a season" to become a closure; it must be a new leap into the unknown, "a leap of faith" (Kierkegaard).[24]

In summary, God tells Cain that he can do better. Not in using a better technique of sacrifice, but in not taking God for granted. Then it may have an impact upon the very performance of the sacrifice as it mirrors the soul of the sacrificer. It is thus a matter of respect, a matter of "reasonable worship," as Paul said (Rom 12:1). If Cain agrees to do well, there will be a "lifting up" (*śe'eth*; 4:7). The term is ambivalent; it means that Cain's face that "fell" (4:5) will be uplifted again, but also that his sacrifice will at last "elevate" the offering to the level of transcendence. Unfort the only "lifting" on Cain's mind is of the "weight" of his puni (*minneśo'*; 4:13).

At any rate, Cain and Abel's sacrifices strike a taut paradox rest of the story. Nothing, as a matter of fact, could have better ce their communion with God and with each other. This, in additio blood kinship of the brothers, contributes to the story's false start

22. Ibid., 88.
23. Bakhtin paraphrased by G. S. Morson and C. Emerson, *Mikhail Bakhtin*, 42.
24. Kierkegaard, *The Concept of Anxiety*; note that Kiergegard speaks rather of a "leap to faith."

J's drama is set in sharp relief through his insistence from the start upon the brotherly intimacy between Cain and Abel. Already almost twins by birth, they are also co-worshippers of the one God, "one flesh," the two faces of one unit.[25] J's refraining from demonizing Cain displays once more his anti-dualism. Were his Cain character a total monster, he would cease to be paradigmatic. We, the readers, would always identify with Abel, never with Cain. But we are Cain as much and even more so than we are Abel. Wisdom demands that I recognize my "degradation"—as Louis-Ferdinand Céline says[26]—(not monstrosity) in Cain. In us, Cain is never without Abel, nor is Abel ever without Cain.

Now, what Paul Kahn says of Eve, namely that she constitutes herself as a separated individual when entering into the dialogue with the serpent in Genesis 3,[27] applies as well to Cain when he cuts himself off from his "Siamese" brother with whom he formed a unit up to this point. Insistently, Abel is said to be his brother, and this redundant qualification of Abel stresses the essential inseparability of the brothers. To Cain, therefore, there was indeed only one way to deconstruct this fact of nature: to "denature" it, to kill Abel.

J was a master "singer of tales." He began the present story with a false start and, before the resumption of the genealogy v. 17 (started in vv. 1–2), the narrative in a way also ends on the false exit of Cain. Cain building a city (Enoch) indeed solves nothing as far as his fate as a fugitive is concerned and as regards the contamination of humankind to violence. Enoch-city is a forerunner of the city of Babel in Genesis 11.[28]

The affair of the brothers' sacrifices allows us to stress another level of understanding that I only suggested above, namely, that we find here a reflection of the socio-cultural reality prevailing at the time of the myth composition by J. Cain and Abel's occupations indeed represent "the two components of Middle Eastern society—farmers and pastoral nomads—[which] have always maintained an interdependent economic relation-

---

25. The brothers-become-enemies illustrate what Freud called the "narcissism of minor differences"; *Civilization and Its Discontents*, 72.

26. See Céline's trilogy, *D'un château l'autre* (1957), *Nord* (1960), and *Rigodon* (1969). Michael André Bernstein writes, "Indeed, to be abject is never to have experienced the monster's single-mindedness"; "The Poetics of *Ressentiment*," 222.

27. Kahn, *Out of Eden*, 40.

28. "That murder fails to right things is a great discovery communicated and explored in art"; Eigen, *Rage*, 3; reference is made primarily to the *Iliad* and, further, to *Hamlet*.

ship, even if there was sometimes tension between the two groups."[29] In our tale, they are brothers, but they also personify the atavistic north-south rivalry. Palestine archaeology has shown that there were always two types of population divided roughly by a line running horizontally between Jerusalem and Shechem (between the southern Judah and the northern Israel). In the north, people were heavily dependent on settled agriculture, while in the south, people tended to be migratory pastoral, two "always distinct and competing territories."[30] (Sheep eat earth-produced vegetation). Cain thus represents a northern community stubbornly considered as sinful by the southerners in Jerusalem. Cain leads Abel-the-shepherd into the "field," that is, into his northern turf. There, true to historical fact (as interpreted from a Judahite point of view), Cain kills Abel. Historically, as a matter of fact, indeed from the ninth century on, Israel's power had marginalized the rural-pastoral kingdom of Judah. In the J story, the two brothers are not really twins, or, if even they are, Cain is the elder one, and this again corresponds to historical reality: the northern highlands were "settled earlier than Judah."[31] They shared a consciousness of priority as is clear, for instance, during Sheba's rebellion (2 Sam 19:41—20:22).[32] Note also the fact that Saul the Benjamite was a farmer (1 Sam 11:5), while David the Bethlehemite was a shepherd (1 Sam 16:11).

On the contrary, when the northerners seceded from the Davidic dynasty, they followed the motto "everyone to their tents" (2 Sam 18:17; 19:9; 1 Kgs 12:16). The expression could have originally meant simply "to their homes," as Josh 22:4 attests, but the textual opposition to the "house of David" constitutes an emphasis that cannot be missed. In this case, however, the "tents" are less an indication of semi-nomadism than an anti-dynastic rally cry (perhaps even with the utopian hope that the seceded north would have no king).

It remains true that, in the Israelite/Judean mentality, shepherding kept an aura of autonomy and *différence*. The Patriarchs, Joseph, Moses, David (see esp. 2 Sam 7:8) are all at first shepherds. In Egypt, the Hebrews

29. Finkelstein and Silberman, *The Bible Unearthed*, 117.

30. See ibid., 155. Ideally "brothers," as our myth recalls, for both populations were worshipers of Yhwh.

31. Ibid., 159.

32. Note that in the Sumerian myth, there is a divine favor to the farmer over the pastoralist: Enkimdu the farmer-god is preferred by Inanna over Dumuzi the shepherd; see *ANET*, 41–42, a tablet from Nippur of the first half of the second millennium BCE.

tended their flocks in provocation of the autochthones, "for every shepherd is an abomination to the Egyptians" (Gen 46:34). The land is where
"milk and honey are flowing" (not where vegetation is growing!). Whether
or not Israel originally was a semi-nomadic population, they symbolically saw themselves that way. They "romanticized," for instance, their
wilderness periods (see Deut 26:5; Jer 2:2; Hos 2:14–15). Yhwh himself
is a shepherd, says Psalm 23; a tent dweller, says 2 Sam 7:6; and Jesus is
called "the good shepherd" in John 10:11–12. Cain's eventual wandering,
notwithstanding, is the hollow side of the ideal of "nomadism."

Typically, Cain's offering is deemed ritually questionable (not necessarily because of its composition but because of the impurity of the offer-
er), and the sacrificer's jealousy toward Abel is found typical (according
to the Judean J). But Cain-"Israel" is not fated to sin. He is not shackled
by determinism, which is a piece of news that is both good and bad, as it
emphasizes Cain-"Israel's" complete responsibility—a responsibility Cain
does not acknowledge. When, in punishment for his fratricide, Cain is
condemned to be "a fugitive and a wanderer on earth" (naʿ wa-nad),[33]
what is alluded to here is the disastrous dispersion of the Israelites at the
hand of the Assyrians in the eighth century, an event generally interpreted
by the Judeans as a divine punishment sanctioning the north's waywardness. Cain settles "in the land of Nod [Vagrancy], east of Eden [= east of
the land of Israel],[34] away from the Yhwh's presence [= in Jerusalem]"
(4:16).[35] While Zion is the city where the Name of the Yhwh resides, Cain
builds a city that he calls by his son's name, Enoch.

All the same, when our inquiry shifts to the psychological and anthropological levels of understanding, there is no need to speculate about Cain's
past before he offered a sacrifice (as many ancient literary sources do).

33. Vawter translates "a restless wanderer"; *On Genesis*, 92. Friedman renders it as
"roamer and rover"; *The Hidden Book in the Bible*, 73.

34. See Isa 51:3. Moye has seen the perfect parallel of Eden and the promised land;
see "In the Beginning," 598. See LaCocque, *The Trial of Innocence*, 64–66.

35. As McEntire has pointed out, the theme of one of two brothers compelled to leave
is frequent in the Bible. And "the brothers who depart always move to the east (*qedem*),
away from the land of the promise"; *The Blood of Abel*, 28). Let us note that Lot, "of course"
(Moye, "In the Beginning," 592) is also going east (Gen 13:11). The "east" is an important
marker in J's narratives on the primeval era; see Gen 2:8; 3:24; 4:16; 10:30; 11:2.

Suffice it to mention that God does not automatically and indiscriminate-
ly welcome human offerings. He is not bound by any "politically correct"
etiquette to welcome the sacrifices of Cain and Abel without discernment
or free will.[36]

It remains retrospectively true that Cain's temporary reversal of fortune brought out in the open his fundamental character. The affair of the
sacrifices provided the occasion that appears to have driven him to murder, but this simply revealed what was already "crouching at the door" of
his heart. As said above, Cain's crime is not to be seen as an access of temporary insanity. And as for Abel, it is true that the text nowhere says that
he had been "innocent" and "righteous" (as do, for instance, Matt 23:35;
1 John 3:12; see also Philo *Q.G.* 1.59; Josephus *Ant.* 1.53; *PRE* 22;[37] etc.),
but the test of the offerings accepted/refused did suggest his fundamental
blamelessness.[38]

The Introduction of Sin into the World

It must be emphasized once more that God does *not* reject Cain—and
certainly not arbitrarily as some postmodern commentators intimate—
for God continues to dialogue with him,[39] and, most importantly, Cain
is marked with a divine sign of protection (v. 15).[40] What God declares

36. Both Cain's and Abel's sacrifices are offerings later ordered by the Law (see Exod
23:16, 19; 34:22, 26; Lev 23:10–14; Deut 26:2; note the mention of the "first-fruits of the
ground" in v. 10 in a text claiming an original "nomadism" of Israel). As such, this type of
sacrifice is celebrating the divine benediction in the past and praying for the abundance
in the future. One of the chastisements on Cain is the curse "from the ground" (4:11–12)
after Cain has sterilized Abel's bliss by killing him. The sacrifice never preempted the
ethical in the Hebrew Bible (see 1 Sam 15:22).

37. *PRE* in eighth–ninth century.

38. Whatever may have been the kind of existence previously led by some among
the millions slaughtered by the Nazis, they *are* innocent victims (so in Ps 10:8, where,
incidentally, innocence is expressed with two different terms). Neher said, "Even if we
posited that Cain was righteous and Abel the wicked one, Cain's killing of Abel is enough
for God to side with Abel" (Lecture at the University of Strasbourg, Sept. 1956).

39. God speaks to Cain, not to Abel! But to conclude from the divine silence that
Abel is "rejected" would be ill-advised.

40. Westermann sees as a "modern intrusion" critical judgments in terms of "election" and "rejection"; *Genesis 1–11*, 297. However, concerning 4:5b (Cain's falling of
countenance), Westermann insists upon Cain's attitude as reacting to his *rejection* (sic!)
(ibid., 298, my emphasis). One wonders whether the *persona* Abel would react the same
way as Cain if put in the same situation; a murderous Abel is simply unthinkable. Against
the idea of rejection, see Alonso-Schökel, *Donde esta tu hermano?*, 29. Ellis comments,

to Cain is that the episode of the sacrifice is just that, an episode.[41] It
is not determining the future: "if you do what is right [from now on],
will you not be accepted [as today Abel is accepted]?" God exhorts Cain
to *interpret* the event and to draw a lesson for the future.[42] It is not so
much the discrete occurrences but their integration that may decide what
kind of person he is able to become. The tragedy that ensues is not to be
blamed on God's alleged exclusion of Cain, but on Cain's rejection of the
openness of tomorrow; he perpetuates a setback into a fateful repetition.
As Franz Kafka said, the gravest sin is the sin of impatience, or inability
to learn from our pain.[43]

It is to be noted that it is the first time that the word *sin* appears in
the J text. The term he uses here is *hatta'th*; it is statistically the most
often used term designating sin in the Hebrew Bible. But one may wonder
whether translating the term here by "sin" is the most accurate, for its
basic meaning is "missing a target," the very antithesis of "torah" coming
from the root *yarah*, that is, aiming at a target (see Judg 20:16). *Hatta'th*
is the transgression of an obligation. It entails guilt and shame. With this
term at this place there occurs a stricter definition of the ethical. Genesis
3 envisaged human disobedience in general, but Cain's wrong is a specific
and aberrant crime. A better rendition in 4:7 is perhaps "culpability." Guilt
is lying at the door of Cain's heart, as it is true of all humans according to
J. It is "pandemic in the human race," says Robin C. Cover.[44] Whether it
is intrinsic to human nature is not apparently J's concern. What interests
him are the divine non-indifference and the human *capability*, "you can
master it." It is the human impotence by default that provokes the divine
wrath: impotence becomes guilt.

"My guilt," says Cain, is unbearable. So says Ps 38:4, which parallels Gen 4:13 so neatly. It reads "my guilt feelings are like a heavy load"
(*'awonothay . . . kemassah kabed*) to be compared with Gen 4:13: "my

---

"it is clear that for an Israelite the Yahwist's recounting of punishment for sin would not
be interpreted as a sign of rejection but as a sign of educative love (see Prov 22:15)"; *The
Yahwist*, 157.

41. See Jerome on 4:6: "Nonne si bene feceris, *dimittatur tibi omne delictum tuum*"
(my emphasis).

42. On the crucial notion of *interpretation*, see below chapter 3, the section "God's
Power."

43. "Perhaps, there is only one capital sin: impatience. They were expelled because of
their impatience, and because of their impatience they do not return"; Bernanos, *Journal*,
"1.16.1922," 530). Bernanos, "All human sins are impatience."

44. Cover, "Sin, Sinner in the Old Testament," 32.

guilt is too big to bear" (*gadol ʿawoni minneśoʾ*). If we translate *ḥaṭṭaʾth* with "guilt" in Gen 4:7, and *ʿawon* by "moral guilt" in 4:13, the contrast with Abel's guiltlessness is emphasized. Innocence dares facing God and its offering is received kindly by the God of innocence (*ṣaddiq*). Cain's "not doing well" jerks him, as it were, to the antipode of innocence and hence to be driven from the face of Abel, the face of the earth, and the face of God (4:14).[45] The guilty Cain remains without a dialogical partner, and this is the essence of his wandering. He is like a space capsule lost in the emptiness of the universe. A man without God, without "other," without ground, he would be floating aimlessly without end, were it not for a gracious divine remission.

Now that Cain is cursed from the very ground he used to be rooted in, the whole world becomes foreign and hostile. His crime, a manifestation of his destructive instinct (*Destruktionstrieb* = Death instinct directed outwards, says Freud), is eventually directed both against the external world as well as against himself (*Selbstdestruktion*).[46]

Guilt then is not lying at the door any more. It has entered Cain's heart. His next move is a repetition rather than a learning from experience and he finds sham moorings in the land of Nod, the land of Roaming, "east of Eden," that is, still more eastward than his parents had to go (3:24). "East of Eden" from an Israelite point of view, is the desert and, beyond, it is Mesopotamia, the land of exile par excellence.[47] Contrary in appearance to God's sentence in 4:12, Cain "settles" and he builds the first city. He calls it Enoch, after the name of his son whom he begat with a "nobody" like himself, so that it may be the name of a ghost town, with no inhabitants and no history; unless we see in Cain's genealogy a description of the inhabitants of Enoch, that is, a society cursed with violence (4:17–24; 5:28–29).[48] Violence begotten by the debilitating feeling of emptiness!

45. Note this J theme of separation, more radical here than in Genesis 3, for J follows a general pattern of progressive evil manifestations in Genesis 2–11. In Genesis 11, humanity becomes an archipelago.

46. See Freud, *New Introductory Lectures on Psycho-Analysis*, 106.

47. To recall, the people who built the Tower of Babel were on the move westward coming from the east (Gen 11:2; Shinar is an ancient name for Babylon.) They also, like Cain, are building a town (11:4). When their plans peter out, they, like Cain, are "scattered" in the whole wide world; see Ellis, *The Yahwist*, 133. Perceptively, Patrick D. Miller sets in opposition the builders of Babel convening in one place, and the movement in the next chapter where "Abraham is sent out"; "Eridu, Dunnu, and Babel," 160.

48. But see below another interpretation of Cain's building the city of Enoch, which may indeed be a sign of rediscovery of love and hope on the part of Cain (chapter 4,

What a vast perspective is opened up here by J! He will expand on the theme in Genesis 6–9 and 11.

That Cain contravened God's sentence by settling in the city of Nod is compounding the gravity of his sin. The apparent inner-contradiction in the narrative between the original divine sentence and its remaining temporarily unfulfilled is not a first in J's narrative. Already (and blatantly) in Genesis 3 he had imagined Adam and Eve giving the lie, so to speak, to God's threat expressed in 2:17: "you shall certainly (or: immediately) die." Furthermore, within the chapter 3 of Genesis there is a taut paradox between the serpent's promise that the humans will know good and evil, on the one hand, and the apparent confirmation given by God in Gen 3:22 that "they have become like one of us knowing good and evil," on the other.[49]

Paradox is an appropriate term to characterize J's narrative. We could also think of a *dialectical* tension. The genius of the bard is manifest here. What he tells may be uncomplicated, but it is certainly complex—because life is complex. In life, extremes meet.[50] After the "fall," Adam and Eve do not die—but something dies. They are mortal and live all their days with the debilitating consciousness of their mortality. Another illustration is provided by the correspondence between the serpent's promise that the humans would become "like God" and a certain truth of the matter. But it is a narrowly contingent truth. The human likeness with God is in fact an adulterated resemblance, the one of an apprentice sorcerer with his master. The paradox goes even deeper, for Adam and Eve indeed used to be like God before their blunder. They now choose to be like God according to a different definition. Genesis 3:22, as a matter of fact, is susceptible of two contrasting interpretations: either God says, "See, the man has become like one of us" (NRSV), or he states, "Now, the human used to be (*ha-ʾadam hayah*, not *wayyehî-haʾadam*) like one of us."

The recourse to paradox continues. J emphasizes the uprooting of the murderer, who is nowhere at home and feels estranged from ground, people, and God. At some point, notwithstanding, he is said to settle, and this is quite unexpected. Not a sign of conflict between two traditions,

---

section "Cain, a Tragic Figure").

49. But see an alternative interpretation of this text in LaCocque, *The Trial of Innocence*, 251, and its summary below.

50. The realization of this fact constituted an important breakthrough in Freud's thinking.

the motif is true to life for the wanderer has no stronger desire than to find a place "to lay his head." Besides, J immediately shows the inanity of Cain's attempt: he settles in the place of "No-Settlement" (4:16). And, when he builds himself a city—presumably after being disillusioned with the emptiness of Nod[51]—one might wonder what its purpose is and who will inhabit the city of Enoch. The latter may be more a scale model than a true-to-life town.

Such is J's dialectic. The first city ever (not counting the ghost city of Nod) is built by the first vagrant. The first fruit of the womb, the first child who is immediately called a "man" (4:1), is also the first man-slaughterer. The first ground tiller after Eden is also the first cursed from the ground. The first worshiper of God (4:3) is the first to be estranged from the face of Yhwh (4:16). The first murderer is also the first, at least in hope, to inaugurate (Enoch means inauguration, dedication of something new) a fresh course in the history of humankind.

He is the first in many a circumstance, but nevertheless, he comes always second after Adam his father, whom he tries so hard to obliterate along with his brother Abel. The lesson seems to be that all those who are "first" among us are in reality always too late. Oedipus may believe to be the first in his wife's bed . . . and Columbus to be the discoverer of the Americas.

A Crux Interpretum—Verse 7

Otto Procksch says that Gen 4:7 is, "the most difficult verse in Genesis."[52] It literally reads, "And/But if you do not do well, at the door sin [fem.] is crouching [masc.] and toward you his [note the masc.] desire." The difficulties must be enumerated.

1) First, the sequence must be taken seriously: only *if* Cain does not do well, he will be the sin's [or guilt's] prey. "Doing well" or "not doing well" is to be understood from within the sphere of ethics, not primarily of the ritual.[53] Not doing well is, in Cain's instance, being possessed by

---

51. That is, in a land that, from its origin and essence, is one of meandering, "this Nowhere land, which is not a place but a lack of place," says Ellul, *The Meaning of the City*, 1.

52. Procksch, *Die Genesis*, ad loc.

53. *Contra* Karl Budde, see, among others, Westermann, *Genesis 1–11*, 300.

anger.[54] Soon after God's exhortation, Cain kills his brother (Gen 4:8; see Jon 4:4; contrast with Isa 53:9).

2) The grammatical conflict between "sin" (*hatta'th*, a feminine form) and the verb "crouching" (*robes*, a masculine form) is partially solved if "sin"—like the earth in 4:10—is seen as some sort of personified demon. Westermann thinks of the Assyrian *rabisum*.[55] Earlier, Gerhard von Rad had suggested that the last letter of the word "sin" in Hebrew (which makes of the term a feminine form) be attached to the following verb ("crouches") as a pronominal prefix; this way, "sin" becomes masculine (*hét'*).[56] But then the verb becomes feminine (*tirbés*) while the subject is masculine and the grammatical conflict is just displaced. Rather, the feminine form *hatta'th* is to be maintained and this "ungrammatical" use seen as discreetly alluding not only to Cain's sin/guilt, but to his *sin offering* (something the masculine *se'et* never does). Besides, Victor Hamilton calls attention to "nouns that are feminine morphologically [and] are sometimes treated as masculine" (noting GKC §122r). An example he cites is the word *Qoheleth*.[57]

3) Sin is crouching "at the door," presumably of Cain's heart.[58] It is described as constantly ready to get in and prevail. Its externalization "at the door" was required by its personification. But this begs the question: Is sin an objective power striving to take possession of Cain? The question is complex. On the one hand, J wants to make clear that Cain is not deterministically required to "not do well." His sin is not congenital. On the other hand, however, sin is close to his heart. Paraphrasing the antipodal conception of the law in Deuteronomy, we could say: Sin "is not far off.

54. The idiom *harah le* is one degree below full anger *harah 'aph*, and could lean to the sense of depression (see Gruber, "Was Cain Angry or Depressed?"; and idem, "The Tragedy of Cain and Abel." A psychological approach to the story of Cain and Abel finds an invitation for analysis here.

55. Westermann, *Genesis 1–11*, 299–300, following other critics. See already Speiser, *Genesis*, 33. Let us note that *robés* is not necessarily ominous, but it certainly is in Gen 49:25; Deut 29:19 [20], and (perhaps) Deut 33:13; see Waschke "*rabas*," 303. Van Wolde translates, "to lie in wait for, to prowl"; "The Story of Cain and Abel," 31.

56. Von Rad, *Genesis*, ad loc.

57. Hamilton, *Genesis*, 227. *Pace* Deurloo, for whom the masc. pronoun designates Abel (!); see "*tešuqh*, 'dependency,' Gen 4, 7."

58. For *b. Sanh.* 91a, it is rather the "gate of the womb," meaning "from your birth on." Sin here designates the bad impulse. Rashi's commentary says that it is the "gate of the tomb," meaning "until your death."

It is not in heaven . . . not beyond the sea . . . but nigh unto you, in your mouth and in your heart."[59]

The localization of evil is a constant problem (internal/external). We must certainly, with Edward P. Shafranske, distinguish between human fallibility and evil. He writes,

> In expressing fallibility, one's relation with others in the human condition is not severed; in evil, it is. It is the willful destruction and disregard for the other that fractures the bond with humanity and the future possibilities of personal existence.

He adds that the evil persons "are aware of the nature of the crime that they commit. In their disavowal of evil, they disavow their victims' ontology as human persons."[60]

In J's stories of Adam and Eve and of Cain and Abel, evil is metaphorically somehow external. Either with the serpent of Genesis 3 or the *rabiṣum* of Genesis 4 that is crouching at the door of Cain's heart, the representation is the same. Of primordial importance, of course, is that neither the serpent nor the *rabiṣum* has any power as long as the door of the human heart is not flung open to take them in. In modern terms, the externality of evil is the potentiality of evil. As Paul Ricoeur says, it is always already there.[61] Carl Jung spoke of a realm of archetypal evil.[62] But affirming such a human atavism of sorts must not become a way of exoneration. More existentially true to the dialectical externality and internality of evil is the Buberian diagnostic that sees anthropological evil as the failure to enter into relation. Maurice Friedman, the great presenter of Buber's thinking, writes,

---

59. See Deut 30:12–14.

60. Shafranske, "Evil," 6. At this point, an attempt at defining evil will be useful, I believe. Peck's formula has the advantage of being short and sharp: evil, he says, is "that force, residing inside or outside human beings, that seeks to kill life or liveliness"; *People of the Lie*, 43.

61. See, for instance, Ricoeur, "Evil, a Challenge to Philosophy and Theology," 636.

62. Jung, *Answer to Job*. While psychologically determined, pain, for instance, is experienced as happening *to* the ego, "as it were, the victim of external forces," says Bakan, *Disease*, 74. Freud, as is well known, spoke of a "death instinct" with the hypothesis that all living substance is bound to die from internal causes; *Beyond the Pleasure Principle*, 59. Even psychosomatic diseases are nowadays seen as often having their nucleus in the individual's "defense mechanism," "in the same way as in the psychological context the individual is not better 'defended' by his neurotic defense mechanisms"; Bakan, *Disease*, 23.

> If it is entering into relation that makes the human being really
> human, it is the failure to enter into relation that in the last analysis
> constitutes evil, or non-existence, and it is the re-establishment of
> relation that leads to the redemption of evil and genuine human
> existence.[63]

Adam and Eve's failure was to not keep up the *I-Thou* relationship
with God, and replacing it with the *I-It* relation with the serpent. Cain's
sin is a duplicate of his parents' failure. But this time the broken relation
is with the fellow human being. In the background of the J diptych of
Genesis 3 and 4, there is the storyteller's equating the love of God and the
love of the neighbor.

Sin is thus both objective and subjective. Martin Buber says of Gog,
"He can exist in the outer world because he exists within us."[64] As a matter
of fact, there is a confluence of inner and outer sinfulness. State, society,
environment, can be corrupt and, as "outside" deleterious conditions,
trigger an evil response in us. So are the serpent in Genesis 3 and the
rabiṣum in Genesis 4. Sin's subjectivity is stressed by the commandment/
promise: "(you shall) dominate over it" (Gen 4:7),[65] while its objectivity
underlines its universality.

Cain's "door" is opened to the demonic when his disposition is not
"to do well." For the human being is called to buttress the "dikes" against
the flooding of evil. If happens just a relaxation of the necessary con-
tinual vigilance, soon the deluge of evil reaches an uncontrollable level, as
Cain's fratricide shows. The danger is all the more ominous in that the evil
crouching at the gate of the heart appears as familiar—as intimately close
as a woman is to her husband (see 4:7 and 3:16: "his desire" [*tešuqatho*]
and "your [her] desire" [*tešuqathekh*]). Cain surrenders to the evil's "desire" and this in turn opens up the path to a collective violence that fills
the earth (Gen 6:12).

---

63. Friedman, ""The Human Dimension of Evil," 30.

64. Buber, *Good and Evil*, 65. Edmond Jacob arrives at the same conclusion in *Les
Thèmes essentiels d'une théologie de l'Ancien Testament*, 228). Although Stratton has
pointed out that the crisis is not due here to "the machinations of another character";
Out of Eden: Reading, Rhetoric, and Ideology in Genesis 2–3, 221). The external face of
evil/sin in Genesis 4 plays the role of the Genesis 3 serpent.

65. The alternatives of imperative and future of the indicative have been deftly han-
dled by John Steinbeck in *East of Eden*.

4) The image of "crouching" indicates a permanent condition; it is reinforced by the use of the present participle ("is crouching"). It points to premeditation in Cain's crime.[66]

5) Why did J personify sin as a male rather than a female as required by the gender of *ḥaṭṭa'th*? Cain has eliminated, he thinks, all masculinity around himself: his brother, his human father, and, hence, his diety.[67] In his own eyes, he is the only man standing. But now, God's address reveals the omnipresence of an unexpected male whose desire parallels in reverse the feminine one in Gen 3:16. From Eve's desire for her male partner, we pass to sin's desire for Cain. Note here again the textual substitution of Cain for Adam of Genesis 3, that is, the substitution of someone much more frightening; and the substitution of "sin" for "woman," a much more dangerous threat.

6) A new contrast is set between Adam's "rule" over Eve (*yimšol bakh*, Gen 3:16) and Cain's "mastership" over the crouching sin (*thimšol bo*). In the former case, Adam's power of attraction leads the desiring woman to submit herself to a sexual intercourse that is endangering her integrity and well-being.[68] In the latter case, Cain is said to be *capable* of overcoming his propensity to sin.[69] At this point, the realm of desire is not sexual—although the same power of attraction seems to exist between the humans and their sin, as between the sexes. Along this line of thinking, it is possibly in order to emphasize the shift of meaning that J used the masculine gender form.

---

66. In the words of William P. Brown, "[Cain's] predatory beast within is the source of premeditation"; *The Ethos of the Cosmos*, 166. For the image, see Jer 5:6. The language is manifestly symbolic. If the human allows the "beast" to enter, simplicity becomes duplicity: the "animal" perverts the human, as in Genesis 3. True, there is no concretization here of an evil spirit, but the gate opening on the personification of evil predisposition is dangerously ajar, under the influence of surrounding cultures. On premeditation, see van Wolde, "The Story of Cain and Abel," 35.

67. In many ways, regicide, for instance, is a camouflage of patricide and of deicide. In 1652, Pierre du Moulin published a pamphlet protesting the execution of England's Charles I: "Regii Sanguinis Clamor."

68. See LaCocque, *The Trial of Innocence*, esp. 220–22, on Gen 3:16.

69. The contrast with Greek characters is stark. Rachel Bespaloff writes, "Clytemnestra, Orestes, and Oedipus are their crimes; they have no existence outside them"; "On the Iliad," 58.

The First Crime

In one respect Cain is an unprecedented first: through his use of violence. He is first but he is far from unique. Cain foreshadows an innumerable posterity of violent people, starting with Lamech and spreading fast to the point when it is reported that "the earth was corrupt in God's sight, and the earth was filled with violence" (6:11 [NRSV]). Sad precedent that occasioned the quasi-total destruction of the world (Genesis 6–9; Gen 6:13 reads, "I have determined to make an end of all flesh, for the earth is filled with violence because of them; now I am going to destroy them along with the earth" [NRSV]). One may surmise that it is also the violence inaugurated by Cain that will some day entirely destroy our world.

It is remarkable how J has not only imagined the occurrence of the first slaying in history, but also the horrible vacuity in the guilty soul. For, if murder in its external aspect is always fratricidal, its internal side is suicidal. In *Beyond the Pleasure Principle*, Freud states that sadism is the deviation of the [self] death instinct. The latter, he says, "is forced away from the ego and has consequently only emerged in relation to the object."[70]

In its complexity, the crime is the blotting out of the face to face with God. This is properly what the Bible calls death. Death is then truly the outcome of sin.[71] That is why God has to put a sign on Cain to commute the sentence. Ironically, Cain, who was not the keeper of his brother, is put at the benefit of God's keeping.[72]

But, before giving the sign, God asks Cain, "Why are you angry?" and it behooves us to listen to the psychologists who invite the raging party to verbally identify and name their pain.[73] God *gives a voice* to Cain, a feature that becomes more and more prominent in the narrative. So, Cain speaks to his brother in v. 8; he answers to God in v. 9. As for Abel, he finds his voice only beyond death (v. 10). In short, Cain is not manipulated by God. There is due process before the judgment (vv. 11–12). The communication between God and Cain is not cut off after a botched sacrifice, not even

70. *SE* xviii, 54. In Thornton Wilder's *The Skin of Our Teeth*, Cain says: "Listen, it's as though you have to kill somebody else so as not to end up killing yourself"; Act 3, p. 131.

71. Cover cites Num 18:22; 27:3; Deut 24:16; 21:22; 22:26; 2 Kgs 14:6; 2 Chr 24:5; Ezek 3:20; 18:20; and Amos 9:10; "Sin, Sinner in the Old Testament," 39.

72. "Keeping" (*šmr*) plays an important role in J's primeval stories. In Gen 2:15—a crucial text in the creation narrative, see LaCocque, *The Trial of Innocence*, esp. 83–89; 272–76—the human is called to *keep* the garden.

73. See Rosenblatt and Horowitz, *Wrestling with Angels*, 55.

after the murder of a brother. When the dialogue ceases, it is more the feat of Cain than of God (v. 16), and there is a vestige of the communication in the form of a divine sign put on Cain (v. 15).

As a further confirmation of his "death-wish," Cain compounds his denial with defiance: "Am I my brother's keeper?"[74] Cain responds to God's question with a question of his own. He feigns surprise: Is God really concerned about human affairs? Does he really call the human to accountability? True, the question may be merely rhetorical and amount to a summarily brushing away denial ("I don't know"). If, with James Crenshaw, we distinguish between three forms of evil (moral, natural, and religious), Cain's response—as we saw above—belongs to the "religious evil," which is "presuming indifference, remoteness, or blindness on the part of God."[75] In fact, Cain's query raises that sort of problem: If Cain is not his brother's keeper, who else is? The answer is God, of course; but if so, God is construed by Cain as an external force that dispenses the human with all responsibility. It is as if Cain were a Homeric hero, say like Agamemnon or Achilles, always speaking of themselves as though some god or other was in control of all of their moves and thus the real accountable party.

This depersonalization of the self is not without damage to the self and to others. Cain addressed by God, like Adam and Eve in Genesis 3, is thereby affirmed in his personality and moral autonomy. Until then, the non-rejected Cain is still a full partner with God, as is any human by creation and vocation. The question of God becomes only provocative the moment Cain retorts with his aggressive counter-query. Then, the partnership between Yhwh and Cain becomes, *on the part of Cain*, hostility. Genesis 4:9 can, therefore, be seen as the hinge-text, the "midnight" text, when time is split between a dialogical past, and a solipsistic future. "Am I my brother's keeper?" cuts all ties with the world and, eventually, with God. The "curse" of Cain is to be isolated from everyone and everything. J serializes the bonds that Cain destroys: the bond with the soil (with nature), the bond with his father and more generally with the others (with society), and the bond with God (with spirituality).[76]

---

74. The record of Cain's retort to God is typically put within quotation marks, and it offers the reader an unmediated access to its content, as it happens with monologs or dialogues on a theater stage.

75. Crenshaw, *Defending God*, 15.

76. Remarkably, Ivan Karamazov declares that he is no keeper of his brother Dmitri,

All this is epitomized in the rejection of the brother. When God asks Cain about the whereabouts of Abel, it is the narrative penultimate occurrence of the name Abel. The latter is in the mouth of God and later in Eve's (4:25). Cain never calls his brother by name, but only by a periphrasis that stresses his own egocentrism: "Am I *my brother's* keeper?" In the eyes of Cain, Abel is reduced—as he already was, it seems, in Eve's eyes—"to a scheme of relations and hierarchies, in a universe of meaning and value which is all-encompassing. Totalization has a quality of violence. . . . The Same attempts to erase the Other by taking away its difference. The ultimate expression of this is murder . . . literally."[77]

Cain counts on the alleged blindness of God (see Ps 10:11; 94:7, associated with human murdering; and Ps 94:11, which dubs human thoughts as empty *hebel* "breath"). Crenshaw calls this "practical atheism."[78] He also refers to Psalm 14 (= Psalm 53), in which I would call attention to the condensed summary in v. 1: "The fool says in his heart: There is no God," a practical atheism that is immediately translated into (v. 3), "They are corrupt . . . no one is doing well," a striking parallel with Gen 4:7, "If you do well."[79]

Cain's question reveals much about Cain's soul. M. Scott Peck writes, "[A]ll sins are reparable except the sin of believing one is without sin." This is a characteristic of what he perceives as "scapegoating."[80] While the Adam and Eve myth has shown that the human freedom makes also wrongdoing possible, the Cain and Abel myth "extends to the possibility of denying the existence of the wrongfulness of one's action."[81] What is more, implied in Cain's cynical question is the appalling consequence that, as Abel is not under his care, he can do violence to him, indeed kill him and feel guiltless. This is, in Levinas's view, what is fundamentally unethical. Cain is first unable to speak with his brother in the field because addressing him with whatever (even small) talk would acknowledge his otherness, that is, says Levinas, his intrinsic demand not to be harmed.[82] In fact, Cain has absorbed the otherness of Abel instead of acknowledging

---

or of his father Fyodor; *The Brothers Karamazov*, book 5, chap. 3.

77. Edgerton, *Speak to Me That I May Speak*, 64.

78. See Crenshaw, *Defending* God, 28.

79. See Rom 3:12. See Crenshaw, ibid., 40: "The clear association of practical atheism with gross immorality."

80. Peck, "Reflections on the Psychology of Evil," 9.

81. Ibid., 11.

82. See Levinas, *Totality and Infinity*.

his irreducible alterity. Because it is irreducible, Abel's blood now cries out and up to God. As I have written, Cain, the one man who was co-created by the divine and the human, brings down the creation of another man, his brother, to de-creation.[83]

Cain occupies the center-stage all along. Abel is narratively (as well as ideologically) eclipsed by his brother, or so it seems. But, on the other hand, the ghostly Abel is omnipresent, like the whale in Melville's story. Ironically, Cain is constantly considered in his denied relation with his brother. It is ironical because Abel has been repeatedly called Cain's brother and has appeared as having no history of his own. To this strange feature we now turn.

A French proverb says, "Les gens heureux n'ont pas d'histoire" (contentment breeds no story). Abel's rectitude and innocence cannot really be narrated. Suffice it in the narrative to say that Abel's sacrifice was agreeable to God. By contrast, the anti-Abel calls for description, although, paradoxically, it is a story of terrible emptiness.[84] The obliteration of the face of God leaves Cain without a face of his own. But, as far as Abel is concerned, his dialogue with God is rapture, and it costs him his life. From the point of view of the so-called "real world," Abel's option is aberrant. It is a bland world in comparison to Cain's world, where there is action: the elimination of competition, the building of a city, the feeling of jealousy, anger, guilt, shame—a whole complex of sentiments and moods much more attractive to a story-teller than the uncomplicated and complex-free world of Abel.[85]

But this exciting "Nietzschean" adventure is based on ruthlessness and on sheer crime. Cain, the man of "substance"—or of possession, as

---

83. LaCocque, *The Trial of Innocence*, 13.

84. As Amos Oz writes, "If Shakespeare had written plays about, let us say, the expansion of the navy . . . in Elizabethan England, who would watch them today? . . . But cruelty, suffering, madness, death—these are not self-evident. They call for some sort of justification or illumination or compassion"; *Under This Blazing Light*, 28.

85. *Mutatis mutandis*, the eating of the fruit of knowledge in Genesis 3 also inaugurates human history as we experience it, and this unfolding is not without exhilarating moments! Regarding the use of "world" here, both the Jewish tradition and the Quran teach that killing an (innocent) human being is same as killing the whole world (see *m. Sanh.* 4:5; in the Quran, see 5:32 [but note the proviso]: ". . . anyone who murders any person who had not committed murder or horrendous crimes, it shall be as he murdered all the people. And anyone who spares a life, it shall be as if he spared the life of all the people"; see also 17:33).

his name signifies by popular etymology[86]—deals in reality with sand and ashes. His world is founded on blood and is marked by death. The mark on Cain makes one think of the ancient and modern decorations displayed by warriors as a record of their prowess. But in Cain's case, the allusion would be deeply ironic. Cain's "prowess" is murder, and the "decoration" is granted, not by the tribe or the military "brass" but by God, with a rationale that is different from the need to impress or scare others. There is here, nonetheless, some remnant of the folkloric in the fact that the "shield" of Cain implies that his potential slaughterer would be punished sevenfold over.

By contrast, the man of the "ephemeral"—a mere vapor, a mist—as he is considered by his mother and his brother, is seen by God as a pleasant interlocutor, whose voice is potent even beyond death.[87] Does J mean that the two brothers' names have been mixed up at their birth?

A Woman's Glory and Her Sons' Competition

A remarkable shift occurred in Gen 4:1 inasmuch as God, from "father" of Eve (and of all existent) became her "husband." In Genesis 3, something dysfunctional had happened in God's family, but now Eve claims to have redressed the dysfunctional through her miraculous co-creation of life. The matter here is one of cooperative function, of course, not a genetic one. The woman's procreation changes the divine rapport with humanity for the better, which shifts from fatherhood to husbandry, that is, as the further development of the *Heilsgeschichte* will demonstrate, a relationship based on "covenantal nomism" (E. P. Sanders). Genesis 4:1, therefore, expresses the hope that, with this new beginning in the God–human relationship, things will fall again into their (created) place. If Adam plays here a quasi-insignificant role, it is because he is *replaced* for all practical purposes by Cain (in the eyes of his mother) as the new

---

86. The anal-sadistic personality comes to mind. "Possession" is what prevents Cain from being an integrated personality. Such integration is, in the words of Bakhtin, "not the unity of my having and possessing, but the unity of not-having and not-possessing, not the unity of my already-being, but the unity of my not-yet-being" (see "if you do good," 4:7); "Author and Hero in Aesthetic Activity," 126.

87. For innocence, says Kierkegaard, is "something which properly speaking does not exist [in the sense of *Dasein*], but only comes into existence by the very fact that it is annulled [the French translation says "destroyed"], comes into existence as that which was before it was annulled [destroyed]"; *The Concept of Dread*, 33.

beginner of humanity.[88] Later on, in the course of Israel's history, there will be a succession of children of the promise, Isaac, Jacob, Joseph. . . . But Cain is the first, the prime, the child of hope. In the evolution of the story, however, the hope that Cain incarnates will be shattered to pieces, and the finality of the catastrophe is stopped only because hope survives on account of God's compassion.

Given the immense import of the birth of the first woman's first child, it is evident that all following child bearings must be considered as mere repetitions of the first, minus some of its distinction.[89]

Because of the passivity of his *persona*, textual criticism sometimes considers Abel as a secondary character in the narrative. There is no expression of joy at his birth in contrast to Cain's, and he is designated in the story as "the brother of Cain" seven times. Indeed, his birth comes as a kind of afterthought in Gen 4:2. Whatever may be the original content of the tale, Abel's effacement confirms the psychological view that he is the weak member among the siblings, younger, non self-assertive, dependent—a breath carried over by someone else's breathing (see Ps 39:6–7, 12; 144:4; Job 7:16; Qoh 1:2). No one in the Bible appears to be as innocent as is Abel; he is like the "firstling of his flock" he offers, and Cain, who initially had offered "the fruit of the ground" (v. 3), slaughters and spills his blood like that of a lamb.

True, the motif of fraternal rivalry is wide-spread in world literature. The history of religions stresses the theme's frequency, including the sub-genre of fratricide. One parallel frequently called upon by scholars is Anubis and Bata in Egyptian folklore, or the murder of Remus by Romulus at the foundation of Rome. The patriarchal stories in the Pentateuch are replete with such stories of controversy between brothers and between sisters. Clearly, this literary motif echoes a deep universal psychological drive.[90] Ernest Becker condenses thusly the psychological analysis on the subject,

88. The obliteration of Adam in the tale may be also the psychological sequel of the reversal of gender roles witnessed in Genesis 3. There, to recall, Adam ate the forbidden fruit as he "was with her" (v. 6). Did Adam at that point stir contempt in his wife's eyes?

89. Note that Eve does explain once again the name of her third son, Seth (4:25). Seth is a new beginning, after the hope attached to Cain was destroyed along with the person of Abel—and the human paternity of Adam is restored (5:3), ricocheting on 4:1 as expressing hubris on the part of Eve; see Bloom, *The Book of J*, 188.

90. Even in the *Iliad*, the Trojans were related to the Mycenaean Greeks who attacked them. Alfred Adler has studied in-depth how being a second born child has a psycho-

The child needs to be an object of *primary* value, and by definition only one person can be primary; and one can only establish
primacy in relation to those around him. The parents are out of
the contest since they already enjoy supreme power; their task is
to dispense it, and in dispensing it they also serve as judges. So one
concentrates on his peers before the tribunal.[91]

But, if we follow the lead of Philo, for example, the text of Gen 4:1–2
may be deceptive. True, Eve emphasizes God's gracious intervention in
the procreation of Cain, the first child ever, while saying nothing about
baby Abel.[92] But the verb *yada*ʿ (Adam *knew* his wife, v. 1),[93] Philo says,
is used for natural births, while the children who are the carriers of the
divine promise are said to be "begotten" by God, a fact that the relevant
texts indicate one way or the other. The Jewish philosopher invokes Gen
21:1 (Isaac); 29:31 (Reuben); especially 30:2, 22 (only God can beget a
child from Rachel); Exodus 2:22 (Moses).[94] Abel is not "born of the flesh
and the blood" (John 1:13), but of a divine intervention that surpasses the
one hailed by Eve at the birth of Cain. For Philo, of course, Eve's paean in
4:1 is wrong as far as the identification of the "son of God" is concerned.
Her blindness is corrected by the text of 4:2: Abel's birth is the outcome
of the divine-human co-creation, not Cain. Furthermore, a characteristic
of J's composition is the exaltation of the second born child above the
elder one: Abel over Cain; Isaac over Ishmael; Jacob over Esau; Rachel

---

logical impact on his/her personality. Even upon the parent of the same gender, he says,
the child's birth provokes less excitement than the first-born child did. Hence the second-
born tries to compensate by being as good as the first-born [Abel, "he also," sacrifices
. . . (4:4)], so as to feel equal in the family; see Hans L. and Rowena Ansbacher, eds., *The
Individual Psychology of Alfred Adler*. Also of interest is Freud's analysis of the first-born's
jealousy because he sees in the second-born a competitor. Already in 1900, he spoke of
"the child's death-wishes against his brothers and sisters"; *The Interpretation of Dreams*
= *SE* IV–V, 255–56. Adler's authority on the topic, however, is shared by Otto Rank, who
in 1926 spoke of the birth of a sibling as of a "disturbing third" in the competition for
the mother's love; see *The Incest Theme in Literature and Legend*, 487, cited by Rudnytsky,
Reading Psychoanalysis, 75. In the story of Cain and Abel, Cain acts out his disdain toward Abel, as he feels backed up by his mother (even if her message remains nonverbal).
As to Abel, although second-born child, he does not look for competition.

91. Becker, *The Birth and Death of Meaning*, 78.

92. But in v. 2, the text states that *Eve* continued to give birth, this time to Abel, and
Adam is bypassed.

93. Or should we understand the accomplished mode of the verb as a pluperfect?
Had Adam known Eve in the Garden? If so, there is continuity from "before" to "after."

94. See Philo, *Cher.* 48, 49; *Post.* 78. Other biblical texts could be adduced, Gen 3:25;
1 Sam 1:6, 11; Isa 7:14. On procreation as creation, see also Ruth 4:12; Isa 53:10.

over Lea; Perez over Zerah; Joseph over his older brothers; Ephraim over Manasseh.

In short, such a reading of Gen 4:1–2 faults Eve for "looking on the outward appearance, while God looks on the heart" (see 1 Sam 16:7). Eve bore Abel, so to speak without Adam (4:1).[95]

This, Eve could not have known at the time of her conception of Cain, short of intuition or revelation. In Genesis 4:1, the text itself becomes pregnant with meaning. Eve, "the mother of all living" (3:20) triumphantly proclaims her unique prerogative as a woman: "I have brought forth [or created; or acquired] a man with Yhwh." After the anonymous mention of her husband as "the man" (*ha-'adam*) we expected some praise for, or at least some acknowledgment of, Adam, but the latter plays decidedly a minor role in the story, and if later on Abel's birth appears to be an afterthought, Adam himself is quasi nonexistent, like a surrogate father. Yhwh as the creator/genitor of the universe is so, in particular, of the human progeny; and Eve, as the female procreator, becomes *ipso facto* some kind of *paredros* for Yhwh.[96] Inasmuch as she is the woman par excellence, her mothering is paradigmatic and inaugurates all women's unequaled glory, according to J. No biblical author went that far in the proclamation of a "feminist" program. The co-creation with God by "bringing forth" life is *not* the prerogative of the mother-goddess—as in Ugarit, where the same verb *qanah* is used to designate her mothering of the gods—but the one of the human mother, of all the human mothers.[97]

95. Bloom, one recalls, understands Eve's exclamation in Gen 4:1 as "an ironic, narcissistic mistake on her part."

96. Clearly, the eclipse of the father runs in favor of the mother. Eve says that she has created "a man," for her domination over the child continues only until "it grows into a man or a woman, a new and complete person . . . . There is no intenser form of power"; Canetti, *Crowds and Power*, 222. Rank's interpretation of Eve as the wife of the sky-god Yhwh goes too far, but is not without some foundation ("Völkerpsychologische Parallelen," 43–81). Note the parallel in the "Infancy Gospel" about the non-role of Joseph in the birth of the "Son of Man."

97. J's implicit polemics against the fertility religions, according to Gardner ("Genesis 2.4b–3: A Mythological Paradigm of Sexuality or of the Religious History of Pre-exilic Israel?" esp. 14), is conspicuous in Genesis 3's statement that Yhwh, not the goddess, controls women's fertility. A Deutero-Pauline passage in the New Testament in 1 Tim 2:15, says that woman "will be saved through childbearing," which is not an abusive restriction of the woman's social and religious role but, on the contrary, the reiteration, after Gen 3:20 and 4:1, of her unique and incomparable glory as co-creator—quite a distance from Pandora (see Hesiod *Works and Days* 100; *Theogony* 585–92). From this perspective, we better understand the despair of biblical women when deprived of progeny ("Give

About the verb *qanah*, let us note its rich meaning in Hebrew. For *qanah* with the sense of to create, see Deut 32:6; Ps 139:13. [98] John Van Seters finds here a perfect correspondence with a late version of the Babylonian myth called *Marduk's Creation*: the goddess Aruru declares having created "the seed of humankind together with him [Marduk]."[99] In my judgment, the correspondence is only approximate.

As regards the difficult construction of the phrase with the Hebrew preposition *'eth*, the latter simply means "with," like in so many other texts (see Gen 14:8; 17:4; 2 Sam 16:17, etc.). Eve exclaims, "I have [co-] created a man [*'iš*] with Yhwh." There is no syntactic reason to look for an inexistent grammatical dilemma, as do so many exegetes of this text. In fact, the translators' reluctance to render literally the Hebrew formulation is due, I think, to a misunderstanding of the *metaphorical* language so characteristic of biblical discourse. Traditional rhetoric has imposed the idea that reality must be expressed in a univocal way, and it considers the metaphor as "ornamental" only. Yet, metaphor is plurivocal and is the principal language in the Bible; it leaves open a wide margin of interpreta-

---

me children, or I shall die!" Rachel says in Gen 30:1). In Gen 2:22, the verb "build" is used: frequent in ancient myths of creation but rare in the Bible, it appears in a transitive form solely in Amos 9:6, and in the passive form (*nibeneh*) in Gen 16:2; 30:3. The idea in these texts is that making a woman have children is to "build" her. Rilke once wrote, "The artist's task is to discover himself. The woman's fulfillment is in the child" (*Tagebücher aus der Frühzeit*, 118–19). On the J's process of de-mythologization, see also the familial rivalry between Cain and Abel occurring on earth, not "in the underworld (Nergal–Ereshkigal–Ishtar) or in heaven, as in the Egyptian tale 'The Contending of Horus and Seth'"; Damrosch, *The Narrative Covenant*, 124–25. Similarly, the mention in 4:11 of the ground's mouth, that is, the Sheol's, is to be contrasted with the mythological god of Death, Mot, Maweth. See also the human invention of arts and crafts in Gen 4:17ff., whereas in Mesopotamia, their origins go back to the gods (see Castellino, "The Origins of Civilization," 93); in Ugarit the god Kathar wa-Ḥasis is the patron saint of the metalworkers. In Genesis 4, however, metalworking is inaugurated by human beings.

98. *Qanithi* may either mean "to produce, to create" (see esp. Deut 32:6; Ps 139:13; see Gen 14:19, 22; Prov 8:22; contrast with Gen 5:3) or "to buy, to acquire" (see Gen 25:10; 33:19). See Paul Humbert, "*Qânâ'* en hébreu biblique." Philo says that Cain had been *bought* by his mother and God had been utilized in the process (see references above). The Gaon of Vilna (eighteenth century) stresses this statement of Eve regarding her "acquisition," which he understands as identification, "I have acquired for myself"; see Shapiro, ed., *The Gaon of Vilna's Adereth Eliahu*. The irony is that the one who was called "acquisition" or "substantial" lost his face, while the one whose name is "breath" ("nothingness" as Josephus says, see *Ant.* 1:54) prevailed over his brother. Some scholars appeal to the Akkadian *ablu/aplu* = son, as a generic term for "mankind" (like Adam; Enosh); see Hicks, "Abel," 4.

99. Van Seters, *Prologue to History*, 123–24.

tion. In Genesis 4, we find again the metaphorical discourse in v. 9 where Cain rejects the idea that he be the "keeper" of Abel. Furthermore, the language throughout is metaphorical when speaking of God's sentiments, speeches, and interventions (see vv. 4–7, 9–11, 15). Indeed, all theological discourse—and, in a certain sense, all complex language—is by necessity metaphorical, that is, a discourse with an indirect intent or, as Paul Ricoeur says, with "a surplus of meaning," for all such communication both expresses and veils its object and is "polyglossic" (Bakhtin).

The primordial mother is a human being rather than a goddess, but her most powerful desire is now fulfilled: she is "like God" (see 3:5). While her former disobedience led her, not to bliss but to exile (3:23–24), the birth of Cain is a homecoming. Eden again. Eve returns home, close to God, *with* God (*'eth Yhwh*), says 4:1.

The Oedipal Cain

Eve says that she has brought forth a man (*'iš*), and the word is totally unexpected for describing a baby. With Ilana Pardes, we should be sensitive to Eve reversing here the thrust of the man's discourse in 2:23 [J]. In the latter text, Adam exclaimed, "she shall be called woman (*'iššah*), because she was taken from a man (*'iš*)." Now, Eve retorts, "I have made a man [*'iš*]" (who, therefore, is not taken from man, but from woman). [100]

It is to be noted that J had used the word *'iš* in Gen 2:23, where it designates the male side of the human being (*'adam*). Together with the female side (*'iššah*), Adam achieved the plenitude of an anthropological entity. Now, in Gen 4:1, Eve proclaims that she has brought forth the *'iš* as intended by the Creator in the first place. By this, she comes with an exorbitant claim:[101] her son is not only "promising," he is the very achievement of Yhwh's creation. This, by the way, explains why Adam, the first *'iš*—of whom Eve is the *'iššah*—is bypassed in the narrative. He is not even acknowledged by name, but is just *ha-'adam* (a generic term) and serves the

100. Pardes, "Beyond Genesis 3." Commenting on Gen 4:1, where Eve exclaims after her first maternity, "I have acquired a man," *Gen. Rab.* 22.2 says that here "man" refers to Adam: "behold my husband is now in my possession!" At the end of the chiastic story of Genesis 4, Seth, the "man" that Eve engenders, himself sires an *'enoš* (man) and Seth *calls* the child by that name (4:26), while the instrumental "Yhwh" of 4:1 is also *called* and becomes the titular Yhwh of the *Heilsgeschichte*.

101. Neher sees in Eve's statement the "sin made explicit." It consists in utilizing God as a means instead of acknowledging that he is the cause of everything; Lecture at the University of Strasbourg, Sept. 1956); see 29 n. 38 above.

sole purpose of begetting the child—the child who will substitute for him in Eve's eyes. But, if Cain is as it were the "eschatological" 'iš, who is his 'iššah? Could it be his own mother Eve?

Contrasting with Cain's "creation," Eve salutes the birth of her son Seth in 4:25 in a very different way. She now refrains from stressing her part in the new event but rather attributes it solely to God.[102] It behooves us at this point to remember the Philonic point that the children of the promise are shown in the texts as coming directly from God. (We shall note also, by contrast, the promotion of sorts of ha-'adam in 4:1 to Adam as a proper name in 4:25.)

Thus, Eve occupies a central position in both the myth of "Adam and Eve" in Genesis 2–3, and of "Cain and Abel" in Genesis 4. In fact, she is the cementing element that "glues" the two stories and makes them one, so that it is ungrounded to separate them but for the sake of scholarly analysis.[103] It is not a surprising elucidation, therefore, when the text of Gen 4:3 says that Cain came with his offer miqqeṣ yamim, "after some time," for the Hebrew expression "describes a continuation of the event, never a beginning," says Westermann.[104] It serves as a hinge binding the preceding narrative on the human transgression of God's command, and the following development on Cain's fratricide. Thus, it does not introduce a beginning per se, but it definitely announces the expiration of a transitional era between two catastrophes.

Moreover, there is an uncanny parallel between 4:1 and 2:7 about the "collaboration" between God and the ground (the 'adamah) in the creation of Adam.[105] The tally of these two J texts shows Eve substituting for the earth in begetting Cain. To wit, the parallel between the earth and the feminine is universally found. In Genesis, the earth is "fecundated" by Yhwh to create Adam; Eve is "fecundated" by Yhwh to create the first 'iš. Eve in lieu of the 'adamah implies that when Cain's link with the 'adamah is broken (4:11), it is also broken with his mother (see 4:25). There occurs,

102. On this, see also Hirsch, Genesis.

103. In my book The Trial of Innocence, on the story of Adam and Eve, I make clear that I am dealing only with a fragment of a complete work by J. Brueggemann calls the movement from Genesis 2–3 to 4 a "move from a vertical crisis to a horizontal temptation"; Genesis, 55.

104. Westermann, Genesis 1–11, 294.

105. As L'Heureux writes, "There is an intrinsic relationship between the human creature and the ground from which it comes, a relationship which, ideally, should result in mutuality and harmony"; In and Out of Paradise, 12.

in other words, a breach between Cain and the feminine. Even when Cain begets a son, it is with an anonymous woman, in sharp contrast to his own birth that conjugated the divine and the feminine (4:1). From the outset, there is between the 'iš Cain and woman (Eve or the earth) an ambiguous relation. This needs further examination.

A number of readers of the myth of Cain and Abel find puzzling the selective absence of God during the clash between the two brothers, but do not seem to be sensitive to another perhaps more troubling absence, namely of Cain and Abel's father, the upholder of the law, whose role implies also the adjudication of justice between the members of the group. In fact Cain claims for himself a "fatherly" omnipotence, and no one in his family challenges him. That is why God has eventually to intervene *instead of Adam*. Thus, the story is less about the eclipse of God than of Adam the representative of humankind.[106] Already in the preceding myth, on Adam and Eve, the role of Adam in the scene of the temptation was so minimal as to be almost insignificant (see Gen 3:6, Adam was "with her [Eve] and he ate").

What are we to do with this utter failure of fatherhood? Is there, perhaps, some kind of reminiscence of a mythical matriarchal line, as exemplified in ancient Greece by Gaia?[107] The parallelism with Greek mythology may even take us one step further. In the legend of "Oedipus Rex," the elimination of the father Laius leaves mother and son facing each other—with delight, and then with horror when a third party is introduced in the person of Tiresias, Creon, or the shepherd-witness. Oedipus kills his father and unites with his mother, thus claiming to be born from one, not from two—or even perhaps born from himself?

In the Cain and Abel myth, it seems clear that Cain has replaced Adam in Eve's dedication (something like this will again occur in the relation of Rachel with her son Jacob instead of with her husband Isaac). There is a primal insularity of mother and son. It is disturbed by the birth of Abel, changing as it does the duo into a triangle in which Abel is made the unwitting witness of the (inchoate) crime of an incestuous relationship.[108] Abel's subjective disruption—which is also an objective return to

106. As Malbim says, the definite article that accompanies "Adam" in 4:1 ("the 'adam knew his wife") shows that he "is the whole humanity."

107. See also the mention above of the Ugaritic mother-goddess mothering all the gods of the pantheon.

108. Significantly, Thornton Wilder (*The Skin of Our Teeth*), has "Mrs. Antrobus"

sanity and order—is subtly forecast by his birth not being attributed by
the mother to divine paternity (as was Cain's), but set under the shadow
of his elder brother, as if Abel's life were accidental and subsidiary: "She
bore also his brother Abel" (4:2). Besides, while Cain as a name is given a
(popular) etymology, Abel lacks one in the text as if he was not important
enough to bother with invoking upon him a programmatic hope. From
the outset, Abel is the intruder. If there is later on an apparent divine
favoritism as regards the sacrifice of Abel, it has been preceded by Eve's
appalling rejection of her baby in favor of Cain, a feigned ignorance motivated by an undisclosable reason.[109]

But Abel in a potent way is to Cain a father-substitute, the unwelcome
presence of paternity, divine or human. For "a brother also is a reminder
of contingency, as the universal reaction of young children to siblings
shows," says Herbert Schneidau.[110] Abel's elimination is to be spliced with
the eclipse of Adam. Cain, like Oedipus, wishes to be his own genitor; he
wants to abstract himself from the contingent, to be autonomous.

Oedipus, the murderer of his father, goes into exile, and Jocasta has
lost both her husband Laius and her son (her son-husband). Similarly,
when Cain kills his brother Abel, he goes into exile, and Eve has lost
both of her sons. The auto-generic incest has come to a tragic dissolution. Jocasta commits suicide; but Eve's fire produces a last spark: "she
bore a son and named him Seth [meaning: "set, appoint"] for she said,
'God has set for me another son *instead of Abel, whom Cain killed*'" (4:25).
Noteworthy is that, in the beginning and at the end of the tale, Eve fills a
role of interpreter, and her interpretation is consistently narcissistic. From
her point of view, the whole drama turns around her, an indication that

---

(= Eve) doting over Henry (= Cain) even after he killed his brother. Further, Henry tries
to destroy every achievement of his father (such as the wheel, the alphabet, the lever)!
The rivalry between father and son goes so far as to have Antrobus (Adam) being ready
to gun down Henry (Cain) and to have Henry try to strangle his father (Act 3). Antrobus
says to Henry, "I shall continue fighting you until my last breath . . . I shall pursue you to
the far corners of the earth" (129).

109. Van Wolde ("The Story of Cain and Abel", 39) says of Abel, "He is . . . never
[referred to] as a person in his own right, with a value of his own." Note that, in the
genealogy of Cain at the end of Genesis 4, there is an uncanny parallel in v. 11: Jabal's
brother's birth is reported in the words, "And his brother's name was Jubal"—it runs in
the family!

110. Schneidau, *Sacred Discontent*, 244.

unwittingly she considers herself as the prize of the competition. To no avail, for after 4:25, Eve entirely disappears from the Hebrew Bible.[111]

In the Field

It is worth our while to compare how J treats the problem of evil in Genesis 3 and 4, and beyond. First, it is remarkable that J never comes with a definition of evil in the eleven chapters of Genesis dedicated to primeval time, while nonetheless dealing with nothing but this subject matter. In the Adam and Eve tale, he shows that the root of evil is human hubris. In the Cain and Abel narrative, the human sin becomes envy and violence. In Genesis 6, sin is confusion of categories. In Genesis 6–9, we return to violence and in Genesis 11 to hubris. This ABCBA construction is very powerful. Evil throughout is strictly in the realm of ethics; it never deviates to the ritual and the magical. This makes the contrast to other Near Eastern myths of origin as stark as can be. True, the ritual is not out of place here, but only as catalyst of a human existential ethos. While in the history of religion, the altar and sacrifice belong to a process of microcosmization, in Genesis 2–11, sacrifice is less a mirror of the cosmos than of the human soul.

So, whether evil is hubris as in Genesis 2–3 or brutality as in Genesis 4—and even when it is described as a shrewd pouncing animal, which is a way to state that evil is always already there—it is an "enemy within." It belongs to the realm of human capability and its origin cannot be blamed on an external element, the societal environment for example, or the State.[112]

Indicating premeditation to murder, Cain leads Abel to his own turf: the field (4:8).[113] No doubt, Cain would feel estranged in the pasture, but Abel does not feel estranged in the field. The sentiment of estrangement

---

111. Significantly, the *Genesis Rabbah* (fifth century) on Gen 4:8 reports the saying of Judah ben Rabbi, "their rivalry was about the first Eve." Another conception is R. Huna's who states that the rivalry was about a twin-sister of Abel. In *PRE*, "the field" refers to a woman, that is, Abel's twin-sister and wife. The same idea may be in the background of *Jubilees* 4. Josephus says that Cain is the embodiment of greed; *Ant.* 1:52–66.

112. Rousseau wrote, "It is the spirit of society alone, and the inequality it engenders, which thus change and alter all our natural inclinations"; *The First and Second Discourses*, 180; such a wrong stance has been adopted by Marxists.

113. Contrary to Kass's opinion (expressed in *The Beginning of Wisdom*, 141 n. 25), śadeh means an (open) field; so already in Akkadian, Phoenician, and Ugaritic. In the Bible, see Josh 21:12 (//1 Chr 6:41); Judg 20:6; 2 Sam 9:7; 19:30. Qoheleth 5:8 specifies that the śadeh is cultivated.

has much to do with the discrimination between good and evil, and with the feeling of alienation (from the good). Here in 4:8, the environment is favorable to Cain. It cannot be blamed for causing his fit of rage. On the contrary, he should feel at ease and at peace. But his brother's presence makes him uncomfortable and alienates him from his own land. Before being later banned by God, Cain is already like a "wanderer" in his own domain. He was ready to say something to his brother, but he can't speak! Words could not express his overpowering feelings, only blows will do.

The absence of Cain's discourse to his brother in 4:8 is, of course, puzzling. In general, commentators see in this gap a sign that the text was tampered with in the process of its transmission. But, such a "solution" reveals a misunderstanding of the biblical *langue*. Contrary to modern expectation that a composition be complete and well-rounded, the biblical text, in the image of the whole creation as it conceives it, begs for interpretation. The text is therefore co-created by its composer and its interpreters. Without interpretation, it resembles the consonantal Masoretic non-vocalized writing before it is read aloud. Biblical literalism amounts to a little more than zero (as even literalists must by necessity use a minimal interpreting).

As it now stands, Gen 4:8 tantalizingly invites the reader to fill the vacuum with something that is now missing. Genesis versions in Aramaic, Syriac, Greek, Latin, have added the expected words, "Let's go to the fields." More interestingly—although no better textually grounded—the Midrash, to recall, reads the word *field* as designating Abel's wife. Cain kills Abel to take his wife, that is, either a twin sister of Abel, or Eve [!]; the story then resembles the adultery of David with Bathsheba.[114]

In fact, the absence of discourse after "and he said" is not unique in the Bible. Both Ibn Ezra (twelfth century) and David Qimchi[115] refer to Exod 19:25 where the same situation obtains, and say that what is implied here and there is what precedes "and he said" (*wayyomer*): Cain reports to Abel what God had told him.

No such gap-plugging is retained by scholars, as they rather opt for an accident in the text copying. But what if it is not so? We may then see here what psychoanalysis calls "repression," which, according to Norman O. Brown, is the very key word of Freudian thought.[116] In such a context,

114. See *PRE* 21 (the opinion of R. Zaddok).
115. Also called Redaq (twelfth–thirteenth century) and so designated hereafter.
116. N. O. Brown, *Life against Death*, 3–5.

it is interesting to note that Cain eventually inaugurates the urban life, that is, according to the later Freud, the deliberate imposition of self-repression through culture and society.[117]

Beyond the purview of the biblical texts, the abruptness of the textual break in Gen 4:8 makes one think of the mid-verse narrative interruption in *Odyssey* 13.187 (about the Phaeacians' sacrifice to Poseidon). I mention this classic parallel because the issue for the critic in the *Odyssey* is akin with our problem in Genesis 4. Gregory Nagy, who discusses the conflicting versions about the Phaeacians' fate after the sacrifice, raises the fundamental question that is also valid for the story of Cain and Abel: Is Homer's poetry "merely a static text," or do "we view Homer's poetry as a living system," in which case there is no need "to choose whenever we see a variation"—for instance, for us, between the LXX with other versions and the MT of Gen 4:8.[118]

As it now stands, the gapping presents the advantage of precipitating the course of action. It is perhaps also suggesting "the deceptive nature of Cain's actions" by having the latter "whisper" in the ear of his brother.[119] We can also imagine that the silence, which here replaces the serpent's enticement in Genesis 3, meant something like the silence that prevails between Priam and Achilles at the end of the *Iliad* epic, when "both remembered . . . ." Cain's silence is similarly heavy with the mental din of conflicting sentiments unable to come to expression. But, in Cain's case, those feelings are hatched by rage and murderous impulse, while in the killing machine Achilles, rage and murder at last have subsided.[120] He discovers in himself with Priam, the enemy until a moment ago, an ineffable fraternity.

At this point, the two stories are uncannily parallel and antithetic, since Cain's speechlessness happens before the enormity of what he dares feel and intent: the severance of one of the most sacred physical and spiritual bonds, and the destruction of the reflection of his own image. Following a central principle in the Bible, Cain's subsequent silence after God's remonstrance (4:16) does mirror his initial silence when he

117. Ibid., 9; and Freud, *Civilization*, 141.

118. Nagy, "Reading Bakhtin Reading the Classics."

119. See McEntire, *The Blood of Abel*, 23.

120. It seems that for Plutarch *orgē* (ire) with added power becomes *phonos* [murder] (in *Ad principem ineruditum* 6, cited by Harris, *Restraining Rage*, 62). Already Aristotle had made a distinction of anger from hatred "by the very ephemeral nature of the feeling" says Gaylin in *Hatred*, 35. See Aristotle *Rhetoric* II.4:1389.

planned to say something to Abel and balked lest the excessiveness of his words betray the excess of his sentiments.[121]

The silence of murderous Cain is stressed by the verb "he said." Without it, we would not even know about the silence itself. But now it "shouts" for our attention. Another notable text on the theme of silence is 1 Kings 19: There God is not present in the grand natural and cosmic storms, but in a "sound of a light silence." Cain's heavy silence is of another kind, of course; it is as ominous and lethal as God's epiphany to Elijah is soothing and enlivening. Cain's is an aborted discourse that would be shameful to broadcast; God's is pregnant with the Word. The latter is entrusted to a prophet who will spread it loud and clear.

In short, the gap in the text of v. 8 is food for thought. For, whatever may be the suggestion of the literary critics to explain the gap in Gen 4:8, it so happens that, in the text as extant, the act of murder appears as appallingly simple, something like the "banality of evil" Hannah Arendt spoke about.[122] This very simplicity has the intended effect of showing that,

> Evil is not an aberration—a failure—in a world otherwise ordered
> by reason. Rather, it is an effort to make the world anew, to create
> meaning on a new basis. That new world—the world of evil—is
> one in which death is projected onto another.[123]

"And he said": suspension points! He opened his mouth to speak but said nothing, for, as Canetti states, "People become silent when they fear transformation."[124] Besides, there was no way that Cain could be shown as carrying the *logos*, that is, what is "man's primordial state, which is word, discourse, and reason."[125] As rhetoric is the art of persuasion, Cain's

---

121. See Bespaloff's essay "On the Iliad." She praises the moderation of Homer in describing excess (78).

122. Arendt, *Eichmann in Jerusalem*.

123. Kahn, *Out of Eden*, 11.

124. Canetti, *Crowds and Power*, 294.

125. Ricoeur, *History and Truth*, 257 (= *Histoire et Vérité*, 270). Audet, in turn, says, "By and large, it is tradition, mostly propped by language, which sets us free"; "La Revanche de Prométhée," 11, my trans.). Cain as tradition-killer could not speak to the brother he intended to murder. Philosophically and psychologically speaking, what sterilizes dialogue is called "relativism." For, as Bakhtin says, relativism makes dialogue "unnecessary" (as all stances are equally valid anyway). Cain's relativism is flagrant in his absence of judgment on his own offering. Such relativism is well documented in the below-mentioned Midrash on the disputation between the brothers as to whether there is such thing as justice (see below on the Targum and note 137). Strikingly, Bakhtin describes such an attitude as *tsennostnaia-pustota* ("value wilderness" or "axiological

attempt at speaking to his brother is aborted as he realizes that his point is not to persuade Abel (of what?), but to eliminate competition. Doing this, of course, Cain isolates himself from the human community (God's speech to him will merely spell out a *fait accompli*) for, as Paul Kahn says, "there is no speech apart from a community of speakers."[126]

When all is said and done, whatever Cain may have actually said according to an "original" version of the tale, it could never have been as profound as the present silence, perhaps due to an accident in the text transmission—*felix casus*!

It is not by chance that J traces a logical sequence starting with Cain's incapability of speech with his brother Abel, via Cain's recourse to a mendacious discourse with God in which he denies knowing Abel's whereabouts, to finally becoming a "political animal" in a city whose name is an oxymoron and a lie, Nod, the city of No-City, the dwelling of No-Dwelling. Cain is the man of mendacity. He is the builder of the first political entity, its inaugurator (*hanokh*), that is, the initiator of a discourse based on what Plato calls "flattery," which in turn is "the art of inducing persuasion by means other than the truth."[127] The moment Cain kills Abel, his "id" (*das Es*) does take over. The "id," says Freud, is "a chaos." "It . . . has no organization, produces no collective will."[128] In short, Cain becomes incoherent. In this sense, God's exhortation to Cain is to "sublimate" his energy.[129]

Thus, Cain as a character is not permitted to master the *logos*. For if his later statement "I do not know" is not a pure lie, then it is a *Verneinung* (a negation), that is, a repressed idea that is not permitted to reach consciousness.[130]

We may think of the "as-if-it-had-never-occurred" calm and harmony between parents and child after the latter's chiding. The human

---

desert," an expression which designates a "merely physical world," as Clark and Holquist say in *Mikhail Bakhtin*, 75.

126. Kahn, *Out of Eden*, 41.

127. Ricoeur, *History and Truth*, 257.

128. Freud, *New Introductory Lectures* 1933 (= *SE* xxii), 73.

129. Freud, *The Ego and the Id*, 1923 (= *SE* xix), 3, 46.

130. See Freud, "Negation" 1925 (= *SE* xix), 235. Jung said, "Believing one's lies when the wish is father to the lie is a well-known hysterical symptom" ("After the Catastrophe" in *Jung and Evil*, 191; see also 188). Gandhi said that lying is "the mother of violence"; *Essential Writings*, 104. But at least this move by Cain saves him from *ressentiment*; see Scheler, *Ressentiment*, 29–31. Cain is not Haman.

capacity of psychological blocking is indeed arresting. Cain's response is typically narcissistic. As Erich Fromm writes,

> If he [the narcissistic person] is the world, there is no world out-
> side which can frighten him . . . . When the one protection against
> his fright, his self-inflation, is threatened, the fright emerges and
> results in intense fury. This fury is all the more intense because
> nothing can be done to diminish the threat by appropriate action:
> only the destruction of the critic—or oneself—can save one from
> the threat to one's narcissistic security.[131]

Along this line, earlier in the story, Cain displayed a characteristic depression; his ego collapsed ("Why is your countenance down?" Gen 4:6). Cain's conclusion that his offering—his *oeuvre*—was refused has triggered in him the feeling of his finitude. His reaction that eventuates in fratricide may appear to some as exaggerated, but we are reminded by Ernest Becker that the human primary repression is precisely the denial of our finitude. For Becker, evil is the outcome of our existential frustration of needs.[132] In other words, Cain sees himself as the victim, hence, when God demands his reckoning after the murder, his response ("Am I my brother's keeper?") reveals his shock: my brother is not the victim, I am!

What expectedly follows is Cain's attempt at escaping God, who here plays a role comparable to the super-ego in psychoanalysis. Yet, with-drawn into his denial, Cain will be unable to totally silence the voice of God—and to forget the divine sign of presence stamped upon him.

Freud had come to the conclusion that a certain sense of guilt may *precede* the perpetration of the crime, "and is therefore not its result but its motive. It is as if it was a relief to be able to fasten this unconscious sense of guilt on to something real and immediate."[133] I believe that this is readily applicable to Cain as it explains the temporary gap between the warning he gets from God in 4:6–7 and the actual homicide in 4:8.

We may speak of a preceding sense of guilt, for Cain's feelings toward Abel are not unalloyed. Rather they are "ambivalent," a term of psycho-analysis that describes "a battle between love and hate."[134] Had Cain not

131. Fromm, *The Heart of Man*, 75.
132. See Becker, *The Denial of Death*; *Escape from Evil*; and *The Birth and Death of Meaning* (see 44 n. 91).
133. Freud, *The Ego and the Id*, 1923 (= SE xix), 52.
134. Freud, "Notes upon a case of obsessional neurosis" 1909 (= SE x), 191. Amos Oz reminds us that "Thomas Mann wrote somewhere that hatred is merely love with a minus sign attached to it"; *Under This Blazing Light*, 163. Gaylin says, "Hatred . . . requires

spoken at all to his brother, the ambivalence principle would have remained unexpressed. Fundamentally speaking, Cain's ambivalent feelings are directed toward God (who, he believes, has refused his offering). But, as is usual in the case of phobia, he displaces one of the components, hate, toward a scapegoat, his brother Abel. In psychoanalysis this deviation of anger is called "displaced aggression," that is, the redirection of the rage to a substitute target less threatening than the original one. As Willard Gaylin so perspicaciously states, "The 'cause' does not generate the rage. The rage demands locating a cause."[135]

Interestingly, jealousy is also called the *Cain's complex* in psychology. In an adult, it is recognized as a sequel of the infant's oedipal possession of its mother. For the young child, as is well known, all persons sharing the mother's care are usurpers. A case in point for our present study is the "jealous paranoid" ones who feel abandoned and humiliated. They readily project upon their beloved companion their self-hatred and may go so far as to kill him/her.[136] They are impervious to reasonable exhortation. Cain, of course, fits the bill perfectly. His aborted speech "in the field" speaks volumes.

Cain is not just the type of the jealous man like Othello; he is also the reemergence of his parents' shame reported in Genesis 3. Not being recognized at a crucial time, namely, after the episode of the offerings, he finds himself drawn to face his own finitude, a consciousness that produces shame. His sacrifice is a "flop" (while the sacrifice of someone else is "successful") and he realizes that his failure is a mirror and a foretaste of his mortality. Death is the ultimate failure. It can be transcended

---

an attachment to the hated person or population"; *Hatred*, 28. But hatred, he continues, "is a psychological disorder—a form of quasi-delusional thinking. It is designed to allow the angry and frustrated individual to disallow responsibility for his own failures and misery, by directing it towards a convenient victim" (dust cover of *Hatred*). Eigen, in his turn, sates, "Rage is partly a special hope for intimacy"; *Rage*, 35.

135. Gaylin, *Hatred*, 136. Of course, there is aggression and aggression, that is, an aggression for the well-being of the organism (e.g. eating) that fights for self-preservation. The other type of aggression is sadistic, that is, a neurotic reaction of the weak and insecure (Adler) at the expense of a scapegoat. Earlier in his book (99), Gaylin had come with the accurate definition of the scapegoated, namely, "a neutral person or group . . . with whom one can be angry without fear of the consequences"; see also Canetti, *Crowds and Power*, 49. Note that Cain later fears becoming a scapegoat to "everyone." God protects him with a sign to the effect that there would be "consequences" in doing so to Cain.

136. The French film "L'Enfer" provides a graphic example, directed by Claude Chabrol, 1994.

either by love or by murder. Loving is "doing well," murdering is "not doing well," but at least with the illusion of "passing the buck" to someone else. By killing Abel, Cain thought of grasping life for himself, "You die, I live!" Freud saw in sadism the transformation of the death instinct into the desire to kill.[137] The outcome, nevertheless, is the reverse of the one dreamed. Cain is excluded from the company of the living. He roams the desert as a "brother of jackals and a companion of ostriches" (Job 30:29), like the man "possessed by an unclean spirit" in the Gospel (Mark 5:1–16). The pattern culpability—*poena* goes beyond the judiciary, for the fact—which constitutes a major triumph of hope for humanity—is that "[e]vil bears within itself its own contradictions and in them the seeds of its own destruction."[138]

Cain's "denial of death" is already evident in his response to God's query in 4:9, "I do not know." His denial of responsibility reflects a willful psychological blockage: he does not want to know, that is, to remember what he did. That would take him to reflect on the appalling death.[139] Abel's death is the sacrificial substitute for his own death. Symbolically one death obliterates the other. One for another maintains the status quo. "I don't know what you are talking about, God. If an account must be kept of life and death, *you* keep it, for am *I* my brother's keeper?" If Cain were, there would be no substitution for his shame unto death.

137. What a stroke of genius on the part of J to start his story with the brothers' sacrifices! From the outset, the issue is one of death denial. See Freud, *Collected Papers*, 2:256. Along a comparable line of thought, Nietzsche spoke of the "will" as "essentially the affect of superiority in relation to him who must obey: "I am free, 'he' must obey"; *Beyond Good and Evil*, 25. Canetti states, "The lowest form of survival is killing"; *Crowds and Power*, 227. We remember that some members of the Bundsen family (Addie and her son, Jewel) feel alive only through violence (Faulkner, *As I Lay Dying*). There is perhaps a relationship to Cain: an act of violence to achieve awareness.

138. Ortiz-Hill, *The Roots and Flowers of Evil in Baudelaire, Nietzsche, and Hitler*, xvii. Baudelaire, one may recall, speaks in *Les Fleurs du mal* of a familiar demon that, like the very air he breathes, burns his insides. It takes him "far from God's face" to "the deep and barren plains of Ennui . . ."; *Baudelaire, Oeuvres Complètes*, "La Destruction," 105). In another "fleur," Baudelaire exhorts Cain to "go up to heaven and throw God from there to the earth"; "Abel et Cain"; ibid, 116).

139. Cain's alleged "unfreedom of the will" is, as Nietzsche rightly said, a wish "not to be answerable for anything, and owing to an inward self-contempt, seek[ing] to *lay blame for themselves somewhere else*" (*Beyond Good and Evil*, 29). We shall contrast this with the legend about Rabbi Suszia who is said to have carried as his own all the sins of those he met. So Rabbi Israel of Rizhyn said, "And if all of us were like him, evil would long since have been destroyed, and death overcome, and perfection achieved"; Buber, *The Tales of the Hasidim, The Early Masters*, 237.

In a way, in the image of the partial success of the serpent in Genesis 3, Cain's rage also is in part successful. After God's disregard for his offering and the collapse of his countenance, he has won God's attention. God speaks to him. He is not an object but a recognized subject. "If you do well" in God's mouth should restore his pride and lift up his self-respect.[140] That it does not is a sign of obstinacy: Cain morbidly wallows in his shame. Only blood, he thinks, can wash it out. The choice of violence instead of repentance and humility characterizes Cain and his line, down to Lamech and beyond. After Cain, "if you do well" remains historically by and large a rejected possibility. And even the present "Abels" are not without blemish; in the image perhaps of the first Abel?

For there is perhaps another dimension to the textual gap left by the text in 4:8. *Targum Pseudo-Jonathan* fills the gap imaginatively: After the "rejection" of his sacrifice, Cain says to Abel that there is no justice and no judge. Abel adds insult to injury by affirming divine justice.[141] This alleged conversation, of course, could be thought of as no more substantial than a simple marginal anecdote without real textual basis. But the midrashic construction is not innocent. For one reason or another, *Targum Pseudo-Jonathan* raises suspicion in the reader about the assumed impeccability of Abel and, more importantly, about the rationale behind Abel's offering in the first place. In which case, some aspects of the biblical text in Gen 4:3–4 need reevaluation. To wit, the very sequence of events is perhaps a clue not to be missed. First comes Cain with an offering unto Yhwh. But, in the wake of this and with a striking emphasis, v. 4 tells us of Abel, that *he also* brought a *minhah*. A second arresting element concerns the ingredients of Abel's offering: they are taken from "from the firstlings of his flock" (*bekoroth s'ono*). Now, the word for "firstlings" happens to be of the same stem that designates "the right of the first-born" (*ha-bekor* and *mišpat ha-bekorah*; see Deut 21:17). In the Israelite legal system, the firstborn among humans and animals, as well as the first fruits, belong to God. The firstborn sons must be sacrificially redeemed through an offering of a lamb (see Exod 13:13; see further Neh 10:36–37).

My point is that Abel here may not be simply imitating his elder brother. At the very least, Cain had some ground to construe Abel's move

---

140. Remarkably, God appears to have changed tactics since the preceding story. There, God gave a command; here he resorts to a question, "Why?" and to a dilemma, "If . . . and if not . . ." (4:6–7).

141. See Ginzberg, *The Legends of the Jews*, 1:108.

as an overstepping of his status of second-born son. For normally, offering the sacrifice is the prerogative and the duty of the first-born son, as he only is the full representative of the *paterfamilias*, who, *ex officio*, performs the ritual. As an illustration, J shows the patriarchs offering sacrifices (Gen 8:20; 15:9–10; 22:1–14). Before the institution of the priesthood—which is evidently the case during the ostensible primal time of the story of Cain and Abel—the sacrificer is the head of the family. He is invested with authority, which he transmits to the first-born in the form of a special benediction (see Gen 27:29, 37).

Cain is the firstborn and as such he belongs to God to whom he is *ipso facto* consecrated (Exod 13:2, 12; 34:19; Num 3:13; 8:16–17). The firstborn children will be substituted for by the Levites (who, by the way, are the ones who actually slaughter the animals according to Ezek 44:10–11 and 2 Chron 35:5–6). Because they belong to God, for instance, the elder sons are the selected victims in human holocausts (severely prohibited by the prophets, see Ezek 20:26; see Exod 13:13; 34:20). The basic principle is that they are endowed with the "might and prime" of their father's "strength" (Gen 49:3; Deut 21:17). That is why Cain becomes an agriculturalist like his father and inherits the family land,[142] while Abel, as the second-born son, naturally becomes the herder of sheep and goats and has no claim on the land. The first-born, says Johannes Pedersen, "has claims on the blessing of the father: it is his birthright."[143]

Abel, strictly speaking, may have had no business in offering a sacrifice after his brother had officiated as the family "priest." (Note here again the surprising eclipse of Adam before his death by his son.) Especially with the mention by J that "he also" did come with the *bekhoroth* (the firstlings) of his flock, such an ambiguous initiative of Abel invites the somewhat malevolent interpretation that he is claiming the birthright of his brother. And, of course, as in the famous case of the rivalry between Jacob and Esau, such claim of Abel's is bent on stirring Cain's jealousy or worse. All the more so in that God is said to agree—one way or the other—with Abel's "usurpation."[144]

---

142. Note the play of words having Cain binding himself (*'bd*, 4:2, 12) to the *'adamah* in the image of his father *'Adam*. But reckoning with the context, what could have been a happy succession becomes usurpation.

143. Pedersen, *Israel: Its Life and Culture*, 1:193.

144. Thus, the story is of a double usurpation!

Such is the background against which J comes with a subversive tenet that we find illustrated time and again in his tales: the birthright does not invariably belong to the first-born. Repetitively J emphasizes the transfer of the right to someone who is born later, so Japhet (Gen 9:18–27, rather than Ham); Isaac (Gen 21:9–10, rather than Ishmael); Jacob (Gen 27:19, 22, rather than Esau); Perez (Gen 38:27–30, rather than Zerah); Ephraim (Gen 48:14–19, rather than Manasseh); Joseph (Gen 49:3; 1 Chron 5:2, rather than Reuben); Judah (Gen 49:8, rather than his elder brothers).[145] Perhaps J was himself a later-born child to his parents, but more profoundly the reader is invited to reflect on the priority of the covenantal election over the natural accident. The "first-born" in the eyes of God is not always the "opener of the womb" (see Gen 29:31; 30:22; Exod 13:2, 12; 34:19). In other words, J destroys all natural determinism. True, the natural occurrence is a message and a pointer, but it is not the ultimate articulation of God's will. There is, in the parlance of Levinas, a "beyond essence." The becoming transforms the being.

In the story of Cain and Abel, things turned ugly. To the extent that Abel was occupying for a while the place of the first-born, his "primogeniture" was short-lived. Cain, after all, is not to be compared with Esau. He was the "possessor," as his name indicates, and he was not disposed to sell his birthright. Rather than conceding it to Abel—whose unwitting claim,[146] to recall, is backed up by God himself—he killed him, thus denying in a second move God's rights to prefer Abel's offering.

If what precedes here makes any sense and if we adopt for a while Cain's point of view, how does Abel come out as a character? Not less innocent and just, unless we should also condemn Isaac, Jacob, Joseph, and so forth. But Abel then appears to be a more complex personality than it seemed at first blush, something that does not surprise us coming under the pen of so fine a psychologist as is J. Abel is not without backbone; his innocence does not make him a moron, not any more than his parents' innocence in the Garden of Eden had made them ignoramuses. We do not have any detail of what happened "in the field," but chances are that

145. See above in chapter 1 the same idea underscored by Philo. Note that in all the occurrences involving the transfer of the primogeniture, reasons for God's selection are not given, as it has been the case here with the favor/ disfavor of the brothers' sacrifices.

146. There is no clue whatsoever in the text and in its "foreground" that the elements I have singled out to "explain" (but not excuse) Cain's reaction to Abel's sacrifice are more than coincidental.

Abel was not just passive. His martyrdom does not require any masochistic non-resistance on his part.

So, be that as it may of what precedes, the empty space left in the text extant of 4:8 after the announcement that Cain was about to speak, was respected by the traditionists to whom we owe the MT. The literary absence of discourse—of the Word—on the part of Cain reflects another absence: the eclipse of God. Falling in parallel with a similar phenomenon in Genesis 3, Cain's murder of Abel happens in a comparable vacuum. J's intent is clear. Mixing God and such disturbing situations was abhorrent.[147] As there is no coexistence of God and the serpent, there is no collusion of God and "sin," especially when the latter is murder. But the absence of God tells us more. It emphasizes J's conviction that the humans are endowed with free will. They are capable of discriminating between good and evil.[148] There is therefore no divine interference in the human options (but only in terms of a pressing invitation, see Gen 2:17). Cain had been told that much when God said to him: "*If you* do well . . . and *if you* do not do well . . . *you* must master." J's God is no puppeteer. Even the killer Cain is still respected as a human being by his Creator after "not doing well." Yhwh "put a trace on Cain" (4:15), the trace of His presence and of His regard.[149] God had done something similar in favor of Cain's parents, when He "made clothes of skins for Adam and his wife, and dressed them" (3:21).

Alienation

"Am I my brother's keeper?" (4:9). Cain's fundamental alienation is clearly expressed in this escapist answer to God's rhetorical question, "Where is your brother Abel?"[150] "The first [i. e., primordial] question," says Canetti,

147. In *The Blood of Abel* (chap. 2), McEntire notes the absence of Pharaoh in Exod 1:20–21, where God is the narrative subject [and] God is absent from vv. 11–14, where Pharaoh's people are the primary narrative subject" (38–39).

148. Aristotle in his *Politics* writes, "For this is special to men alone in relation to the other animals, having alone the awareness of good and bad, just and unjust, and the rest"; 1253a 3–19, quoted by Kass, *The Beginning*, 228. This Aristotelian statement finds a useful complement in Fromm's reflection on freedom as "acting on *the basis of the awareness of alternatives and their consequences*"; *The Heart of Man*, 145 (his emphasis).

149. In Ezek 9:4–9, the divine sign to provide protection is also given in a context of groaning, sighing, and bloodshed.

150. No longer "Where are you?" as in Gen 3:9, for "God's question is now raised from a social angle" (Vischer, *Jahwe: der Gott Kains*, 45. With Gerhard von Rad (ad loc.) we are struck by Cain's response that makes him harder in wickedness than the first

"concerns identity, the second is about place."[151] In God's question, both aspects are simultaneously present. Something like: "You are Cain for 'Abel [is] your brother.' Now, 'where is he?'" The questioner starts with elementary queries and, certainly, intends to pursue with more complex and searching questions. Cain, therefore, feels the need to cut short the dialogue with a question of his own. Answering a question with a question is, of course, a way to impede the questioning process. *It is also only possible between equals.* Cain's arrogance is self-evident. Cain's reply conveys a clear resentment of being supposed to take care of another one who is a brother but also a competitor in life. He says, "I do not know," and his denial is evasive and even cynical.[152] Biblically speaking, all "natural" or bloodline relationships demand a willful confirmation. Cain must decide whether Abel is his brother or his rival. No choice was easier to make. Abel was no unknown quantity to Cain. He obviously and uncontrovertibly was his younger brother, and his imitation of Cain's sacrifice was innocent.[153] Cain, however, chooses to disregard all this and, hence, relinquishes his "guardianship" and, indeed, his "brotherliness."[154] His lack of remorse shows that he keeps his grudge beyond the point of the crime perpetration—that finally has solved nothing. The act is premeditated and post-meditated.

Cain's ironic question to God may even hide an appeal to magic. He is blaming God because He is not manipulating history, even against him, Cain. God should have been the keeper of Abel. Here is another parallel with his father's reproach to God in Genesis 3, "The woman whom you gave to be with me . . ." (3:12). Both chapters are closely knit.[155] Genesis 3 tells about a crime against God; the chapter 4 about a crime against the fellow human. Such correspondence is again vividly illustrated in the

human couple in Genesis 3.

151. Canetti, *Crowds and Power*, 287.

152. See Bar-Efrat, *Narrative Art in the Bible*, 75; he draws a parallel with Ahimaaz's answer to David in 2 Sam 18:29.

153. Even within Cain's malevolent interpretation of his brother's sacrifice, it remained up to Cain to reclaim his birthright (to be "uplifted" says 4:7) by "doing well."

154. Kass is right in stressing the word "your brother" in God's response to Cain. "Am I my brother's keeper?" "*Your brother's* blood cries unto me"; *The Beginning of Wisdom*, 142. St. Augustine said (about Adam and Eve's transgression), "The unrighteousness of violating the prohibition was so much greater in proportion to the ease with which it could have been observed and fulfilled"; *Concerning the City of God*, 205.

155. See Fishbane, *Text and Texture*, 26–27; Hauser, "Linguistic and Thematic Links."

duality of the law tables (Exodus 20 [E] and Deuteronomy 5 [D]), with
the reverence due to God and to the neighbor.

Regina Schwarz draws another parallel, this time, expectedly, with
the story of Jacob and Esau. Esau also intends to kill his brother (Gen
27:41).[156] But the parallel is weakened by the fact that Esau was actually
flouted by Jacob, while Cain was not spurned by Abel. Important is precisely the contrast between the two stories. Esau's rage is for revenge and
his feeling, while not condonable, is understandable.[157] But Cain's wrath
is truly against God. Killing Abel is, by all intents, killing God. The only
thing Abel is described doing in the story is mentally dialoguing with
God through his offering. In the whole story, he does not even speak out;
only his spilled blood restores to him a voice he never had while alive
(v. 10). James Williams says that the Bible is against victimization: "all
humans have a voice before the God who creates all."[158] Williams's statement finds an echo in what Hans Jonas says about Yhwh's statement "The
voice of thy brother's blood cries unto me from the ground":

> Should we not believe that the immense chorus of such cries that
> has risen up in our lifetime now hangs over our world as a dark
> and accusing cloud? that eternity looks down upon us with a
> frown, wounded itself and perturbed in its depths?[159]

So far, I have interpreted Abel's voice beyond death as clamoring for
justice and vindication. Yet, another aspect must not elude us. For Abel
is *saying* something; he is not just crying. Abel's insignificance during his
life, his muteness of sorts, is now changed into a discourse, the discourse
he has been pregnant with all along: the message of his being. For the
death of Abel is the whole of Abel. His voice is at last claiming his death
and his life. From insignificance to meaningfulness, from anonymity to

---

156. Schwartz, *The Curse of Cain*.

157. Iamblichus, already in the third century (in *Mysteries* I.11; see III.9), theorized
about the necessity of an outlet for the human passions (he recommended the theater as
an excipient!). No one can blame Cain for being annoyed by his sacrifice's lack of success.
His annoyance, however, becomes murderous rage, which is quite another matter.

158. Williams, *The Bible, Violence, and the Sacred*, 4. Robert McAfee Brown, speaking of the "wretched of the earth," says that they are "the poor, the oppressed, the marginalized, the voiceless, the exploited, the victims. . . ." In this list, at least four terms
apply to Abel. Brown continues, *"they have been denied a voice and have been without
hope; they now demand a voice and that gives them hope"*; *Theology in a New Key*, 25 (his
emphasis).

159. Jonas, "Immortality and the Modern Temper," 129.

fulfillment. Paradoxically, Abel's fulfillment was to be killed.[160] Such was his historical vocation. Dead, he is "such as into himself eternity changes him" (Mallarmé), and his voice, gagged during his short existence, is now loud and clear; it goes up unencumbered to God (4:10).

Paradox indeed: During his life, Abel lived in the shadow of other people; he was known as the brother of someone else, more illustrious, issued from the thigh of Jupiter (see 4:1). Later, Abel died of an inflicted death. He died "before his time," the first human to have his life cut short by someone else; and, in the image of his existence, Abel's death is without luster. Or so it would be but for the astonishing divine preference for the living Abel's grand gesture of his offering, and for the dead Abel's word. Then, the transformation is total. Abel is resurrected. Or perhaps should we say that he is quickened for the first time. His innocence fills the horizon as his voice "is still speaking" (see Heb 11:4).[161]

In the world of the "visible," as the author of the letter to the Hebrews puts it, Cain is the living one and he begets a progeny. So J, like a modern journalist would do, follows Cain's escape into the wilderness, where he wanders aimlessly so long as it is away from God and man. It is a "journey to the end of the night" (Céline) for nothing ever will assuage Cain's need for redemption. In spite of some rebound of activity (see 4:17), he is eventually swallowed up by night and fog, leaving behind only ominous traces of his trail. His progeny, bloodthirsty like its forebear, runs head on into disaster and is wiped out in the Flood along with the inherited guilt of its ancestor.

J's tale is not guileless. It presents the reader with the ever-recurring choice between Cain and Abel. J's narrative art does not make it easy. It describes Cain's destiny at length and readily shortchanges Abel's. In a similar context, the Nazarene uses the metaphor of the highway and the narrow path (see Matt 7:13–14). And a disciple of the Nazarene will conclude that "God chooses what is foolish in the world to shame the wise" (see 1 Cor 1:27).

---

160. An uncanny parallel is offered in the Gospel about the death of Jesus.

161. In Gen 4:10, the verb is "crying out," but Heb 11:4 renders it as *laleō* (to speak), for had the text been too literally like the model, its effect would be the reverse of intended: Abel's blood is still *unsuccessfully* crying (for justice).

Abel, man of *skandalon*, is scandalously killed by another man, cursed for being "the one by whom the scandal comes" (see Matt 18:7). They were two brothers.

Cain's motive for killing his brother is perhaps not exhausted by explaining it as the outcome of sheer jealousy. Abel is clearly virtuous. He is pious and he offers a choice sacrifice to God; he is humble and contents himself with being called Cain's brother; he is naïve and lets himself be lured into "the field;" finally, he is the innocent victim of an act of utter violence. Abel before Cain embodies innocence and purity. It is precisely these virtues that offend Cain. Like Versilov in Dostoevsky's *The Adolescent*, Cain feels the urge to soil purity.[162] Dostoevsky has perceptively unveiled the morbid desire in all the Cains of history to deface beauty; Versilov even tries to commit the act that cannot be forgiven. Cain's killing of Abel is the paradigmatic onslaught against innocence.[163] Max Scheler writes,

> Precisely because this kind of hostility is not caused by the "enemy's" actions and behavior, it is deeper and more irreconcilable than any other. It is not directed against transitory attributes, but against the other person's very essence and being.[164]

What Alain Badiou writes of the Nazi "Final Solution" (in guise of a summary of Emmanuel Levinas's thinking, which he criticizes) can be transposed to Cain's fratricide, "As the supreme negative example, this crime is inimitable, but every crime is an imitation of it."[165]

---

162. Versilov humiliates Sonia.

163. Golgotha is the appalling but not unfathomable last event in the life of the Nazarene. It continues to be disfigured or trivialized in many ways, which include novels and films. As Jacques Madaule writes, "toute beauté est une provocation, un défi, une offense" (all beauty is provocation, defiance, offense) in *Amour et Violence*, 69.

164. Scheler, *Ressentiment*, 55.

165. Badiou, *Ethics*, 63.

CHAPTER THREE

The Theological Dimension

Kinship Relations Belong to the Sacred

KINSHIP RELATIONS BELONG TO the sacred—this point is emphasized in our narrative by God's constant presence and concern for domestic affairs, which are elevated thereby to a superior level. And this deserves all our attention, for the natural brotherly kinship is transcended. It receives a special divine confirmation and is the object of a special divine care. J, who had already stressed the oneness of husband and wife in Genesis 2–3, now shows the sacredness of the family ties. Cain's fratricide will not just be unnatural, but blasphemous. A crime against nature is a grievous thing, but a crime against God is unforgivable. Cain's murder transgresses the limits of legality, so that we may not construe the event as a private and internecine affair, not only because it is originary and paradigmatic, but because it is a religious perversion, "satanic." Cain's exile "from the face of Yhwh" is embodiment of the formula "Get behind me Satan" in Jesus' mouth (see Matt 4:10; see also Job 1:12b; 2:7).

Does Cain's fratricide actually belong negatively to the sacred? Yes, but also and concomitantly to the mundane. It is an act of desecration and of profanation. In God's creation the sacred and the profane are one. We need no Prometheus (or modern technology) here to snatch secrets from God he never kept to himself in the first place.[1] Getting away from the face of God, the murderer Cain could believe that he is now in a "death of God" domain. But everywhere he goes Cain is carrying the mark of God. Not a tattoo; not a branded stamp; not a tribal emblem (at most, something like Zeus's aegis); but rather, perhaps, just his humanity, in the image of God.[2]

1. On Gen 3:22, see LaCocque, *The Trial of Innocence*, 247–54.
2. True, the *imago Dei* is a priestly concept (P), but it is clear that J's thinking agrees

An interesting Midrashic reading of Gen 4:15 (in *Gen. Rab.* 22) has God setting Cain in person as a sign of warning not to kill him or as a sign addressed to all people willing to repent.[3] From a syntactical point of view, this Midrashic translation is not without foundation; the GKC grammar refers to the construction of Isa 5:20.

But the Midrash at this point is wrong. Cain is far from repenting. On the contrary, it is psychologically a common defense mechanism for the guilty to cast themselves as victims, as we saw. "You have driven me away," says Cain, and thus he turns the condemnation into a miscarriage of justice. He persists in refusing to acknowledge his responsibility—which, incidentally, is a frequent feature among psychotic people. Rather than repenting, he is withdrawing into self-pity, feeling that he is "banished from the face of the earth—the mother—and the face of God—the father."[4]

In short, Cain instead of accepting the blame has recourse to the lament. As Paul Ricoeur reminds us, "blame makes culprits out of us, lament reveals us as victims."[5] Cain deflects God's condemnation into victimization. The evil inflicted becomes, impudently, an evil suffered. Before the crime, Cain felt he was a victim; after the crime he still claims to be a victim. The act of murder is thus bracketed. The insignificant Abel in life would remain insignificant in death.

The impudent Cain belongs perhaps to those to be forgiven "for they do not know what they are doing." When Cain expresses fear that, being away from God he will be exposed to slaughter by "anyone," he is told: "Not so." God sets a permanent mark on Cain, meaning that Cain can never be without God. Cain, however, does not seem to be impressed,

---

with it, see Gen 2:7; 3:22; 4:1; etc. Benno Jacob wrote, "Language transposes psychological causes through metaphors into physical effects; compare Lev. 18, 25 'the land vomits its inhabitants'"; *The First Book of the Bible interpreted by B. Jacob*, 36. As Kass writes, "Respect for the brother, reverence for the father, and awe-and-reverence for the Lord are part of one package"; *The Beginning*, 448.

3. According to Jewish tradition, Cain repented (see *Lev. Rab.*, Tsaw, 10.5; *Tanh.* Bereshith, par. 9, fol. 12b). There is more here below on Cain's mark (chapter 4, section "Violence and the Sign upon Cain").

4. Rosenblatt and Horwitz, *Wrestling with Angels*, 58.

5. Ricoeur, "Evil, a Challenge to Philosophy and Theology," 636. Cain's attitude makes one think of the "noble morality" à la Nietzsche (see *Beyond Good and Evil*, Part 9: "What is Noble," par. 260, 204–8). Did he not say, "The evil of strong people hurts others without thinking about it—it *must* have a release" (*Daybreak*, par. 371). Surely, in Nietzsche's eyes, Cain is a strong man daring to do what the weak condemn. Cain is a "daring traveler and adventurer" (*Beyond*, Part 1, par. 23, 31–32), who is ready again and again to "Break, break the good and the just"; Kaufmann, *The Portable Nietzsche*, 324–25.

unless we read the text as saying that he ran with the prize, for we learn that he departed from the face of God and started his wandering in total solitude (4:16).

Soul Murder

With his reply to God, "Am I my brother's keeper?" Cain kills a second time; he compounds his murder with an onslaught against the "surplus" of Abel. "If man is more than his life, violence will attempt to kill him even to the retrenchment of the *more*; it is eventually this 'more' that is seen as too much," says Ricoeur.[6]

J's report of Cain's question uses the same keyword that appears in Gen 2:15 (Adam's vocation was to *keep* the Garden). Cain's rhetorical question about keeping his brother implies that to him there are limits to God's demands. He cannot require the keeping of the brother! So, Cain plays God, like his parents had done before him (see Gen 3:12, 13); he teaches the Creator a lesson. But God does not honor with an answer a question that Cain must realize is simply stupid. God's demands are not subject to humans drawing any line: here and no further.

In fact, Cain's rejection of responsibility is far-reaching. It not only denies the actual crime of fratricide, but more generally speaking, it euthanizes all morality.[7] With the irresponsible Cain, there is a return to the issue debated in Gen 3:1–6 between Eve and the serpent, with the purpose of making "good and evil" a notion purely relative. The "non-guardian of his brother" Cain has already at this point cut himself from the human fraternity. His subsequent ostracism is a self-exclusion from the community. Without morality, there can be no sociality, let alone civility. The price to pay for amorality is anti-sociality. On this score, few

---

6. Ricoeur, *History and Truth*, 227 (I have revised the translation). Let us note that this qualifying distinction between the "plus" and the "surplus" in human life was not missed by the "death specialists" of the Holocaust. Terrence Des Pres says that "if something within him [the victim] remains unbroken . . . something has escaped [the destructive powers'] reach, and it is precisely this something—let us call it 'dignity'—that must die"; *The Survivor*, 60, cited by Phillips, *The Problem of Evil and the Problem of God*, 66. Let us note that Henry A. Murray extended the definition of aggression to include belittling, harming, ridiculing, and accusing maliciously someone else (see *Explorations in Personality*; and "What should psychologists do about psychoanalysis?").

7. See above *Tg. Ps.-J.* on Gen 4:8 with the midrashic sharp intuition of having Cain tell his brother that there is neither judge nor justice, before killing him.

writers have been as insightful as Dostoevsky in his chapter on the "The Grand inquisitor."[8]

As is typical of someone who believes that he/she knows good and evil, Cain both transgresses the limit of the sacred—indeed of sheer decency—and sets a limit to God's "acceptable" behavior. By contrast, he claims the right to set for himself pliant and malleable limits. He may kill Abel, but not keep his brother! The keeping is not his responsibility but God's, and the latter has forfeited it (v. 9, "*am I* my brother's keeper?" [the emphasis is present in the Hebrew text wording]). In short, the culprit is not the human murderer but God who has not fulfilled his task as Protector. Cain adds insult (to God) to injury (to Abel). At his own convenience, he shrugs off the blame and accuses the Creator who allowed the perpetration of crimes in his creation. The motif sounds familiar. As R. F. Holland writes,

> To credit the one true God with having a moral reason for doing anything is to conceive Him . . . as a one among many . . . subjectable to moral judgment; and within a moral community of course it would make perfectly good sense for the one by whom, or let us say the chief one by whom we are judged, to be submitted to our moral judgment.[9]

The truth is that Cain's murder is a premeditated crime. The affair of the sacrifices has only provided motive and opportunity. Innocence works as a lightning rod: it calls for "offense and humiliation," or worse. Cain is the name of human morbidity; "all were not dying of it, but all were hit by it."[10]

The exoneration of Cain by some modern discontented critics is arguably the type of conclusion J as the author of the myth in Gen 4 wanted to defeat. As Westermann says, "[T]he purpose [of J] is . . . to ascribe full responsibility to Cain."[11] Besides, ironically, there is actually a divine

---

8. *The Brothers Karamazov*, chapter 5.

9. Holland, "On the Form of 'The Problem of Evil,'" 237–38, quoted by Phillips, *The Problem of Evil*, 149.

10. La Fontaine, *Fables*, Bk. VII, fable 1, "Les animaux malades de la peste," line 7. See Versilov's foiled murder of Akhmakova in Dostoevsky's *The Adolescent*.

11. Westermann, *Genesis 1–11*, 300. In Gnostic literature, a stream called "Cainist" said that Cain was the good character; he was born from the (good) serpent of Genesis 3. A brand of Jewish mysticism considers the preposition *'eth* in Gen 4:1 as introducing a direct complement after the verb *qanithi*, that is: "a man who is Yhwh in every aspect," an immanent but unborn Yhwh. "Cain is Yhwh incarnate." Some day, "Cain will

rebuttal of such scholarly twist in the biblical text itself: while Cain implicitly blames God who disregarded his sacrifice and suggests that God should have been a better guardian of Abel, God readily speaks of Cain's *sin* and of its necessary control (see v. 7). In spite of its over-pious character, St. Augustine's statement is to be meditated upon: "You [God] are innocent even of the harm which overtakes the wicked, for it is the result of their own actions."[12]

Furthermore, let us note that the attempted exoneration of Cain flies in the face of a structural analysis of the tale. According to this approach, one may distinguish, with Heda Jason for example, the units "action-slot/action-filler" and "role-slot/role-filler." Villainy, the action-slot is concretized in the action-filler of the fratricidal Cain. The role-slot of the villain is the role played by the murderous character.[13]

Besides, if the roles of villain, donor (God in 4:1), helper (Adam in 4:1 as regards Cain), dispatcher (Eve in 4:2 introducing the future hero), punisher (God in 4:10–12), are easily recognized, who fills the role of the hero if not Abel? Second, many of the Proppian functions can be spotted, including trickery, spatial transference, struggle, punishment, branding, and others, but here again the pattern demands the main ingredient, namely, the hero. After all, Cain does not kill a ghost.

This is not to say that the story in Genesis 4 fits the model of the heroic fairy tale (Propp) or the one of the romantic epic (Skaftymov). While there are similarities, there are more differences. But there is at least one dimension remarkably common with the "fairy tale, innocent persecuted hero or heroine," developed by Jason and her students.[14]

---

be infinitely higher than Abel" for Genesis 4:8 ("Cain rose up against Abel") is read as meaning: "Cain was exalted over Abel." He kills in Abel his own "animal-soul." Abel is vanity, that is, "conditioned existence." See Suares, *The Cipher of Genesis*, 134, 135. A modern author, Ernst Bloch, says about the intervention of the serpent in Gen 3 that it is better to die than to remain stupid; Bloch, *Atheism in Christianity*, 116–20; 231–37. In Milton, *Paradise Lost*, however, it is Satan who says, "Better to reign in Hell than serve in Heaven" (I, 263). During the Romantic era, some saw Satan as a Promethean hero in conflict with an unjust God.

12. Augustine *Confessions* II.6.

13. See Jason, "The Narrative Structure of the Swindler Tales," cited by Milne, *Vladimir Propp and the Study of Structure in Hebrew Biblical Narrative*, 114.

14. See Milne, ibid., 117–18, 112.

God's Favoritism?

But against the Augustinian theodicy, for which human perfection was obtained only in the prelapsarian past and is seen as a *stasis*, biblical anthropology is dynamic and teleological. God and the humans are working together toward the fulfillment of God's creative purpose. Adam and Eve were not created *in* perfection (see, for instance, Gen 2:7a) but *toward* perfection (see 2:16); in **P**, the word *ber'eshith* that opens the creation narrative is dynamic: "*for* a beginning," or "*for* perfection"). Within this perspective, Cain can "do well" and thus respond to God's expectation. If he does not, he acts not only against himself but against the Creator. Blaming God for Cain's failure implies that God *could* but *did not* stop Cain's hand (as he restrained Abraham's hand on the Mount Moriah). But Abraham was "doing well," and the reported divine intervention is figurative. Abraham, *in extremis*, realizes that, while Isaac as the substitutive holder of the primogeniture does indeed belong to God (see again Exod 13:13) and, as such, must be returned to God through sacrifice, this terrible "privilege" is assorted with its redemption. At the very moment Isaac is about to be slaughtered, a ram is "caught in the thicket by its horns" (Gen 22:13). Abraham credits this "coincidence" as the angel of God's intervention. Thus, Isaac is both offered to God and spared: life is granted twice to him.

In contrast, the *deus ex machina* imagined by Cain is a far cry from the scene of Genesis 22. At any rate, rewarding a meritorious deed in some fashion is very different from preventing a free human act. Abraham's hand is diverted from one (human) victim to another (animal). Along the trajectory of this same paradigm, God the hand sacrificing Abel conceivably could have been voluntarily deviated (like Abraham's). Cain in that case would have regarded his own offering as the acknowledgment that all life belongs to God: his own, Adam's, Eve's, Abel's. The potential animal in Genesis 4, like the one in Genesis 22, would have been substitutive. But Cain's hand is not materializing such an acknowledgment; on the contrary, it robs God of the life that belongs to Him.

I do not imply that confronting God with criticism and expressions of incomprehension about his "behavior" is taboo. On the contrary, I believe that such human demand for intelligibility is a sure sign of taking God seriously. True, God is not answerable to us as if we were his judges (see Job 9:32; Hos 11:9; Zeph 3:1–5; Ps 92:6–8; Sir 15:11–12), but his actions or inactions can be deplored, even questioned. This was clearly the case when God decided to wipe out Sodom and Gomorrah (Genesis 18), or with his outrageous demand on Abraham to commit infanticide, or again with his non-intervention in favor of his "Son" on the cross, or of his "sons" in Auschwitz. "Why have you forsaken me?" (Matt 27:46) is a universal cry. But, the heart-rending question of Psalm 22 shows the right framework for the human protest, namely, the lament. Lamenting, we question. Lamenting, we complain. Blaming God is no theologian's business, only Job's and those in a like position. There is, I say, an obscene—because complacent—accusation of God. Some of the post-modern attempts at excusing Cain are imposing a self-serving, self-exonerating agenda on the text regardless of content and context. I fail to see on what basis God could be blamed for Cain's fate in the myth we are dealing with. God's non-intervention before Abel's murder is God refraining from manipulating human history, a manipulation that would sterilize history or, at least, reduce the human drama to a puppet show.

Moreover, the romantic irritation on the part of God's critics in this case emanates from a theological conception very close to magic: God the Great Magician who can at will metamorphose Cain into a cherub (and presumably Abel into a devil). The opposite of this is the dialogical God of Genesis 4. He is not indifferent, listless, impassible, but his intervention is not with a magic wand. God speaks with Cain and makes his will perfectly clear, although without coercion: "*If* you do well . . . ." Actually, God speaks more than any other character in the story, and what he says is far from being non-committal. There is no inkling here to a "God who hides" (Isa 45:15), or to a God who does not care (see Ps 10:4). In fact, God requites the blood shed and "does not forget the cry of the humble" (Ps 9:13).

The fundamental problem is not whether God does well, but whether the human in relation to God does well. There is a certain criticism of God that hides—like Adam and Eve hidden behind the tree in Gen 3:8—a sheer refusal of responsibility. Does a criterion of legitimacy exist in the human questioning of God's conception of justice? I think there is. The criterion consists in keeping a balance between critique of God's rule and compassion for the suffering God.[15] The criterion is respected when we

---

15. Fretheim reminds us that God's act of creation is a self-limitation that "might be described as a divine *kenosis*, a self-emptying, an act of self-sacrifice . . . the beginning of the passion of God"; *The Suffering of God*, 58. I have developed a similar idea in *The Trial of Innocence*, see esp. 84–85.

cry unto God, "Why do you allow such suffering as I am undergoing, and why do you allow such suffering that you are sharing with me?" Logically, this implies that things could/should be different, that is, in a world without my pain and without his pain. But then I am not any longer myself and God has ceased to be God (that is, the creator and redeemer God of the world). Then the cross is an aberration and so is the one who is nailed on it. In the critics' zeal to blame God for the terrible waste carried over by human history, they have wasted the *Heilsgeschichte*.

God is no magician, and he is no juggler. A large part of the postmodern theological misunderstanding about evil emanates from the conception of *creatio* as *ex nihilo*, that is, of an act of creation that leaves nothing uncovered by the Creator's power. The biblical myth of creation, however, does not warrant such an understanding. Here, God is described as creating out of a preexisting chaos, a cadaver-like mass. Nowhere in the Bible is it said that God created the waters, for instance. Moreover, other texts show God overcoming chaotic monsters (see esp. Ps 74:13–17; Isa 51:9–11).[16] This "suggests that the 'material' from which our world was created had some power of its own,"[17] that is, a power of inertia, hence of resistance (Gen 1:2 P). In the J creation story, the resistance of the "material" reveals itself in the animal rebellion headed by the serpent.[18] True, the chaotic matter is not evil, but it is lifeless and thus to be submitted to a quickening by the God of life, the "Ground of Being" (Tillich). Genesis 1:1 tells us that "in the beginning" there happened a "surrection" (which foreshadows the final resurrection: "primeval time becomes end-time" ("Urzeit wird Endzeit," Gunkel). As for J, he comes with the vivification of dust into Adam (= "the human"). In Genesis 1, universal life is created by the Spirit of God; in Genesis 2, the human life is created by the breath of God. Evidently, "spirit" (*ruah*) and "breath of life" (*nešamah*) are in full correspondence. As dust at the core of the human being emphasizes fallibility, the chaos at the basis of the cosmos emphasizes its fundamental

16. The classic treatment of this theme remains Hermann Gunkel's *Creation and Chaos in the Primeval Era and the Eschaton*. See also the remarkable study by Jon Levenson, *Creation and the Persistence of Evil*.

17. Griffin, "Creation out of Nothing, Creation out of Chaos, and the Problem of Evil," 108. He cites Gerhard May, who, he says, has demonstrated that the doctrine of *creatio ex nihilo* is not biblical, nor found in the Intertestamental literature (including 2 Macc 7:28, "out of non-being") and the New Testament; see May, *Creatio ex Nihilo*. See earlier, Fisher, "Creation at Ugarit and in the Old Testament".

18. See LaCocque, *The Trial of Innocence*, esp. 151–53, 188–89, 197.

weakness. Eventually, the human returns to the dust whence it came, and eventually the world returns to the chaos (i.e., the "non-being") whence it came. The tally between the microcosm and the macrocosm is perfect.[19]

Meanwhile, between *alpha* and *omega* so to speak, Cain is capable of being either *the* man (see Gen 4:1) or the prototypical fratricidal murderer that he became. Would he be all "living soul" (*nepheš ḥayah*), he would be the former and nothing else; but he is also "dust" (*ʿaphar*) and thus Cain—like everyone else—finds himself wavering between "doing well" and "not doing well." The decision, based on his capability, is all his, without divine interference.

"If you do well" is a most remarkable statement. It emphasizes God's willingness (not incapacity) *not* to interfere with the human moral decision. Cain is fully respected as partner by God. The latter's "omnipotence" consists in relinquishing all total control and manipulation in the dialogue with the humans.[20]

God's "omnipotence" surrounds the human potency to choose any way they choose. *Absolutely* anything is possible in this state of affairs. There is *absolutely* nothing that prevents the humans from doing what they please. Even the fratricidal Cain is embraced by God's potency. Even Gomer is still Hosea's wife. Even wayward Israel is still God's people. In the wake of this logic, Paul said that "neither life, nor death . . . nor anything in all creation, will be able to separate us from the love of God . . ." (Rom 8:38). Even "deadwood" Cain is not separated. What this means is that God's impotence is still part of his omnipotence.

The subjunctive "if" in the sentence "if you do good" open a large margin of negative possibilities, still multiplied in the statement's sequel, "and if you do not good."[21] Cain's only restraint, if he accepts it, is God's

19. A Jewish mystical document (the oldest mss. date to the tenth and eleventh century) called *Shiʾur Komah* ("Measure of the Body") describes Adam as filling the span of the whole cosmos.

20. My position on this problem displays a certain kinship with Bishop Charles Gore's "*kenotic*" theory (nineteenth century) according to which God's omnipotence includes God's divestment of his omnipotence. "God declares His almighty power most chiefly in such an act of voluntary self-limitation for the purposes of sympathy"; "A Kenotic Theory of the Incarnation," 167.

21. Let us note incidentally that speculating about God creating a being that would always freely choose well in every circumstance is a self-contradiction in terms of the dialogical relationship between God and the human creature. By transposition, it amounts to a sham relationship between two lovers who would just be essentially unable to be unfaithful or in mutual disagreement. Love and faith are thus emptied of all

commandment, which expresses God's expectation. God's lordship over history is not by might and coercion, but by wager (Job 2:3–6) or by election (Genesis 12).[22] True, according to some texts, God thunders and rages against enemies, but only the saints hear him—and more often than not retrospectively.

Indeed, many a biblical statement about God's power and victory must be understood as a prayer. At the risk of being misunderstood, I would say that it is expressing a wishful (= a prayerful) thinking. Israel's faith in God is ultimately because there is no one and nothing else to turn to: "to whom else but you should we go?" (John 6:68).

In a real sense, it is the human acquiescence that makes the divine triumph.[23] True Israel chooses to interpret life and history in a certain way, and her interpretation is performative: it makes true what it says—at least for the interpreter. After the creation of the universe, nothing is happening in the ethereal Valhalla; all is happening "down" here, on earth, among the humans, by the humans and for the humans. They are called to be the knights of God. The faithful are made privy to God's will and wish. Not only are they willing to "do well," but they trust the "foundation of their hopes, the evidence of happenings not seen" (Heb 11:1). They echo God's wager with their own: love is the ultimate victor (Song 8:6; 1 John 4:7–21).

So God's address to Cain in Gen 4:7 is an invitation to join the historic people of the saints by "doing well." The other alternative, exemplified by the "wrong" choice of Cain, is murderous. Is this perhaps J's Middle Eastern exaggeration? Hardly. J at any rate is consistent. Genesis 2–3 described the alternative to God's bliss as mortality (2:17). In Genesis 4, it is death-inflicting. From the outset of biblical literature, the human choice amounts to an existential option between life and death (see Deut 30:15–20). Siding with God ("If you do well") brings about life; not siding with God ("If you do not do well") brings about death. Again, it is a mat-

---

substance. There is no dialogue possible as all the rejoinders would be totally superfluous and desperately monotonous. Then Ernst Bloch would be entitled to contrast dying and being stupid (see above 71 n. 11).

22. Biblical dualism belongs to the *moral* order, not to the ontological. The human culpability does not reside in the fact of being human. The human evil is evil-making (killing one's brother, for instance), but where evil-making is possible, there is unbound freedom—a freedom to *act*.

23. See Isa 53:10.

ter of interpretation (living is interpreting),[24] which empirical experience does or does not back up. The bottom line is that, for Israel's interpreters, a "life" away from God's face (Gen 4:16) is simply no life at all, and conversely, a "death" occurring "on the mouth of Yhwh" (as Deut 34:5 literally says) is really life (see John 11:25–26).

Cain apparently felt unable to accept this paradox of paradoxes, scandal and folly for all people, Jews and non-Jews (1 Cor 1:23). So, he seizes the *skandalon* (=stumbling block) and with it he smashes the head of one who is a living reproach to him. For, this at least he understands: all considered, there is no more ultimate decision set before the human than this "either/or" choice: to be a saint or a rogue in a world that abusively favors the latter over the former. Why then would Cain choose to be a "loser" when his very name proclaims the virtue of winning, of possessing, of greed, of earthiness?

If there is a "Cain complex,"[25] it consists in the stubborn pursuit of the destructive choice that entails a "curse from the ground" as it sterilizes everything around and uproots the human from the very concrete world in which he/she claimed to be rooted. A "Cain complex" is the same complex encountered in Gen 3:12–13 where, there as well, we find no repentance and no return to innocence.

The capable Cain is Cain "become like one of us," says God, "knowing [intimately, experientially] good and evil" (Gen 3:22). Such knowledge sets him at the crossroad of one and the other. God—who is also "one of us" with Cain—knows good and evil, and he bets on good to bring the whole world to its intended prime, to its *rešîth* (Gen 1:1), to its status of Eden (Gen 2:8). Cain, partner of God in the drama, is endowed with the enormous capability to "elevate" (*śe'eth* in Gen 4:7, in contrast to his countenance that unduly "fell," in Gen 4:6). This is how he would activate, as it were, the ability as co-creator with God that is within him.

Instead of this, since Cain is also capable to "not do well," he "fells" his brother Abel. The initial quickening is reversed. God's breath (God's *hebel*, God's "abel") is choked to nothing. *The human has just proved that he/she can "de-create," deconstruct the world.* On the individual scale, the murder of Abel is what violence on the universal range will bring up, that

---

24. Michael Holquist writes, "In Bakhtin's philosophical anthropology, to be human is *to mean*"; *Art and Answerability*, xli.

25. See Hughes, *Theology and the Cain Complex.*

is, the Flood. The former crime leads naturally to the latter. And in both, God "is hanging here on these gallows."[26]

He has been hanged, that is, victimized in the person of Abel sacrificed. For, in the act of Abel's murder, precisely against the background of his offering that Cain looked on with jaundiced eyes, there is a striking prolongation of his sacrifice. Abel did start with offering the prime of his flock; he eventuates by being himself the victim—and also the prime of innocence. What had started by being a sacrifice (*minhah*) becomes a holocaust (*'olah*). Wittingly or unwittingly, Abel has offered himself in sacrifice. Therefore, if Cain is the first murderer, Abel is the first martyr (= [God's] witness).

Sacrifice Revisited

Of course, the boundary between slaughtering and sacrificing is fuzzy. Abel's murder is a slaughter perpetrated by Cain. But by virtue of the fact that Abel's blood cries out and is a message-carrier, the slaughter is transcended into sacrifice as far as the victim is concerned. Slaughter and sacrifice being in dialectical tension, one easily becomes the other, in both directions. The victims of Auschwitz, for instance, were killed in an enormous slaughter. But their very humanity and our present communion with them—that is, our choice to be among the victims rather than among the victimizers—change the slaughter into an immense sacrifice, and make of them an innumerable cloud of martyrs.

Paul Kahn states, "Ultimately the object of the sacrifice must be man himself, for it is man who must realize an ultimate meaning."[27] He adds, "We know the person as a saint when he sacrifices his own life."[28] As a matter of fact, no one is a saint before her life is completed. Whatever may be the (non-) historicity of Judas, there is always symbolically the possibility of an existential reversal before death, one way or the other.[29]

Within the perspective of Abel's self-offering, his blood was supposed to be poured upon the altar. Actually, it is shed upon the earth, which thereby is the universal altar absorbing the blood of the paradigmatic vic-

26. Wiesel, *Night*, 71. The human capability for evil underscores the miraculous nature of God's *creatio continua*.

27. Kahn, *Out of Eden*, 191.

28. Ibid., 204.

29. On the "two fundamental attitudes: self-sacrifice and murder" (ibid., 140) or love and evil, see esp. ibid., chapter 3.

tim. With the first historical murder history has missed the advent of the Innocent. For the one who might have been *the* "man" according to God's desire (rather than the one so mistakenly hailed in Gen 4:1) is destroyed, an ominous sign of things to come (see, for instance, Luke 11:47–51, where Abel is mentioned). Not surprisingly, the New Testament uses the paradigm in the context of Jesus' martyrdom (see Heb 12:24).

Matthew 23:35 also speaks of "the blood of the righteous Abel." Note that, retrospectively, this Gospel reading confirms that the veritable type of the "Son of Man" (= the human par excellence) was not Cain, as his own mother initially believed (see Gen 4:1), but Abel, for whom she had no regard in contradistinction to God. Thus, already in this primeval myth of Cain and Abel, a highly paradoxical truth is unveiled: of the two brothers vying for being "*the* man," it is the slaughtered one rather than the slaughterer who is chosen. Cain as "the man" would lay claim to "possession." Abel as "the man" chooses to become so through self-offering. Cain takes the other's life; Abel gives his own. One is driven by an insatiable appetite for "having," the other is moved by the moral demand of "being."

That is why, incidentally, Abel remains mute and is manipulated by others in the story. He voices no claim and does nothing to affirm his "inalienable rights." He is as dumb as "a lamb that is led to the slaughter" (Isa 53:7).[30] From the very start, he is the designated victim, the scapegoat, the *huios tou anthropou* (the "human one") who "must die," the Dostoyevskian Idiot. The clamor of his blood is both a perpetual indictment of a world sick with greed, and a redeeming factor since no one can gag it from being heard in the midst of the world's cacophonous din. "When you make his life an offering for sin, he shall see his offspring and shall prolong his days" (Isa 53:10 [NRSV]).

The Divine and the Human in Reciprocity

It is to be noted that once Cain turns away from Yhwh, God becomes absent from the story. Only with Seth and his son Enosh is the name of Yhwh "made to be invoked" (Gen 4:26, literally).[31] To be invoked *again*.

---

30. It is true that, at some crucial point, Cain also is incapable of speaking. The text of 4:8 says, "And he said . . ." but nothing is said. Kahn is right when he states, "Love and evil are speechless . . . because their symbolic structure is not propositional"; *Out of Eden*, 139.

31. The verbal form in 4:26 is a *hapax*. For the same formula in the negative, see Ps 14:4c, "they do not invoke Yhwh."

In *The Trial of Innocence*, I call attention to Gen 4:1, where the first human being to utter the Name "Yhwh" is a woman.[32] Genesis 4:26, therefore, is not a "premiere" but an "encore." Throughout the story, there is a striking alternation of divine presence and absence. The point, most remarkably, is that such variation depends upon the human (un)willingness to be addressed by God. We already encountered the phenomenon in Genesis 3, with the arresting divine caesura during the dialogue between Eve and the serpent. For J's theology, the reciprocity of human action and divine reaction is important. In the wake of Gen 3:1–7, the eclipse of God in Gen 4:17–25 is the human obscuring of God. Cain is not wicked because God hid himself from him, but Cain's wickedness hid God. At any rate, it is clear that J avoids all promiscuity between God's presence and the violence of Cain and his descendants. The ancient rabbis said that the Shekhinah (divine presence) receded by degrees to heaven, pushed away, as it were, by human waywardness.[33] The Nazi *Nacht und Nebel* (night and fog) was able to draw a thick cloud between humanity and God.[34] For the divine is willingly subjected to human behavior.

Here lies the kernel of truth in the principle of distributive justice: there is reciprocity between the realms of the divine and the human. There is, for instance, a "chosen people" because they choose God; they choose to be chosen.[35] Cain, like the nations in the *Mekilta* just mentioned in the note, turns his back to God's presence—and God is left without a counterpart. But, the Creator God without a human *Thou* is not God.[36] For it is true of the Creator as it is of the creature that the *I* needs a *Thou* in order to be. Jon Levenson comes to the striking conclusion that "God is not yet God."[37] The "not yet" depends upon the human witnesses being truly trustworthy. For, "the elevation of the God of Israel is partly a function of those who elevate him."[38]

32. See LaCocque, *The Trial of Innocence*, 124 n. 151.

33. See *Num. Rab.*, Naso, 13.2; see *Deut. Rab*, Ki Tetse, 6.14; *Sifra* 88d (end).

34. See Mark 15:33; Matt 27:45; Luke 23:45. *Nuit et brouillard* is the title of Alain Resnais's documentary on the Nazi concentration camps (1959).

35. Before the constitution of Israel, Noah, for example, after Enoch (Gen 5:22) "walked with God" (6:9). See *Mek.*, Bahodesh, ch. 5, lines 64–80: all nations are offered the covenant at Sinai but they all refuse. Israel alone accepts the Torah.

36. See *Sifre Deut.* 346 on Isa 43:12: "'So you are my witnesses, declares the Lord, and I am God.' That is, if you are my witnesses I am God, and if you are not my witnesses, I am, as it were, not God."

37. Levenson, *Creation and the Persistence of Evil*, 38.

38. Ibid, 139. By transposition, the "becoming of God" (the title of a book of mine in

The pairing of Seth and Enosh brings a closure to Yhwh's eclipse and resumes with God the relationship that Abel used to embody. Seth, says his mother Eve, is "another race instead of Abel," and he is walking in his footsteps (4:25b). Cain the murderer is lost in space, but Abel the murdered one has come back home (4:25a).

The term "race," (*zera*ʿ) in Hebrew, is literally "seed." J has used the word earlier, in Gen 3:15, with the divine promise that Eve's *zera*ʿ "will strike the head" of the serpent. By hailing now the birth of Seth as "another seed," Eve expresses anew her hope—that she first wrongly uttered about Cain's birth—that Seth, "Abel redivivus," will be the one man after God's desire. This is a favorite theme in J's work. We find it again expressed in Gen 5:29 (J) about the birth of Noah (who, incidentally is made a descendant of Seth and not of Cain as he is in P). All these more or less fulfilled hopes become pointers to Genesis 12.[39] Eventually, only Abraham will actually start a new humanity en route toward Eden retrieved.

The insistence of the text on the humanity of Eve's progeny, echoing the magnificent exclamation of Adam about her in Gen 3:20, is remarkable. First, the tale starts (and also ends) with "Adam"; then Lamech speaks of "a man," and "a child"; now Seth's son is called Enosh, that is, "man," like Cain had been called (*'iš*) = man in 4:1. Eventually, J emphasizes that the *human* "began to call on the Name of Yhwh" (4:26).[40] One of the main interests of J's artistic creation is that his theology is inseparable from his anthropology. Inspired by the Yahwist's vision, Abraham Heschel said, "The Bible is not man's theology but God's anthropology," a text that I quote as an epigraph in my earlier book on *The Trial of Innocence*.[41] Any quest of God starts and ends with the study of humanity.

God's Power—To Be Interpreted

None of this detracts from the issue of God's power. But there are different sorts of power. We generally connect potency with coercion and violence. And it is true that the biblical God is not infrequently described as violent,

---

French) parallels the becoming of the self. Bruno Snell writes, "The self does not come into being except through our comprehension of it"; *The Discovery of the Mind*.

39. "The beginning of the story of redemption in Gen. xii.1–3 . . . not only brings an end to the early history . . . but actually provides the key to it"; von Rad, *The Problem*, 65.

40. See also in J, Gen 12:8; 13:4; 21:33; 26:25 (and sixteen more times in the Hebrew Bible according to Hamilton, *Genesis*, 455).

41. Heschel, *Man is not Alone*, 129.

either against collectives or against individuals. There is, however, another kind of power that consists in God's loving self-limitation for the sake of giving space to someone else. *Before* he creates—this is admittedly sheer speculation, but after all there is a *beginning* to the world—God is omnipotent, in the sense of an unlimited power of doing anything at will.[42] But after he creates humanity, God sets himself as inseparable from it and he shares in its becoming. Consequently, the human beings are *capable*, legitimately although finitely, to interpret the One who is so involved in their own becoming. Historically, Israel's pious interpretation of the divine has decanted to a rock solid ore: God is both *just* and *merciful*. The rabbis of old said that the alternation of the divine names within the Pentateuch indicates these two faces of the divinity: strict justice with Elohim, and compassionate love with Yhwh.[43] There is no justice without compassion and no love/compassion without justice. The "impossible" combination of the two attributes demands a reexamination of the notion of power in the sense of being fundamentally non-coercive, non-intrusive, as it "bets" entirely on love to defeat evil.[44]

Again the coextensiveness of the divine and the human implies that any manifestation of love on earth is an echo of love on high. Any manifestation of justice on earth is an echo of justice on high. God *is* love (1 John 4:8) and he *is* justice. There cannot be love or justice on earth that is not originally and essentially divine.

In the vertical relationship that binds God and humanity, the communication is essentially downward: God is said to descend toward the humans (see Gen 11:5, 7; Ps 18:10; 144:5). But, interpretatively, the movement is ascendant, from earth to heaven. Let us take for instance the drowning of the Egyptian chariotry at the time of the Exodus (Exod 14:28). Even if it were historical, the event might have had a natural cause, but the "event" is strikingly interpreted by Israel as a manifestation of

42. A Jewish tradition states that God did create numerous other worlds before the present one. See *Gen. Rab.* 3:7 (R. Abbahu): "God created worlds and destroyed them, until he said, 'This one is good.'"

43. Genesis 22, by way of illustration, has Elohim demand from Abraham the sacrifice of his beloved son Isaac. Yhwh (or his angel) is the one who stops the patriarch's hand and shows the animal substitute "caught in the thicket by its horns" (v. 13).

44. From this point of view, David Hume's famous quandary about evil in the world becomes somewhat spurious. He asks about God, "Is he willing to prevent evil, but not able? Then he is impotent. Is he able but not willing? Then he is malevolent. Is he both willing and able? Whence then is evil?"; *Dialogues Concerning Natural Religion*, Part X, 198).

divine justice vis-à-vis the Egyptian oppressors, and of divine compassion toward the oppressed Israelites. In the interpretive process, the Egyptian drowning is the outcome of a direct divine intervention.

Closer to our topic here, there is a vexing problem in that we are not told how Cain and Abel knew about the favor/disfavor of God. More pointedly, how did J know? It must be confessed that to fathom the divine pleasure or displeasure would be a lot easier were the deity visible. Then he would either smile or frown. But, with an invisible deity, Israel was left with only one possible recourse: *interpretation.*

Let us first notice the striking consensus of the narrative characters regarding the objective divine favor shown to Abel. There is no discordant opinion, not even on the part of Cain as the main interested party. Moreover, the rest of the tale is a clear confirmation of the correctness of what every character has understood. Now, if we were to translate the issue in psychoanalytical terms, I think that the inescapable conclusion would be that even before and during his offering, Cain *knew* that he was not doing well and Abel *knew* that he was. Cain's offering was either half hearted or had an ulterior motive. No one, not even God, needed to say anything to make all the actors know that something was right or wrong. When, later on in the story, God tells Cain in so many words that his problem is to do well—that the human problem is to do well (see Mic 6:8)—we may infer that the thing was already obvious to Cain himself, but was repressed and would continue to be repressed.

The truth is that interpretation is everything.[45] The meaning(s) of any historical or fictional event[46] is/are, like God himself, non-obligatory. The exodus from Egypt, which is considered fundamental by Israel, is only so because it is thus interpreted. Then God's "trace" is seen in the event, including its violent nature, which is deemed to reflect God's violence. For the beloved, the lover is ever and everywhere present; God fills the horizon, he fills history. God is meant to precede the event of the drowning of the Egyptian chariots, as well as to be present during it, and

45. For the fundamentalist, there is practically no need for interpretation. But the price to pay is exorbitant, as all reality demands interpretation. Without interpretation, there is nothing left. As Mason Cooley says, "It is possible to interpret without observing, but not to observe without interpreting"; *City Aphorisms*, fifth selection, cited by Rollins and Kille, *Psychological Insights Into the Bible*, 79.

46. Hence the "double meaning" in English of the word "history," as it designates the past and its record (which is interpretation); see Moye, "In the Beginning," 577.

beyond it. When the Egyptian disaster occurs, there is no other way for Israel than to attribute it to a divine scheme.

There is no gap between an event and its interpretation. Interpretation belongs to the event as message belongs to discourse. Of course, the more complex any given event is, the more numerous are the alternatives to its understanding. But the first thing to be said is that there *is* a message in need of being decrypted. In the Cain and Abel narrative, the issue is presented as fundamentally driving the interpreter to an either/or decision: "if you do well . . . if you do not do well." J is not the only one in the Bible moved by the conviction that there is no third term to the alternative offered by the message; "*tertium non datur*" (a third term is nonexistent).[47]

Life is a succession of crossroads: either Abel or Cain; Isaac or Ishmael; Jacob or Esau; the narrow path or the highway—a life-enhancing or a life-denying kind of interpretation. As we saw above, Seth/Enosh, the antitype of the couple Cain/Lamech, restores the right interpretation of the divine-human relationship that was badly distorted by the latter. With Seth, history is no longer without a name and identity. The divine signature on it is again legible.

47. See Deut 30:15, 19.

CHAPTER FOUR

The Psychological Dimension

Violence and the Sign upon Cain

FOR THE FIRST TIME in the Bible, blood is mentioned, as well as its virtue of epitomizing life that belongs to God (4:10; see 9:4–6). Let us start with a philological note: although the singular "blood" (*dam*) may only at times refer to blood shed by violence (see Num 35:33), the plural *damim*, as we have it here in Gen 4:10, is more specifically blood spilled or blood-guilt (see Num 35:27, Exod 22:1). The expression "man of blood" (*'iš damim*) designates a murderer (see 2 Sam 16:7, 8; Ps 5:7) and "city of blood" (*'îr damim*) a city caught in blood-guilt (see Ezek 22:2). Cain has stolen a life that belongs to God. His fratricide is blatantly an onslaught against God, a deicide.[1] While the animal blood of Abel's sacrifice went "up" to the divine abode, Cain has offered Abel's blood "down" to the ground. The soil has swallowed a life that did not belong to it.

The fact that Cain, in spite of everything, is protected by God certainly does not correspond to strict justice. To see Cain as "rejected" with Regina Schwartz amounts to an overstatement. Furthermore, as a "fugitive and wanderer on the earth," he is surprisingly able to "settle" (v. 16) and even to "build a city" (v. 17), a feature at the antipode of vagrancy.[2] Cain the perpetrator of fratricide may be looked at with horror by others (an anachronism in the story[3]) and could be destroyed by them, were it

1. Taking upon himself the right of life and death, "Cain killed to become God. To kill God"; Wiesel, *Messengers of God*, 68.

2. About this shift from Cain's vagrancy to settlement (Gen 4:14, 16), Rabbi Judah concludes that exile grants half the forgiveness of a sin (*b. Sanh.* 37b).

3. An anachronism or, once again, a synchronism. There is absolutely no need to imagine here the presence of "pre-adamites" of sorts (see in particular Mowinckel, *The Two Sources of the Predeuteronomic Primeval History (JE) in Genesis 1–11*, 25–43, and

not for the sign granted by God. The mark on Cain is, nevertheless, ambivalent. It distinguishes him from any other, thus dangerously breaking his anonymity, while at the same time shielding him from retaliation on their part.[4] In spite of his lifting evil to the level of radicalness, Cain receives a sign that means that "there are no persons whom God cuts off as simply evil and therefore by nature hostile to his purpose."[5] Besides, there is here no need for a third party interceding in favor of Cain, in contrast to Genesis 18 where Abraham intercedes for Sodom and Gomorrah.

This latter point, however, is not to be construed as de-legitimizing the acknowledgment of certain deeds as genuinely evil, for, as J. A. Colombo says, "To deny the possibility of genuine evils is unwittingly to legitimize them."[6] The sign on Cain is not downgrading his murder to a misdemeanor or to less than a genuine evil. It is God's pure *grace*, that is, by definition a totally undeserved divine gift. In a way, the latter is morally as shocking as the crime it "covers" (in Hebrew, *kapper*, hence *kippur*), but, of course, the "shock" at the gracious gift of God is of another nature altogether.

Cain's evil is radical in the sense that Immanuel Kant defined it, "This evil is *radical*, since it corrupts the ground of all maxims," he says. "Yet it must be equally possible to *overcome* this evil, for it is found in the human being as acting freely."[7] "Radical evil" in Kant's parlance means that it lies at the very root of human nature; it is what the rabbis called the *yeṣer ha-raʿ*, the evil inclination in the human heart. However, as Martin Beck Matuštík says, Kierkegaard went further than Kant by calling evil

---

Stade, *Ausgewählte akademische Reden und Abhandlungen*, 229–73.

4. All the texts with the composite *śim ʾoth* ("put a sign [on]") have a negative meaning. A text such as Exod 10:2 is clear: God mentions his signs in Egypt (*weʾeth ha-ʾothoth ʾašer śamthi bam*) where "sign" has the sense of plague. The same situation obtains in Ps 78:43; Isa 66:19; Jer 32:20–21. In Ezek 14:8, a cursed man becomes a "sign" (*ʾoth*) of God's wrath. In regard to Gen 4:15, we are thus led toward the sense of a stigma rather than toward a tribal mark such as a tattoo. A collective interpretation is further excluded when we realize that Cain's mark is set on a murderer, and barely protects him from being killed. Although the rainbow in the clouds (Gen 9:13, "as a sign of covenant" *le-ʾoth berith*) does not belong to the said stigmata, it is also ambivalent: a reminder to humanity of the universal catastrophe as well as of the divine promise. See also Exod 12:13 , for instance. In Wilder's *The Skin of Our Teeth*, the mark is shameful and is deceptively hidden under Cain's (Henry's) hair mop.

5. Friedman, "The Human Dimension," 33.

6. Colombo, "Christian Theodicy and the Genuineness of Evil," 40. Colombo uses the term "genuine evil" where Friedman uses "radical evil."

7. Kant, *Religion within the Limits of Reason Alone*, 6:37.

"a defiance of unconditional love." Then evil is so radical as to become "diabolical," because "there is no rational explanation for a human person who wants to exist in defiance of the loving cosmos."[8] Paul Ricoeur in his turn, in his posthumous book *Vivant jusqu'à la mort*,[9] wrote, "[V]iolent *death* becomes the figure of absolute Evil, of inimicality (of Satan? of God? of which vindictive God? perhaps Wicked?)." And, a little further, "absolute Evil, the Enemy of fraternity." Elsewhere, Ricoeur has said that "we must *never forget* . . . the history of the victims . . . delegates to our memory of all the victims in history."[10]

One other categorization of evil(s) introduces a distinction between "avoidable evils" and "unavoidable evils."[11] This may be philosophically useful. For J, nonetheless, it seems that all *morally* unavoidable evils are in fact always avoidable. Adam and Eve commit an avoidable evil and so does Cain. There is nothing unavoidable either in the other crimes J describes in the remaining chapters of the "prehistory" culminating with the construction of the Tower of Babel (Genesis 11). The notion of "unavoidable evils" is rather to be understood as relating to all the evils the *victim* (like Abel) is unable to avoid.

In short, is Cain's evil substantial? Yes. Is it radical? Yes again. Absolute? No. It would be absolute without God's grace *after the fact*. The divine intervention in human history does not tamper with human freedom, even the freedom of unspeakably obscene acts, but the sign on Cain prevents his evil-doing from being absolute, that is, an evil for which there is no forgiveness or reprieve because it has usurped God's unique absoluteness. In and of itself, Cain's evil is an absolute—he has taken upon himself the power of life and death over another being—which God gra-

---

8. Matuštik, "Violence and Secularization, Evil and Redemption," 45. Matuštik refers to Kierkegaard, *The Sickness Unto Death*, 14–15. The psychoanalyst Willard Gaylin also protests against the de-moralization of crime in modern society. He writes, "It is time to reverse the therapeutic trivialization of morality, where nothing is either wrong or right, only sick or healthy. Where nothing is deemed punishable, only treatable" (*Hatred*, 13). Already Aristotle in *The Nichomachean Ethics* (III.5.6) said, ". . . a man is the author of his own actions, and if we are unable to trace our conduct back to any other origins than those within ourselves, then actions of which the origins are within us, themselves depend upon us, and are voluntary." And in VIII.9.3, "[W]rong is increasingly serious in proportion as it is done to a nearer friend. For example, it is more shocking . . . to strike one's father than to strike anybody else" (62).

9. Ricoeur, *Vivant jusqu'à la mort*, 58, 60.

10. Ricoeur, *Temps et Récit* III, 340–42.

11. See Phillips, *The Problem of Evil*, 235.

ciously downgrades to contingent; if not, the crime of Cain would have brought the end of the world.[12] *The sign on Cain is also on the world.* As long as the latter lives, redemption is still a possibility. But also as long as "Cain" lives (with all the successive Lamechs), the divine shield is ambivalently a sword of Damocles hanging over the heads of all creatures.

God himself is not thereby spared, for God's grace, his patience, is concomitantly God's risk. From a purely economical point of view, Cain's death would have considerably simplified the matter after all—something like a successful assassination of Hitler in 1943. Cain alive is at the immense cost to Creator and creature alike; both are under the threat of annihilation. The sole dike against an impending Flood is in the human repentance, that is, in the human acknowledgment of sin/offense against God as vulnerable. As the creature must constantly reinvent herself through the ordeals of life, she must also constantly reaffirm God, restore God's hope, and vindicate God's righteousness and innocence. James Crenshaw speaks of God's vulnerability as "a divine dependence on reciprocal love that cannot be ascertained unless submitted to radical choice," and Crenshaw brings about the example of the book of Hosea where God is cast in the role of a betrayed husband.[13] The death of the Messiah proclaimed by the Christian branch of the faithful means exactly that. The key to the theodicy—to the extent that it is legitimate to construct a theodicy at all[14]—is not God's omnipotence but God's pathos.[15]

12. Besides, the "absolute evil" of Cain's fratricide can always be overrun by a more absolute evil, for the human imagination "is evil from youth" (Gen 8:21) and is inexhaustibly "creative."

13. Crenshaw, *Defending God*, 82, 84.

14. See the convincing tearing apart of the theodicy by Phillips, *The Problem of Evil*.

15. See the J text of Gen 6:6–7 (an anthropopathism of God). A statement by Wiesel will remain for ever branded on the Holocaust, like the divine mark on Cain: "Where is He? Here He is—He is hanging here on these gallows" (Wiesel, *Night*, 71). In the Talmud, *b. Ber.* 83b declared, "Everything is in the power of Heavens except the fear of Heavens"— that is, except the human freedom to fear or not to fear. In which case, what does indeed remain in the power of Heavens? Except perhaps the natural laws and the phases of the moon? According to a true insight of Nietzsche, the devil told to Zarathustra, "God too has his hell: that is his love of man"; *Thus Spoke Zarathustra* in Kaufmann, *The Portable Nietzsche*, 202. Simone Weil said, "The act of creation is not an act of power. It is an abdication . . . As for the cause of this abdication, Plato expressed it thus, 'He was good.'" Weil, "Are We Struggling for Justice?" 3; quoted by Phillips, *The Problem of Evil*, 179–80. As Peter Berger writes, evil is "a flaw that can only be repaired by God's own suffering, by His participation in the agonies of his creation." *Question of Faith*, 38; cited by Cooper, *Dimensions of Evil*, 13.

In this regard, let us again reflect on Abel's cry beyond death (4:10). To whom is Abel's cry addressed? "Unto me," says God. And Abel's moan deeply affects God. For it "awakens" in God a fatherly trauma falling in parallel with the one reported by Freud in *The Interpretation of Dreams* (= *SE* V:509–10) that culminates in the dead child's plea, "Father, don't you see I'm burning?"

Such is the backdrop of God's painful remonstrance to Cain. It confronts Cain with the question, "What have you done?", that is, what have you done to your brother? What have you done to me as the father of the dead child? Abel is now and for ever crying out to me, so that I shall never be again able to rest, for "the voice of the beloved" will for ever awaken in me the memory of the irreparable loss. "Though dead, he continues to speak" (Heb 11:4).[16]

God's complaint is meant to awaken Cain to Abel's cry. Thus, the "unto me" is also "unto you." The whole future depends from now on upon Cain's receptivity to his brother's call. Either he will hear *with God*, or he will not, against God. Hearing the wretched cry is Cain's "spiritual [existential] worship" (Rom 12:1). Not hearing entails an aimless and hollow drifting, away from the face of God, of the others, of the ground, of the self.[17] J's open-ended story of Cain leaves in suspension any conclusion regarding his "hearing." Is begetting a son and building a city to be interpreted as tokens of repentance? Ambiguity persists to the end, as if J was pragmatically stressing the human existence's "unfinalizability" (Bakhtin).

At any rate, Cain becomes the prototype of human ambiguity. He is after all the first human being born of a woman, like all humans after him. As we are all mythically the descendants of Cain, his violent drive is also our drive.[18] He is the murderer among us and within us, the one

16. Strikingly, the psychoanalytic "seeing" is in the Bible a "hearing."

17. Max Scheler writes about psychological repression (here triggered by God's judgment) that it makes one "no longer feel[ing] at ease in his body; it is as though he moves away from it and views it as an unpleasant object"; *Ressentiment*, 52.

18. Buber, *Good and Evil*, 131, says that the "narrator [J] must have experienced Adam as well as Kain in the abyss of his own heart." Claus Westermann, *Genesis 1–11*, 285, states: "4:2–16 is an elaboration of a genealogical table." Our descent from Cain is only according to J, not according to P for instance (see Gen 5:3). P has no expressed knowledge of the myth of Cain and Abel. Let us note here with Richard S. Hess that the genealogies in Genesis 4, 5, and 11 contrast with the ancient Near Eastern ones as the latter "are concerned with the succession of office holders." He also stresses the absence in Genesis of ancestor worship, ". . . as many negative features as positive are portrayed

"who does not do well" and whose "sin is lurking at the door" of his heart continually. Yet he is also the one with the capability to "master it" (v. 9).[19] Such is our inheritance, since we are not the offspring of Abel, whose innocence—if the following oxymoron be forgiven—materializes in the immateriality of a breath in winter, as his name indicates.

Two in One

Philip Culbertson writes about Abel,[20] "He is nearly invisible to his mother, who identifies Abel as Cain's brother but not as her own son (4:2)."[21] Abel from birth is already the designated victim, the scapegoat par excellence; Abel is innocence continually suppressed by Cain with the complicity of everyone around. There is for him no way to escape. Abel is the Dostoyevskian Idiot; an adumbration of the New Testament Christ. But, although the present humanity does not descend from Abel, Israel as a community decides to emulate Abel, not Cain. James Williams adds, "Israel began to perceive its own origin and destiny in the light of the innocent victim." It is *not* "founded on the expulsion or murder committed by its ancestors."[22]

As is well known, René Girard sees "the hidden generative scapegoat[ing]" as one important aspect of evil in the world.[23] Jesus' passion is "the unconditional refusal of scapegoating, even if . . . it entails that [h]e must be scapegoated."[24] There is, he says, all too often a *mimetic crisis:*

---

in the ancestors named in these [1–11] chapters"; "The Genealogies of Genesis 1–11 and Comparative Literature," 65–66).

19. Unless one understands the phrase in Gen 4:7b as Castellino does, that is, as an interrogation: "Sin will be lying on wait for you, and are you sure you shall be able to master it?"; "Genesis IV 7," 445.

20. Culbertson, "De-Demonizing Cain . . . and Wondering Why?" 3. Culbertson's reading of the myth of Cain and Abel differs from mine.

21. Rabbi Abraham Saba (fifteenth century) said that Cain's birth was too close to the serpent's poison injected into Eve; that is why Abel the Just did not come first and also why Eve disregarded her second son (*Tseror ha-Mor*). Malbim adds that Abel, in his mother's eye, was an unsubstantial addition. But Philo said about Gen 4:2, "to add something is also to subtract something . . . so Cain was subtracted" (*Sacr.*).

22. Williams, *The Bible, Violence and the Sacred*, 29, 30. While a parallel is often drawn between Cain and Abel on the one hand, and Romulus and Remus on the other, the contrast is stark: the Romans claim to be the descendants of the murderer.

23. Girard, Foreword to James Williams, ibid., viii.

24. Girard, in ibid., viii, "This so radically discloses unanimous victimage"—according to the fundamental human tendency to mimesis, a largely *acquired* desire for what the other has or is—that "scapegoating is everywhere uncovered" (ix).

violence—often born from envy or rivalry—creates chaos and must be kept in check by the prohibition in order to restore social order.[25] Cain finds that he is unable to "tolerate the differentiation that God has made."[26] Abel becomes the sacrifice. Cain *eliminates* him; Seth *compensates* for him (Gen 4:25), which is an irenic alternative to bloodshed.

Cain with his mark is "the exception in the process of emerging" (Girard).[27] The sign set upon Cain is a substitute for his expected victimization in response to his transgression. James Williams explicates the function of the sign in these words, "thou shalt not murder Cain as he murdered Abel."[28] A statement that, put in Cain's mouth, would sound like, "Do not kill me, although I am a killer" (see Matt 5:21–22 and its radicalization of the prohibition against murder). While here (as is also modeled in the Joseph story) God sides with the younger victim, the "older brother" is not excluded from God's care; on the contrary he is reintegrated (so Cain; Esau; Joseph's brothers; etc.) while the younger brother is not immune and must undergo a sacrificial ordeal (so Isaac, Joseph, Moses).

So, the distance that separates the brothers—a notion that Mikhail Bakhtin held dear—is both affirmed and restricted. It is necessary but is not allowed to become a divorce. There are an upper and a lower limit to the distanciation. On one hand, exclusivism "kills" Cain, or Esau, or the "brother enemy," and draws a humbugged vanity from its "superiority." On the other hand, inclusivism erases the distance with the other by mimetism, thus triggering a "mimetic crisis."

Regina Schwarz sees the very root of violence in the process of "identity formation" whereby one claims to be what the others are not. Peace would be through some kind of mimesis with others. This, I must say, appears to me rather naïve—no offense intended. Whether or not we agree with sociologists of the Bible that Israel's origin is to be construed as peasant secession from Canaanite feudalist regimes, it seems incontrovertible that Israel's history has been a constant struggle against reverting

25. According to Martin Luther, if God and his angels would cease only for a single day to rule the world, the devil would bring everything to an end in a terrible chaos; *Lectures on Genesis*, in *Luther's Works*, 6:91.

26. Williams, *The Bible, Violence, and the Sacred*, 38.

27. J associates civilization with violence and control of violence. Note that Freud believed that violence is part of our inherited biological nature, only partially transcended by our attempts at civilization (*Civilization*). In this sense, Cain's building a city is sign of a certain maturation consisting in frustrating his drives, especially aggression.

28. Williams, *The Bible, Violence and the Sacred*, 37.

to a *Weltanschauung* marked by polytheism, magic, historical and natural determinism, dualism, and totalitarianism. In particular, the prophetic movement in Israel is to a large extent motivated by the people's temptation to become like the "others" through what Erich Auerbach and René Girard, among others, precisely call "mimesis" (see 1 Sam 8:5, "appoint for us a king to govern us, like other nations").[29] Were not the ancient Hebrews in need of no one less than the formidable visionary Moses to prevent them from returning to the Egyptian slavery? In fact, rather than unilaterally focusing upon the claim—also real, but perhaps as a compensatory face saving—to be different from others, it is probably wiser to speak with Emmanuel Levinas of a "Difficult Freedom."[30]

The "other" of Abel is Cain; the "other" of Cain is Abel. But Cain is not put in a position to define himself as what Abel is or is not; he must not conform with or get rid of Abel in order to be himself, not any more than Abel is himself only without Cain.[31] They are brothers; they have everything in common—but one is innocent, a "poet" of sorts and so, in the eyes of his sibling, he is as "disincarnate" as a breath in winter. The other brother, by contrast, has his feet solidly on the ground; he is an agriculturist, a no-nonsense realist for whom innocence, like poetry, is a vain luxury, soon resented as intolerable because, even unwittingly, it does question all the powers that be.[32] And Cain is powerful; his very name designates him as a possessor; so much so that Abel is just "his brother" and is in a sort of dependence upon him (4:2). Whatever may be Abel's relationship with his parents, he is above all the brother of his brother and the latter's shadow as it were. It is on the model of his brother's offering that "he *also* brought of the firstlings of his flock" to Yhwh (4:3–4). Abel imitates his brother. So much so that he considers himself as second after Cain, as he was trained to think from the beginning. God is the one who

29. When in the early 1950's I was a student at the Hebrew University in Jerusalem, the first murder occurred in the new state. To my great displeasure, not a few articles in the press did celebrate the event. It was, they said, one more demonstration that Israel is like all other nations!

30. Levinas, *Difficult Freedom*.

31. Note that Cain and Abel have different occupations, a fact that should thwart mutual rivalry. The division of labor is, of course, an important element in the story (see here above on "pastoralists" and "agriculturists").

32. Poetry is a lot more "at home" in the meadows than in the soil clods or in the city. Leon Kass calls attention to the literal meaning of the text, as I did myself above, describing Cain's occupation: he is "servant of the ground" (4:2); see Kass, *The Beginning of Wisdom*, 131.

will reverse the hierarchy; [33] the reversal does not originate from Abel's hubris. Malbim advances the idea that it is possible to understand "he also" (*gam hu'*) as meaning that Abel brought his own person as well in sacrifice.[34] This philologically ungrounded conclusion has the advantage of calling attention to a closer relationship between the animal blood and Abel's own than between Cain's vegetables and himself.

Cain's suppression of innocence in the person of Abel—Cain is so powerful that he can wipe out poetry and innocence with one stroke—amounts to the destruction of an opposite that used to be a counterpart, his "other side." Abel's imitation of his brother emphasized their similarity, their mutual "duplication."

The two brothers' "twinness" makes them as it were one person with two faces (like, in Genesis 2, male and female formed an originary unit). In Genesis 4, one "face" is the human belonging to nature as any other animal; the other side is the human distinct from nature. This, Erich Fromm calls a "*contradiction in human existence*" that "*demands a solution.*" It is this very conflict that constitutes "the essence of man."[35] When Deuteronomy 30 exhorts to choose life and reject death, the text is spelling out its conception of the human essence, not just an ethical ideal. By choosing "curse and death" Cain was untrue to his human essence. Both J and Deuteronomy's assumption is that Cain was free to choose one thing or the other. Ricoeur speaks of "l'homme capable" (the capable human). Once, however, Cain has killed his brother, he has cut himself out from freedom. Inclination has become determination. Nothing will annul the murder. As far as he himself is concerned, the only redemption is in repentance, something he shuns.

Thus, Cain kills a part of himself that he has identified as undesirable, his conscience. His crime strips all pretense of guiltlessness; it sets bare his soul. Abel used to be called "his brother," but, ironically, his disappearance makes of Cain Abel's brother (see Gen 4:9) for Cain is now to bear his guilt as "Abel's murderer" for ever. As there is night because there is day, Cain's guilt exists because of Abel's innocence. Saint Paul's

---

33. Shimon Bar-Efrat calls attention to the chiastic construction in 4:1–2 and 4:4–5; *Narrative in the Bible,* 112: Eve bore Cain . . . she bore Abel / Abel was a shepherd . . . Cain a ground tiller/Cain offered a sacrifice . . . Abel also / Abel's offering pleased Yhwh . . . Cain's did not.

34. On Malbim, see 20 n. 10 above.

35. Fromm, *The Heart of Man,* 116–17.

dialectical understanding of the law's *function* belongs to the same logic. Cain without Abel believes that he is automatically guiltless. Abel was the law to Cain. With his demise the law, he thinks, becomes non-existent. All criterion to innocence has disappeared.[36]

The severance between the two halves of the human being (two brothers, like two twins) appears now as complete; it resembles what happened to the positive difference between the genders that eventuated in mutual distrust and denial in Genesis 3. The Adamic humanity has not "kept" the Garden of Eden (Gen 2:15; 3:23), and the Cainite humanity has not "kept" brotherliness as the alternative to violence and guilt (Gen 4:9). The story of Cain and Abel is more generic than temporal.[37]

But things prove not to be as simple as Cain had thought. Abel's blood cries out. As the Garden was not destroyed, innocence is not annihilated; its voice is not extinguished. When there is no Abel left, Abel's God is still there with the same demand upon Cain to "do well." The commandment is indelible as is also the mark on Cain. The latter is not only protecting Cain from the furtherance of violence in retaliation for his crime, but is also, as we saw, a constant reminder to Cain of his sin and guilt. It is as much oppressive as it is liberating, a curse and a blessing. God's mark on Cain is simultaneously the divine rightful claim to being the "avenger of blood" (*go'el damim*) of Abel. The parallel of Abel's cry with Psalm 94 (esp. vv. 1 and 16–17) is striking,

> O LORD, you God of vengeance, you God of vengeance,
>   shine forth! . . .
> Who rises up for me against the wicked?
> Who stands up for me against evildoers?
> If the LORD had not been my help, my soul would soon
>   have lived in the land of silence. [NRSV]

Cain is cursed from the ground (Gen 4:11–12),[38] but he builds a city (v. 17). Now, the city as such is not necessarily a blessing, but the building

36. As Eagleton shows, the criminals, *like the gods,* "demonstrate their freedom from the law by putting it in suspension"; *Holy Terror,* 4.

37. True, however, at some point the myth takes us into the historical time, when the humans mutate nature into culture (building a city, polygamy, arts . . .). About Lamech's bigamy, let us note incidentally this first sociological split in the "Adamic" oneness of husband and wife. It is a foretaste of the grand dispersion of humanity in Genesis 11 (see here below, on "Cain Builds the First City").

38. About the new impotence of the land, William P. Brown stresses the irony of the text, and he contrasts "[t]he impotent figure of Abel [that] has attained powerful

of it is certainly a palliative shift from the agriculturist Cain's tilling of the ground to his urban living. Thus, Cain's flight from the contrasting alternatives of innocence and guilt has yielded an unexpected outcome: a deep ambiguity. Pure innocence is no more, and pure guilt is also thwarted by a divine intervention. Cainite humanity is now living in a hybridized reality.[39]

In our world, nevertheless, even relative innocence is provocative. It is easily equated with weakness, and the world does not like weakness. "La loi du plus fort est toujours la meilleure" (might is right), said La Fontaine, who had a keen understanding of the human soul. [40] Weakness is a vacuum of power, and nature abhors vacuum. Were it not for the God of Israel—as we saw, a character in our story who is much vilified nowadays by exegetes,[41] but a God who sides with the just and the downtrodden—the death of Abel would stir no ripple, like the dissolution of

---

significance in his death" (*The Ethos of the Cosmos*, 169). Shakespeare understood well the tally between murder and the destruction of the natural fabric. See *Macbeth* Act II, scene 3, "And his [Duncan's] gashed stabs looked like a breach in nature" (line 116; see also scene 4, lines 1–24). See, of course, Matt 27:45//Mark 15:33//Luke 23:44. See the section below, "Cain builds a city."

39. St. Augustine and Martin Luther have both insisted that there is no neutral ground between good and evil. Such a stance is not entirely right, however. Good and evil are intertwined and form an impure mixture, like truth and mendacity in the human discourse. As Paul says, "I do not do the good that I want, but the evil I do not want is what I do" (Rom 7:19).

40. Jean de La Fontaine, *Fables*, bk. 1, fable 10.

41. See Blumenthal, *Facing the Abusing God*, 19; Bloom, *The Book of J*, 188; Miles, *God: A Biography*, 40; Moore, *God's Gym*; Brueggemann, *Genesis*, 56–57; Culbertson's paper (see 3–4); as well as others. There is something of the same plea in favor of Cain in Wiesel's *Messengers of God*, 37–68: "Cain and Abel: The First Genocide" (see also of the same, in Philippe de Saint-Cheron and Wiesel, *Evil and Exile*, 179. Wiesel's "Cain" is more a midrashic character than the biblical Cain. On midrashic interpretation transforming textual meaning, see Halpertal, *People of the Book*, 11–44. For Jewish tradition, any human fate is reward or punishment. The principle of distributive justice is here in full force. Abel's violent death is due to some demerit of his, and the divine protection on Cain is reward for some desert (Cain allegedly repented). Such conception of distributive justice is defeated by Second Isaiah's insight that the people's suffering is not a sign of God's rejection, on the contrary. The notion of the Suffering Servant tears apart the disastrous concept of divine retributive distribution of fortune and misfortune, happiness and misery. The book of Job, of course, is another decisive push in the same direction. Retributive justice is the cornerstone of Job's four friends; see, for instance, Bildad's statement in Job 8:3–7, and Elihu's in Job 34:11 (Elihu would certainly have condemned Abel, see 36:21), contrast with Isa 53:4. Moreover, after Isaac, Job, the "Suffering Servant," the Nazarene, the pogroms, and the Shoah, such stance is untenable.

a breath in winter. God is the champion of innocence. As a matter of fact, innocence has no other recourse than God, none whatsoever.[42] The innocent's choice of no-power is choice of divine advocacy. Abel, like the suffering Servant, "does not open his mouth" (Isa 53:7); but unexpectedly the silent Abel shouts beyond death.[43] Innocence crushed "is crying out to God from the ground" (Gen 4:10), and the ground itself curses the one who has cornered the victim to the extreme dereliction of having to find a voice only in death. True, on the tables of Cain's diachrony, the cry of Abel comes too late, that is, when all redress is impossible even if the guilty party was eventually willing to contemplate that closure. The blood of the victim has been sponged by the earth ("swallowed" 4:11), so that no evidence of the murder remains. Cain is in the clear, he thinks. But in God's synchrony, the cry fills time and space.[44] Abel's cry becomes the cry of abused humanity, and Cain is reduced to silence.

No Rehabilitation of Cain

I have mentioned modern negative reactions to God's behavior in our story. Walter Brueggemann, for instance, speaks of "the capricious freedom of Yhwh."[45] But with 4:6–7, we learn from the dialogue of Yhwh with Cain that there is no capriciousness in the divine disregard of Cain's offer. "If you do well . . . if you do not do well," that is the question. It shows that we must "introduc[e] a moral dimension into the incident"; unless of course we surmise that God is not acting in good faith.[46] God has put squarely upon Cain's shoulders the responsibility of the crime. It is only through speculation that we may entertain the thought that God could have intervened and prevented Cain from killing Abel. No less theoretically, we may imagine teaching a psychological lesson to God and coun-

42. From v. 1 on, Psalm 27 states that God is the only trustworthy recourse. The parallel with our story is reinforced by the use in the Psalm of "voice" (v. 7); plus the petition to see God's Face, and not to be turned away (v. 9, see Gen 4:14, 16).

43. Facing piles of corpses killed by the SS at Dachau, Father Sommet evokes "the silence of their presence, which was a kind of silent, immense speech . . . [T]he failure of their existence was indicative of the price that freedom and dignity demand" (Jacques Sommet, *L'honneur de la liberté*, 127, quoted by Ortiz-Hill, *The Roots and Flowers*, 167.

44. Hebrews 11:4 says of Abel slaughtered, "he is still speaking." Using another terminology, Ricoeur distinguishes between the "chronological [or sequential] order" and the "configurational order" of the signifying whole; see his "L'identité narrative," 287–300).

45. Brueggemann, *Genesis*, 56.

46. Ibid., 57.

seling him to pretend to have an equal consideration for Cain's offering as for Abel's. But this would miss the mark. God's statement in Gen 4:7 tallies with God's commandment in Gen 2:17. "If you do well" amounts to the command "Do well!" or to the prohibition "Do not choose not to do well!" Thus, before and after the "fall,"[47] the very bridging of the gap between the Creator and the created is God ordering and the human obeying. Without God's commandment, the universe returns to chaos. God's order is the dike containing its onslaught (see Job 38:10–11). Within the Cain paradigm, leaving the face of God means returning to the soullessness of the clay. And, as there is no disclosure of meaning to draw from the clay he is treading, Cain is wandering aimlessly from field to field, starting with the range where he killed his brother. He strolls without command, lawlessly, but also senselessly. Immersed in soullessness, he becomes himself soulless, "cursed from a ground," which itself is already cursed (Gen 3:17). From being a man of the promise (4:1), Cain has fallen down to being inhuman ("not a man" *lo' 'iš*; see Exod 2:12), like a clod.

That is how Cain's banishment amounts to death, and that is also why Cain had to break the cycle of meaninglessness by stopping his vagrancy and settling somewhere, even though the place of settlement is Nod, "Nowhere." Later, he will build and inaugurate a city, Enoch, a name that means "inauguration." There, the outlaw Cain will be a ruler, the imposer of a rule under his own authority. Cain's law will replace God's law—a pitiful parody that is endlessly echoed in ancient and modern totalitarian states' laws.

J's basic conviction is that the human beings are free. Cain can do well and he can also not do well. Cain can choose innocence like his brother does or he can choose shrewdness and power, even the power of life and death over others.

A more immediate issue than whether "to be or not to be," Cain's existential question is *what* to be. The text of Gen 4:7 reaches a rare summit when Cain hears the divine statement of human capability, sublimely condensed into one word in Hebrew, *timšol* ([you shall] dominate!). About this performative expression, John Steinbeck's *East of Eden* comes much closer to the true purpose of the biblical text than does even a scholar of the caliber of Brueggemann, for instance. As we saw above, Steinbeck writes, "These sixteen verses are a history of mankind in any age or cul-

47. The justification for the quotation marks here is spelled out in my *The Trial of Innocence*.

ture or race," while Brueggemann reads the sentence as pronounced by a God who is a "gamesman . . . playing with this elder son whom he has so easily rejected."[48] We are almost led to believe that God is the sadistic slayer and that, as we are Cainites ourselves, we are the victims! The whole thing smacks like of a *pro domo* argument. We shall note the almost absence of Abel in the commentator's exposition. Eve's outrageous disregard for her second son finds an uncanny echo in some modern scholarship. Brueggemann adds, "God . . . may be an enemy."[49] W. Lee Humphreys goes so far as to speak of God's arbitrariness, which He uses to "destabilize the human condition in what now seems a power play" [*sic*].[50]

On the contrary, the text's emphasis is unmistakably on human responsibility. Cain—that is, humanity at large—is to "dominate." The same idea is expressed in Gen 1:28 where the human ruling is over the whole of creation. True, the verb used by P there is different (*radah*), but the same conception is also present in Ps 8:7, where it is expressed with the same verb *mašal* as in Gen 4:7. The human dominion is therefore as a stand-in of God over the world. The dominion over sin falls in parallel with this in the sense that the world is corrupt and may be called *sub specie Dei*, evil (see Isa 13:11; Jas 4:4; 1 John 5:19).

Be it said emphatically again, a modern "rehabilitation" of Cain misses the mark. After all, we dispose of preciously limited means to judge a narrative character. Robert Alter comes with a useful "scale of [six] means" by which "character can be revealed."[51] If we apply Alter's scale to Cain's personality, we discover that all the textual elements available concur to building up a convincing profile: we know Cain's profession (means #1); the high opinion of his mother about him (means #2); what he did: he sacrificed to Yhwh, he killed his brother, he wandered (means #3); we hear his words (means #4); we know something of his inner thoughts (means #5); finally, the narrator's negative judgment, although sober and typically understated, leaves no doubt as regards this antihero's twisted mentality (means #6). To this scale, it is proper to add, with Humphreys,

---

48. Brueggemann, *Genesis*, 60.
49. Ibid., 61.
50. Humphreys, *The Character of God in the Book of Genesis*, 56–57. Yhwh is here confused with a Mesopotamian divinity.
51. Alter, *The Art of Biblical Narrative*, esp. 116–17.

the contrast set by J between "characters in juxtaposition to each other."[52] Cain's relationship with others is far from exemplary, of course.

"What have you done?" (4:10; the same question as in Gen 3:13) expresses the enormity of the crime in God's eyes and, by ricochet, in the eyes of all decent people. Nothing so appalling was ever done and nothing more heinous will ever be perpetrated than Cain's fratricide-patricide-deicide. Cain's transgression of the boundaries of decency is dwarfing his parents' earlier transgression.[53] Adam, to recall, was not cursed; Cain is cursed (4:11) like previously the serpent in Genesis 3, and as foreshadowing in the future the curse of Canaan in Gen 9:25–27. Even God seems overwhelmed by the crime, and he asks from Cain a confirmation, as it were, of what he witnessed, "What have you done?" As Westermann says, "This is one of the monumental sentences in the Bible."[54] It makes clear that an injustice, let alone a crime, will not remain unheeded by God (Westermann cites 1 Sam 2:12 [Uriah]; and 1 Kings 21 [Naboth]).

Now, this divine unmediated questioning of Cain imagined by J could be construed as wishful thinking on his part, not corresponding to the dire reality of universal indifference, were it not for the fact that Abel's blood, instead of fertilizing the soil, has actually debilitated its vitality. Cain's crime has cosmic repercussions.[55] Genesis 4:10–12 intimates that cosmic evil is due to human sinfulness. Uncannily, Gen 4:12 could be a modern ecological statement.[56]

---

52. Humphreys, *The Character of God*, 13. He insists also upon character-construct by the reader (14–21). Let us add that the reader judgment must necessarily take into account all the means offered by the narrative (= the evidence in a court of law). This does not mean though that Cain's narrative figure remains unaltered to the end. Another aspect emerges *in fine*, when he builds the city of Enoch, as we shall see below.

53. A taut paradox when we realize that Adam's sin was against God.

54. Westermann, *Genesis 1–11*, 305.

55. In both Gen 3:17–19 and 4:11–12, it is said that the ground is cursed *because* of an unethical act of the humans. True, this is not the complete story of cosmic evil, which is "always already there" in the human environment. But the tie between the ethical evil and the cosmic evil is strongly emphasized by J. "The blood [shed] pollutes the land," says Num 35:33 . "The murderer shall be put to death" (35:16–18, 21), for the sole decontaminant is also blood. Only God's commandment (by imposition of a sign) can override the law; see "Thou Shalt not Kill" in LaCocque and Ricoeur, *Thinking Biblically*, 71–110, and my "About the 'Aqedah' in Genesis 22." In *Crime and Punishment*, the murderer Raskolnikov bows to the ground he has profaned with his crime.

56. About Gen 4:12, Waltke says, "Once again earth's ecology is impacted by human morality (see 3:17)"; *Genesis*, 98.

From this ecological perspective, it behooves us to return to the initial motif of Cain being an agriculturist (while Abel was a pastoralist). Cain in the story has clearly a fascination with the soil. He never raises his head toward the sky; he resembles our ape-like four-footed "ancestors." Now, it is important to read the story synchronically, that is, without the determination of the "before" and the "after." The ground tilled by Cain and that provided the ingredients of his offering *could* have been a blessed ground, full of vitality and fit to yield a produce appropriate for the sacrifice—but not automatically so and not unambiguously. It is not the fact that one of the two brothers is a tiller while the other is a sheepherder that matters; what matters is the "souls" of the one and the other.[57] We could speculate that, had Abel been an agriculturist, his offer of the produce of the soil would have been agreeable, while whatever Cain would offer been unpleasant. The old popular image of the smoke of Cain's sacrifice crawling close *to the ground* while Abel's offering's smoke rising straight to the sky emanates from a right intuition. Among the myth-oriented societies, the watching of the smoke rising from the altar was one way to interpret the (in)validity of the offering, like extispicy (the reading of animal entrails).

Cain—A Tragic Figure?

Jacques Ellul says that the divine sign on Cain did not satisfy him, so that "now Cain will spend his life trying to find security," using his own means, not trusting the potentiality of the sign.[58] This way, Cain "is forever the man going somewhere, but where?" In fact, Cain has left the face to face with God and has thereby lost all location, because any other place is no-place, nowhere. That is why, as we saw, being estranged from the face of God means also being estranged from the ground (4:11).[59] For the

57. Those who insist exclusively upon the qualitative difference in the brothers' offerings indulge in a depsychologizing that is uncalled for. As Otto Rank averted in *The Myth of the Birth of the Hero*, myth's meanings must be sought in the human psyche, cited by Rudnytsky, *Reading Psychoanalysis*, 83.

58. Ellul, *The Meaning of the City*, 3. One could even think in Hobbesian terms that the city founded by Cain will serve as a "Leviathan" to control human violence, a natural "condition of man" who is involved in a "war of everyone against everyone"; *Leviathan*, part I, chap. 4.

59. Willy Schottroff stresses the distinction between a curse "which affects the cursed in his own personal life" as in Deut 28:16–19, and the curse "which excludes a person from the community and the land"; "Soziologie und Altes Testament," 62, cited by

face to face with God is a "grounding" into the world, finding one's place in life and in the universe.

Cain went from before Yhwh (*milliphnei Yhwh*). Claus Westermann takes exception to Franz Delitzsch's understanding of the sentence in 4:16 as saying "Cain went away, away from the place of the divine revelation (like Jonah 1:3)." Westermann says that Cain cannot go away "from the place of the divine revelation" because there is no space fitting for a divine revelation in the primeval event.[60] Now, assuredly Delitzsch went too far in one direction; but Westermann went too far in the other, for *liphnei Yhwh* has in many a text a *cultic* meaning. Thus the logic is with Westermann, but J's allusiveness is perceived by Delitzsch. For the cultic is not absent from our narrative, although, as elucidated here below, J's interest in the cultic is strikingly minimal. All the same, both brothers offer a sacrifice and, therefore, go "before Yhwh." The fact that this is not expressly specified by the Yahwist leads Gerhard von Rad to speak here of a process of "historicization" and "secularization," so that J's narrative is "almost wholly devoid of cultic associations." *History*, he argues, has taken their place and is characteristically "directed and ordered by God . . . [along with] every sphere of life."[61] Nevertheless, rather than to follow von Rad here and see this phenomenon as falling in parallel with David's succession narrative in 2 Sam 7; 9–20 + 1 Kings 1–2, the obvious kinship with the prophetic literature is more significant, as J may have penned the succession tradition, if we follow the lead of Auerbach or Hannelis Schulte.[62]

In 4:16 Cain, after doing away with his brother, is stealing away from Yhwh. For Cain, there will never again be a cultic encounter with God.[63] The first sacrificer in human history is also, paradoxically, the first "excommunicated." He is the great wanderer because he wandered away from God's presence. Then Cain's punishment becomes a voluntary exile (like Oedipus'): he takes upon himself to go away from the face of God,

Westermann, *Genesis 1–11*, 307. Cain's wandering sets a paradigm, which Paul Tillich calls the "estranged" condition of the human being (see in LeFevre, ed., *The Meaning of Health*; Tillich, "The Theological Significance of Existentialism and Psychoanalysis").

60. Westermann, *Genesis 1–11*, 314.

61. Von Rad, *The Problem of the Hexateuch*, 68, 71.

62. See Auerbach, *Wüste und gelobtes Land*, 24–33; Schulte, *Die Entstehung der Geschichteschreibung im alten Israel*, 172ff.; 218ff.; see also Blenkinsopp, "Theme and Motif in the Succession History (2 Sam xi 2ff) and the Yahwist Corpus"; Friedman, *The Hidden Book*.

63. So also Ramban [Moses ben Nachman; thirteenth century]: *Ramban (Nachmanides) Commentary in the Pentateuch*, ad loc.

either because the face to face has become intolerable, or because he is still full of rebellious rage. From potential victim of a divine chastisement, he has become self-destructive. Cain is hit with what psychoanalysis calls "unconscious guilt feelings" whose manifestation, among others, is melancholia (narcissistic neurosis). For Cain's profile would remain incomplete without diagnosing him as narcissistic. Only a narcissistic blindness can bring someone to "even gracefully kill a brother since he is not 'me,' therefore less sacrosanct, 'less human' than one is oneself."[64]

As the story of Cain and Abel is inseparable from the previous tale on Adam and Eve, so it is also tied with the next J story in Genesis 6 on the monstrous commerce of angels with human maidens, that is, about a paroxysmal attempt "at abolishing the essential distinction between the divine and the human; hence at violating the sacred order of things," according to Paul Humbert.[65] This remark by Humbert is important, for it stresses the metaphoricity of many spatial descriptions by J. It belongs to the narrative nature of the story to have the angels coming down to come in to human females and begetting "Nephilim," that is, "the heroes that were of old, warriors of renown" (Gen 6:4 NRSV). The same is true when J pictures Cain taking a physical distance from God. In reality, the distance is spiritual (see Ps 10:1; 145:3). John Hick uses philosophical terminology and says,

> The distance must be epistemic, a distance in the cognitive dimension. And the Irenaean hypothesis is that this 'distance' consists, in the case of humans, in their existence within and as part of a world that functions as an autonomous system and from within which God is not overwhelmingly evident.[66]

D. Z. Phillips's statement can be readily applied to Cain's fate after his crime, "[T]o fear God's wrath is not to fear what God will do to one (the external view), but to fear what one will become (the internal view), namely, cut off from God."[67]

Consistent with the lack of repentance on the part of Adam and Eve in the preceding myth, J pictures Cain as relentless. But, in contrast with Adam and Eve being expelled from Eden, Cain goes away on his free

---

64. Becker, *The Birth and Death of Meaning,* 162. Becker refers to Herman Melville's "The Indian Hater."
65. Humbert, "Démesure et chute dans l'Ancien Testament," 70.
66. Hick, "An Irenaean Theodicy," 42.
67. Phillips, *The Problem of Evil,* 253.

will from the face of God. The deepening of the estrangement between the divine and the human is manifest: while the very last word of God sounding in the primal couple's ears was "you shall return" (*tašub*; Gen 3:19), the last in God's utterance to Cain is "shall be avenged" (*yuqqam*; 4:15), a term that underscores the series of violent acts initiated by Cain's fratricide. J develops the theme further on with Lamech's song and with texts such as Gen 6:13 and 9:5–6. The relevance of J's diagnosis needs no demonstration.[68]

Nevertheless, for J, the increasing degree of gravity in human sinning does not supersede the essential priority of hubris.[69] Violence itself is the direct outcome of hubris/arrogance. True, the psychoanalyst Willard Gaylin would discern fear at the root of anger and violence, and he is certainly right to look back at the human response to their survival's threats as fundamental.[70] Yet Cain's angst is real, although he has nothing to fear from Abel for his survival. The only threat he (wrongly) perceives is to his integrity and to his pride. Thus J rather focuses on the latter revealing a common denominator between Cain and Cain's parents (between Genesis 2–3 and 4) that is not fear but hubris, will to power.

Now, the appetite for supremacy is basically a quest for immortality and an escape from death. The serpent says, "You shall not die" (Gen 3:4) and Cain says . . . something that remains inarticulate but is translated into lethal blows: inflicting death to someone else is to escape one's own death. You die, I live. Man's animal fear of dying is commuted into its opposite, namely, to be like God, as in Gen 3:5. The deepest root of human alienation from God is the will to play God (see Genesis 3). Cain's violence against the other is aping the divine ownership of life in creation (see Gen 9:4–6; Exod 13:2, 12; 22:29–30; 34:19), "the god-like empowerment over other human lives," as Chris Hedges says; "the divine power to destroy," he adds.[71] For Abel's blood spilled on the ground is first claimed by the murderer (who, uncouthly or under the cover of a more refined mask, duplicates the savage thirst for appropriating the substance of the

---

68. As strongly stated by Gandhi, "Retaliation cannot end violence . . . . There is no alternative but to adopt non-violence. Love alone can conquer hatred"; *Essential Writings*, 115. "For, through violence you may murder a murderer but you cannot murder murder" said Martin Luther King Jr., "Where Do We Go from Here?" 176.

69. A point that Herodotus, in the fifth century BCE, would confirm historically.

70. Gaylin, *Hatred*, 45ff.

71. Hedges, *War Is a Force That Gives Us Meaning*, 89, 171.

victim, human or animal).[72] It is evident that, in the game of God-imitation, the supreme act of power is the *taking* of someone else's life.[73] That is why there were so many volunteers in the organized crime hordes of the SS, and nowadays so many candidates to be listed among the religiously exonerated massacre gangs.

The result is not the one expected. Finally, what Cain succeeds of doing is killing a brother, killing his own vis-à-vis, killing himself. And his sham imitation of God eventuates in a permanent banishment from God, from ground, from humanity. The "heroic" warrior (or at least the victorious warrior) stirs horror and outrage among his fellow humans (see 4:14), and in the sight of God (see 4:11–12).

The outcome of violence is the destruction of the world by annihilation (Genesis 6–8). The rabbis of old were right when declaring that killing someone amounts to killing the whole world; so does also the Quran.[74] J was aware of the cosmic dimension of Cain's "private" crime. His invitation to his readers to a reflection in this direction has, however, seldom been heeded.

At least in part, Cain is a tragic figure.[75] First he was "king of the hill," acclaimed as the very "man" (*'iš*) that God had in mind in creating Adam. But Cain ends up as completely disoriented; his initial leadership—Abel followed servilely in his steps—would now conduct into the abyss, the abode of death. Hence, anyone in her right mind dreams to do away with him as he did away with his brother. He is spared by the divine avenger of blood, but he is soul-less, without contact with people or with land. Alienated and uprooted, Cain has become a zombie.

Few modern writers are more eloquent than Hannah Arendt on "loneliness" (the loneliness of modern bourgeoisie, atomized into an archipelago of individuals incapable of any social generosity). Loneliness, she says, is "to have no place in the world, recognized and guaranteed by others." There, she adds, "I am deserted by myself."[76] This, I suggest, is

72. Hedges writes, "If you kill your enemy his body becomes your trophy, your possession, and this has been a fundamental part of warfare since before the Philistines beheaded Saul"; *War Is a Force*, 30; see 1 Sam 31:9.

73. This customary phrase expresses a deeply rooted popular feeling.

74. See above, 41 n. 85.

75. The story composed by J corresponds to the Greek tragedy, invented in the fifth century BCE and focusing on violence, punishment, exile or death. Also in parallel with the Greek drama, the Yahwist's tale is imbedded in religious worship.

76. Arendt, *The Origins of Totalitarianism*, 475.

the veritable vagrancy of Cain; it does not conflict with the building of a city. Wherever Cain may be, he is ostracized by all others and lonely in his soul ("deserted by himself"). Arendt says that such isolation led the German bourgeoisie to throw itself into Hitler's murderous arms. In the myth of Cain and Abel, the reverse seems to be true: first comes slaying, then loneliness. But Cain may be thought of as lonely from the beginning, an impression confirmed by his inability to speak to Abel in the field, and his laconic rebuttal to God's question with, "Am I my brother's keeper?" Let us note at this stage that his societal ineptitude is not without relation to a castrating mother (see Eve's possessiveness in 4:1–2).

The story of Cain does not end here. There is an entirely unexpected settling of Cain and the building of a city! This, it must be acknowledged, retrospectively sheds some doubt about how to classify the narrative as a whole. Is it a tragedy (characterized according to Aristotle's *Poetics* by an unhappy ending), or is it a comedy (with a happy ending)?[77] J's narrative remains purportedly ambiguous—and Aristotle's categories are exploded into a mixed genre akin to the so-called tragicomedy. Cain is not irremediably ignoble and he is certainly not noble; he is all too human—like the recipients of J's story.

The rebound of Cain's story is a moment of psychological surprise and of literary suspense. There is here what Ricoeur calls a "discordant concordance"[78] to which corresponds the narrative identity of the character (Cain). And, here again is reversed the Aristotelian model of the plot (*mythos*) being primordial while the characters are secondary. In Genesis 4, the plot is at the service of the characters' becoming. To quote Paul Ricoeur again, "The dialectic of agreement and discord, transferred from the plot to the character, then from the character to oneself, can then begin again, with a renewed hope, if not of success then at least of significance."[79]

77. Aristotle, *Poetics*, 5, 49a 32, 38; 6, 49b 22; 2, 48a 17; 13, 53a 36; Aristotle's categories are reversed in Genesis 4 because, to the Greek *contemplation* of reality, the Hebrew worldview opposes a desire to *communicate* with the real. Therefore, primacy tends to be attributed to characters rather than to episodic occurrences. At some point, the Nazarene said, "I am the Truth" (John 14:6).

78. Ricoeur, "L'identité," 292.

79. Ibid., 300: "La dialectique de concordance et de discordance, transférée de l'intrigue au personnage, puis du personnage à soi-même, peut alors reprendre, avec une nouvelle espérance, sinon de réussite du moins de signifiance."

The Psychology of Abel, the Kin of Cain

Abel is thus sent back, as it were, to his childhood stage, before being eventually pushed further to his prenatal nonexistence. But Cain's move backfires: the ghost has a voice, a will, a meaning. All along the story, Abel appears as not only younger than Cain but also more naïve, gullible, innocent. He follows his brother without suspicion "to the field." He does not detect in Cain any trace of anger or jealousy. All along, he is voiceless (while alive). The news of his birth was shortchanged by his parents, his life is spent far from the hearth, and eventually his death apparently does not create any ripples among his kin. The extremely condensed scene "in the field"—where even a potential dialogue is aborted—is all the same strikingly eloquent. By abducting Abel and cornering him to face his death, Cain has "subject[ed] the victim to a radical and catastrophic infantilization," in the words of Christopher Bollas.[80] Cain has taken advantage of his brother's vulnerability, and now he submits him to the paroxysm of immaturity. Bollas adds that "The structure of evil exploits our primitive belief in the goodness of the other."

The content of the posthumous cry of Abel is too rich to be fully explicated.[81] At any rate, one thing it says is that the nature of any murder is fratricidal[82] and, ultimately, a patricide and deicide. To illuminate this point, the story in Genesis 4 sets in stark contrast Cain's homicidal rebellion against God, and Eve's initial exclamation that God is the veritable father of her child(ren) (4:1). True, the obliteration of Adam in the tale might be for the sake of emphasizing God's role in the lad's birth and, more subtly, of putting paternity out of reach of suspicion and rivalry. But Adam's fading presence gives way to Eve's (and only Eve's) new "acquisition," Cain. The latter, as it were, starts by setting aside his father, all but eliminating him from the unfolding events. Such a beginning is ominous and augurs ill for the future. It is not out of character that Cain be

80. Bollas, "The Structure of Evil," 200.

81. The soundless cry as a theme is fascinating (see 1 Kgs 19:12), as is pictorially shown in Edvard Munch's "The Cry" (1893), and displayed in Bertolt Brecht's play "Mutter Courage und ihre Kinder" (when she is put in the presence of her dead son Schweizerkas). The latter scene is mentioned with great pathos by George Steiner, *The Death of Tragedy*, 352–54.

82. See Cassuto, *Genesis*. Westermann, *Genesis 1–11*, 286, writes: "Every murder, J is saying, is really the murder of a brother." As brothers spring from a common father, "when a man fights with his brother, he is indirectly fighting with his father." Hence, "fratricide is patricide"; Kass, *The Beginning of Wisdom*, 447.

displeased with the "intrusion" of a younger brother—even though without fanfare and almost shamefully on the part of the parturient[83]—whose presence now resuscitates, if not the father himself, at least the situation dealt with originally by mother and son conniving in Gen 4:1.[84]

Cain transgresses the taboo. He kills Abel who becomes the first dead in the history of humanity.[85] We are, of course, reminded of J's preceding myth in Gen 2:17 ("you shall die") and in 3:19 ("you shall return to the ground"), but strikingly the first death is inflicted by a man, not by "fate."[86] The message is clear: all death in human history is harking back to an original human slaughter.[87] God is not taking life. Jean-Paul Sartre was even more right than he knew when he said, that anyone living dies by accident[88]—an accident ultimately provoked by himself or by a "brother." J explicates this by showing a human being introducing violence and murder into history, that is, the extreme of disorder and chaos, the antipode of creation and life.

Remarkable is the stark contrast between the triumphant cry of Eve at the birth of the "man" Cain (4:1) and her being actually deprived by that same man of another man, her second son. Woman gives life; man gives death. By killing Abel, Cain kills all masculinity around him, first in the person of his brother, and second, by implication, of his human and

83. To wit, the name given to the second son: "emptiness, vanity."

84. The plot of Rebecca and Jacob fooling Isaac comes to mind (Genesis 27).

85. Strikingly, the first dead in the Bible is the brother. Thus, the warning of Gen 2:17 regarding one's mortality ominously expands to include murder and fratricide. In *moth tamuth*, one can also detect *moth tamith*, you will bring death—not just to yourself but to others. Transgression will make you a carrier of death. That is why Levinas states that on the human face is written large, "Do not kill me!" Rainer Maria Rilke, in a letter to Lou Andreas-Salomé of September 1914 wrote, "We all are and ever will be the killers of ourselves and of each other. Perhaps this is inevitable but, because of it, our guilt is terribly universal and our sole means of redemption is to accept it as it is, that is, to feel the universality of our guilt"; quoted by Peters, *My Sister, My Spouse*, chapter 9 "Exorcising the Demons"]). In the fourth century, St. Ephrem said that, as Abel is the first dead descending righteous in the Sheol, the latter "would be compelled in justice to cast him forth from its depths," and thus Abel becomes the premises of resurrection; *Commentary on the Diatessaron*, 339, cited by Gary A. Anderson, *The Genesis of Perfection*, 174.

86. So the prayer, "deliver us from evil" may be understood as meaning, "from self-inflicted evil; deliver us from our morbid, suicidal and sadistic inclination to do evil to ourselves and to others" (see Gen 6:5).

87. On the evident parallel with Freud's speculation on humanity's original patricide in *Civilization and Its Discontent*, see below.

88. "tout existant . . . meurt par rencontre"; *La Nausée*.

his divine fathers. He remains for a while the only genitor (4:17: "And Cain knew his wife; she conceived and bore . . .").

The parallel with the Oedipus myth is all the more striking when one re-reads Gen 4:1, which sets the framework of the story with even more emphasis than we have done above: "And the man knew Eve his wife; she conceived and bore Cain (*qayin*) . . . . She said: I have created (*qanithi*) a man with Yhwh." Not only is Adam not named here ("the man"), but Eve is the one who names the child.[89] And she attributes the birth to Yhwh, not to her husband. In other words, at his birth, the male Cain is squeezed between Adam and Yhwh and their conflicting paternities. Hovering over the trio, there is Eve, impregnated by one husband, made a mother by another, and giving birth to a third male. The trio of males she faces will soon become a foursome complex, with the birth of Abel, all of them contributing to a kind of "quadrant": the divine male (the "Magician"); the progenitor ("the man"/the King); the killer/warrior; and the poet/lover.[90] The former pair may communicate since they are both father figures and, as Gen 4:1 demonstrates, they can at points alternate as the genitors of humanity. The latter pair, however, can hardly coexist, unless they gingerly remain in separate corners of the human space. Symbolically, "Menelaus" the warrior and "Paris" the lover clash (*Iliad* 3). Their difficult accord readily becomes conflictive when the idealistic poet starts to walk in the steps of his practical brother the "warrior." Cain offers a sacrifice and Abel should have known better than to imitate him. The warrior takes umbrage at an imitator-competitor. The "poet," of course, may not even realize that his move could possibly be construed as a challenge. Unsuspectingly, he goes with his brother to "the field" that swiftly becomes a battlefield. The issue of the clash raises no doubt: the innocent is crushed.[91]

The foursome complex of males has been short-lived. Cain gets rid of Abel, and through him of Yhwh-the-father, hence of his genitor

89. Contrast this verse with v. 25 where Adam is clearly used as a proper name and where Eve reiterates a similar process with Enosh, v. 26. About motherly comments after the birth of a child, see also Gen 21:7; 30:23–24.

90. In my study of Adam and Eve (*The Trial of Innocence*), I applied the term "poet" to the prelapsarian Adam and I called attention to the absence of that figure from the "archetypes of the mature masculine" (271).

91. See Jean de La Fontaine, *Fables*, V, 2 "The earthen Pot and the iron Pot." The fable starts with the words, "let us go abroad a little" (see Gen 4:8); it continues with, "Having won his friend's compliance, Off they started in alliance." As expected, the earthen pot is shattered to pieces by the iron pot. The story ends with the morality, "With our equals let us mate, Or dread the weaker vessel's fate" (147).

Adam. While Cain had chosen the occupation of tiller of the ground after his father Adam (see Gen 2:15), in itself a possible sign of communion between father and son, in reality, the son's fare is already replacing his father and eliminating him.[92] He takes upon himself to become the sacrificer of the family.

It goes without saying that, in the background of the conflict between kin males, the mother's profile looms large. She is the confessed or undisclosed object of the primordial desire. According to Freud, here lies the very ground of any family conflict, while, according to Girard, the conflict comes first, and the rivalry second. Girard's paradigm, like the one of Freud, is triangular, but it postulates the presence of "the model, the disciple, and the object that is disputed by both because the model's desire has made the object desirable to the disciple."[93] In the context of the uneasiness between Cain and Abel, this makes a lot of sense. The story of their rivalry starts early on with the statement that Abel's sacrifice was regarded with favor by God, while Cain's was disregarded. But let us ask once again: who said so? The text tells only that Cain's countenance fell, hence indicating that the pessimistic conclusion came from Cain's interpretation of the events. Cain is the one who transforms the brotherly communion into an antagonistic competition. Within this twisted perspective, the discrete courting of the favor of God by the brothers appears to be so mutually undistinguishable that it need breeds what Girard calls a "mimetic desire."

Now, of the two brothers, the "model" is clearly Cain, and the "disciple" is the one who is constantly referred to as his brother. But, as the story unwinds, there is an uncanny exchange of roles for, whether Cain is blinded by jealousy, or whether God's favor is really going to Abel's sacrifice, this latter becomes the "model," like in so many biblical stories of birthright. Abel's offering becomes Cain's obsession. This is an important point, for it is on Cain's part a fateful shift in focus (that God tries to correct with his exhortation to refocus on his own: "If *you* do well . . ."). So, whether based on actuality or fiction, Abel has taken the lead—something we earlier contemplated in dealing with the silence of Cain in the field.

The object of desire of both brothers, which they share by mimesis, is evidently God's blessing, but also all that this blessing implies, primarily on the plane of fertility; the fertility of the land (*'adamah*)—the domain of

92. On Cain destroying the Other, see White, "Where is your brother?"
93. Girard, *Violence and the Sacred*, 181.

Cain—and the fertility of the womb—the domain of Abel—the soil and the womb corresponding to each other, as it also did in Gen 3:16–17.

In the brothers' relation turned conflictive, where is *the* womb-object? There is in the story only one named woman: Eve. So far, she has definitely and unabashedly favored Cain and disregarded Abel—like Rachel who also will later favor one of her two sons. But now, Abel unwittingly and innocently becomes supreme, and Cain is not ready to exchange his born supremacy for a plate of lentils! According to God's exhortation, he can regain his status through brotherliness toward Abel, that is, through transcending the evil that lies in wait at the gate of his heart and gnaws his soul. But Cain chooses a more radical solution to the fraternal conflict: the elimination pure and simple of Abel.

Remaining on the stage are only two narrative characters: Cain and Eve, the son and the mother. The broken triangle Laius–Oedipus–Jocasta is again paradigmatic here, and incest is not far off. Psychoanalysis shows the relation of aggressiveness with sexuality. Already Alfred Adler in 1908 had advanced the idea of an autonomous "aggressive instinct."[94] The incest, notwithstanding, is thwarted, like the adultery of sorts between Eve and the serpent in Genesis 3.[95] It is cut short by the unexpected voice of God, whom Cain may have considered as dead, dead like Abel. But even the latter's corpse has a powerful voice.[96] The Oedipal Cain will not have his way after all. Like Oedipus leaving Thebes, Cain "went away from the presence of Yhwh" (4:16)—and also from the presence of Eve for, in a

94. See Adler, "Der Aggressionstrieb im Leben und in der Neurose," 577–84. For Freud, to recall, "incest, cannibalism, and lust for killing" are "born afresh with every child"; "The Future of an Illusion," 189. It is a "constitutional inclination of human beings to be aggressive towards one another"; 336. Nothing runs more strongly against the human instinct than to "love the neighbor as yourself"; 303.

95. According to the *Gospel of Philip* (61:5–10), Cain was begotten by the serpent (see above regarding the "Cainist" Gnostic literature, and 70 n. 11). So, Gen 4:1 is here understood as saying that Adam knew *about* his wife ('s adultery); so also in *Tg. Ps.-J.* 4:1; *PRE* 21. Westermann, *Genesis 1–11*, 285: "[Gen] 4:2–16 follows closely the pattern of Genesis 3."

96. See again Heb 11:4. The speaking ghost in *Hamlet* comes to mind. Paradoxically, Cain is also at the benefit of being granted a "voice." See the divine promise to Cain that his death would be avenged sevenfold! This expression is strictly judicial. Exod 21:21 uses the verb *qum* also with this sense of punishment. Any killer of Cain would be *fully* sanctioned. What good does it do to Cain to know that? The divine commitment is in fact that Cain would find an avenger in God *like* Abel's death did. Thus equanimity between the two brothers is for the first time established, the very equanimity that Cain had disbelieved and trashed.

terribly ironical paradox, by killing Abel Cain has forever lost his mother's love. The story is rounded up with Eve begetting another son, whom she calls Seth (Adam is once again bypassed). Seth is in the eyes of his mother replacing *Abel* "whom Cain murdered" (4:25).[97]

In the country of his exile, Cain finds a substitute for his loneliness; he "knows" a woman, not his mother Eve to be sure but rather, significantly, an anonymous female who does not seem to have fully replaced the object of the quasi-incest, for she is mentioned as if in passing and, somewhat disrespectfully, as a mere genetrix. So, the odd absence of the feminine in the core of the story—a story with three interacting male characters: Cain, Abel, Yhwh—is disconcerting. Let us note at this point that by taking a wife, Cain turns a page in his life and bets on the future at the expense of the past. To this extent, there is hope.[98]

Another message "cried" out metaphorically by Abel's blood confirms an above-mentioned sober statement by Immanuel Kant that the human becomes evil "*as soon as he is among men* . . . it suffices that they are at hand, that they surround him . . . for them mutually to corrupt each other's predispositions and make one another evil"[99]—a corruption and evil more often than once motivated by jealousy. As men make war whereas women do not,[100] it is clear that there will be a hoary atavism of belligerence among males for the conquest of females. Both the Bible and psychoanalysis assume that the humans heave along within their bloodstream, so to speak, the stain and the remembrance of an originary crime: fratricide and/or patricide. Either one is corrupting their being and is all the deeper ingrained as it is repressed to the inner coils of the unconscious. The humans are fundamentally violent; in fact they are the most violent species among all the animals. Their onslaught is primarily directed at their fellow creatures (in French, their *semblables*), thus

97. Devora Steinmetz writes, "A man who cannot live in peace with his brother has no choice but to leave the land, and to leave the land means not to have a place . . ."; *From Father to Son*, 91.

98. See the beautiful note in Kass, *The Beginning of Wisdom*, 447 n. 2.

99. Kant, *Religion within the Limits of Reason Alone* (see 3 n. 7 above). In a letter of Rainer Maria Rilke to Eva Cassirer, the poet exclaims, "What horror to think that the world has fallen into the hands of men!"

100. At least, this has been generally true for thousands of years.

demonstrating time and again that all violence is parricidal, as Genesis 4 shows.

But now we have gone one step further: all violence toward another is, fundamentally, directed against the self. It is a suicide as the other is always an *alter ego*, "someone-like-me," a *semblable*.[101] Abel, as we saw, was Cain's own shadow, the other face of himself, the innocence he shuns after having become weary of the role his primogeniture imposed upon him. The suicidal Cain would thus disappear like a wadi in the sands of the desert,[102] were it not for the fact that he sires a son, Enoch. Now, this is one more sign of God's clemency, and an important one at it, especially in a J document where blessing made effective in the domain of family increase is a central idea.

Conversely, the brutal diminution of a human family was in and of itself a curse. As a result, the ghost of Abel is haunting the survivors and particularly Cain. The murderer steals away from God's presence, but also from remembrance, or rather from remembering. Within this context, there is the realization that, as long as the family remains amputated of one of its members, there shall be no peace, no *shalom*.

Abel's demise demands reparation. Now, in death Abel has not only gained a voice, but in spite of his absence, he remains uncannily powerful. He will not let things go and fade into business-as-usual. Cain the wanderer is pursued by a nightmarish demand for restoration, the "cry of Abel." It "stonewalls" Cain in the town of Nod and, through having a child, compels him to retrieve his humanity. Well, part of his humanness,

---

101. Martin Buber and Franz Rosenzweig's German translation of Lev 19:18 is, "Love your neighbor, he is like you"; *Die Schrift*, vol. 1. Scapegoating Abel on the part of Cain is a showcase of the fact that "Others become the necessary targets to avoid the aggression toward, and hatred of, ourselves . . . Stated more strongly, the killing of others serves as a means of killing our own self-contempt, our mortality . . . *Hatred of others may very well begin with a hatred of ourselves*"; Cooper, *Dimensions*, 103, 132, 157; Cooper's emphasis. "Every murder is a suicide. Cain killed Cain in Abel"; Wiesel, *Messengers*, 61; a point confirmed by Gaylin's analysis, "Hatred is . . . self-destructive"; *Hatred*, 90.

102. Cain leaves a trace of himself in the tribe of the Kenites (see Num 24:21–22), and Seth in the Sethites (see Num 24:17), that is, the Sutu nomads known from Assyrian inscriptions (and perhaps the Shasu among the Egyptians). Here, gentilics can be equated with handicraft guilds. (Unconvincingly) Frank Frick, *The City in Ancient Israel*, says that "Gen 4 is concerned with the origin of guilds and trades, and transfers them to prehistory"; 166 n. 284. As for the city of Enoch and to the fruits of culture and civilization, everything will disappear with the Flood.

for Cain's relationship is with a nameless female, so that the offspring, Enoch, is for all practical purposes a motherless child.[103]

This is indeed the fate of Cain. As his city of refuge, Nod, was a no-city, the mother of his son is a no-woman. Cain has become the man of nothingness. But nevertheless, his son at least is no phantom. Enoch "inaugurates" something. There is definitely a redeeming dimension in Cain's paternity.

For, Cain begetting a child is Cain overcoming his "aggressive instinct" and his drive to Thanatos. Eros is victor.[104] The very child's name Enoch promises a better future—if not in the nomadic way of life, then in an urban one perhaps. The "building" of a city (4:17) may be somewhat illusionary, but it is at the other end of the spectrum from the chaos that Cain had occasioned. It constitutes a dramatic shift from *Gemeinschaft* (community) to *Gesellschaft* (association), but the latter is tempered by a community name: Enoch.

J leaves the story of Cain open-ended. He fathers a son; he builds a city; and . . . suspension points (here again as in 4:8). What we can add about his fate is mostly in the negative form: he is not killed; he is not jailed; he is no longer roaming the desert in search of food and shelter; and he is not sterile or impotent. Furthermore, Cain has inaugurated human culture, whose "crucial function . . . is to make *continued* self-esteem possible. Its task, in other words, is to provide the individual with the

---

103. Cain's fate of being "fugitive and wanderer" deprived him from content and form, for only the meeting of *I* and *Thou*, the meeting of two consciousnesses, creates a personal "directedness from within his own lived life," as Bakhtin says; *Art and Answerability*, 97. That is why, lest Cain's suicidal move become final, he must find a substitute other for Abel in the person of a (here anonymous) mate (4:17). Then Cain's horizon opens up on a renewed future. He sires a child whose name is Enoch, that is, *inauguration*.

104. Freud eventually recognized a human deep-seated destructiveness. This, he thought, is inherent to our nature (see *New Introductory Lectures* [1933]), a stance corrected by Paul Tillich and Reinhold Niebuhr (see e.g. below, 121 n. 134). Already in the Jewish worldview, evil is a *doing* (see Gen 4:7: "If you do well . . ."). In Erich Fromm's parlance, Cain displays a "necrophilous inclination." For Fromm, the Freudian "death instinct" is "a *malignant* phenomenon . . . [that] represents *psychopathology*"; see *The Heart of Man*, 50–51. On the intertwined relation of Thanatos and Eros—as can be seen in the sacrifice in which life and death are brought together—one will refer to the ancient Near East goddesses who are simultaneously divinities of love and of carnage. See Kapelrud, *The Violent Goddess*. Shakespeare's "Othello" takes us to Cyprus, the isle of Aphrodite, but where war (external and internal) is raging.

conviction that he is *an object of primary value in a world of meaningful action.*[105] Quite a program!

Paranoia

Before becoming a father, however, Cain is described as "bargaining" with God. He thinks that God's sentence is too harsh, perhaps incommensurate with the crime.[106] First, Cain lied, "I do not know;" then, he implicitly blamed God who should have been a better keeper of Abel (against Cain himself!); now he displays a callous attitude: for him, taking a human life is not as momentous as God seems to think. The penalty should be lighter as for a lighter misdemeanor. If some readers kept until now any doubt regarding Cain's innate perversity, it has now become flagrant. There is not only absence of regret in the man, but he is here adding insult to injury. His insensibility is such as to have the effrontery of expressing fear of being himself murdered by "anyone"! Cain may be a tragic figure, but he is above all a man of *chutzpah*, impudence.

Among his panoply of authorial gifts, J was a master of irony. Here, it is true, the irony is bitter. Cain is fool enough to ask a question ("Am I my brother's keeper?") that obviously must be answered in the affirmative,[107] whereas he stupidly expects to have silenced God on the issue of brothers' relationship. And now, he cringes before the same fate he did not hesitate to mete out to his brother. Perhaps after all the divine commutation of the death penalty in favor of Cain (4:15–16) was in consideration of the man's obtuseness. Instead, Cain is sentenced to be banned. The chastisement is watered down, to be sure, but is still severe for, as Klaus Koch has shown, banishment was the punishment meted out to the murderer of a clan's member and amounted to a death sentence.[108] Cain has become

---

105. Becker, *The Birth and Death*, 79. See above the quote from the same critic about sibling rivalry motivated by the desire to be *primary* (see 44 n. 91).

106. The Midrash understands Cain's question as an indictment of God: "You carry worlds and you cannot carry my sin?" (See a *Baraitha* in *b. Sanh.* 101b, it reads the text of 4:13 as saying "Is my sin too heavy for you to bear?"). Another interpretation is found in the LXX version of 4:13; Cain is saying, "My guilt is too great for me to be forgiven." The Vg of 4:13 has, "my iniquity is too great for me to merit forgiveness" (see also *Psiqta de Rav Kahana*, Suhbah 11). Along this line, a Midrash cited by Wiesel (*Messengers*, 60) invites to read Abel's blood's cry from the ground as not addressed *to* God but *at* God as an accusation. The citation comes from *Tanh.* (fourth century). Wiesel adds, "Death itself is an injustice."

107. *Pace* Riemann, "Am I My Brother's Keeper?"

108. Koch, "Der Spruch 'Sein Blut bleibe auf seinem Haupt.'" Gaylin's summary of

"infectious," as Westermann says.[109] He must be quarantined or ostracized. Thus, with the banishment motif, the story has introduced the first historic forensic judgment. Cain under ban has become fair game to the blood avengers of the clan. His complaint to God that "anyone . . . will kill me" makes sense within the framework of the vendetta. The spilled blood demands reparation (see Isa 26:21; Ezek 24:7; see also Gen 37:26; Job 16:18). We know that at some point the vicious circle of retaliations had to be interrupted by the legal restriction called the "law of talion (retaliation)" (see Exod 21:23–25), that is, by a required commensurability of the chastisement with the crime ("an eye for an eye"). But, in the story of Cain and Abel (J), we find a legal refinement of the law that goes beyond the talion: Cain is not to be put to death for his terrible slaying. His punishment is strictly in God's hands.[110] Consequently, we cannot fully agree with Westermann when he says that the mark on Cain has "an individual meaning and not a collective one."[111] The collective dimension of this motif in a primeval paradigmatic story is concretized in the cancellation of the law of talion by J, in spite of the fact that Cain's exclamation that he is not his brother's keeper (4:9) shows how the murder of one has broken the community of all.

Freud's contributions "that have stood the testing of time," highlights the point that "we are obligate social animals" and that "[o]ther people are essential to our survival as food, water, and oxygen. Therefore, exclusion from the group is a terrifying concept"; *Hatred*, 81, 82. Frick calls attention to the fact that the death penalty was performed "outside the city"; see 1 Kgs 21:13 . The expression "outside the city" is also dubbed "an unclean place," for instance, in Lev 14:40–47, 54; see Frick, *The City*, 126.

109. Westermann, *Genesis 1–11*, 307.

110. We shall note this clue to J's late dating. See LaCocque, *The Trial of Innocence*, Part 1, and *passim*. Cassuto as well sees in our text a reprobation of blood revenge. He adds that it is a rejection of Canaanite human sacrifices. To refer to the biblical *talion* in our day and age as a support for the infliction of the death penalty is a gross anachronism. If anyone deserved to be put to death for his/her crime, Adam and Eve and then Cain are prime candidates. But in neither case death is the penalty, but banishment and wandering, in spite of Gen 2:17 and 4:14. The ancient rabbis see in the plural of "the bloods [of Abel crying to God]" a decisive argument against the death penalty: with the executed, a whole world vanishes (*m. Sanh.* 5). The sinister Lamech is the one who snaps back the right to avenge himself (Gen 4:23–24), and modern death penalty is more vengeance than punishment. As for Cain, we need note with William P. Brown (*The Ethos of the Cosmos*, 170) that the potential violence against Cain is stemmed by the threat of "the exponential rise of violence." Such is now the world of Cain.

111. Westermann, *Genesis 1–11*, 312. On the collective dimension of Cain's crime, see also a further elaboration here below.

On a psychiatric level, nonetheless, Cain the perpetrator of fratricide has become soulless; he has lost a *self* and has thereby become "abnormal" and therefore unacceptable to others. Losing a sense of self-value, he renders others uncomfortable and willing to do away with him. Thus, after reaching the apex, however contrived, of being—you die, I live—Cain falls to the nadir of existence—I die and the others will live!

Cain's protest to God's judgment falls in an uncanny parallel with Abel's. Abel's blood cries out. *Ṣaʿaq* is moaning; it is "associated with the groans of an innocent victim who is brutalized and harassed."[112] The spilled blood does not only cry for justice through God's intervention, but also for being offered, as it should, to the Creator, while it is now swallowed by the soil as by Sheol.[113]

The lament of Cain is understandable. Although he is expelled like his parents before him from Eden or alternately from the ground (this is a recurrent theme in the Yahwist's literature), his protest contrasts with the heavy silence of Adam and Eve in the same circumstances. Westermann pointedly sets together the cries of both Abel and Cain. As God was receptive to the former one (and will always be), so he is heeding to the killer's lament (and will always be).[114] Cain, banned from the clan, feels that he must hide from God and from man. [115] A fugitive away from heaven and earth, his miserable existence would be the one of a living dead, of a ghost (*not* a nomad) roaming aimlessly in an absence of time and in a space without contour, were it not for God's compassion.

On the model of Genesis 3, here also the divine sentence is mitigated. As Adam and Eve did not die on the spot in spite of God's saying in Gen 2:17, so Cain is himself put at the benefit of a reprieve in 4:15. Incidentally, it is again inappropriate to speak of God's anger here, as do, for example, Cassuto, Ehrlich, and Westermann. In our story, God does not appear moved so much by emotion as by impartiality. The punishment

---

112. Hamilton, *Genesis*, 231; he refers to Gen 18:21; Exod 3:7; 22:21–24; Ps 34:[17–]18.

113. On the motif of spilled blood, see Gen 9:4–6; Isa 26:21; Job 16:18; Matt 23:35. The Sheol or the earth swallowing up, see Exod 15:12; Num 16:31–33; 26:10; Deut 11:6; Job 7:9.

114. And this is another decisive rebuttal of the principle of the death penalty.

115. Beside the judicial aspect of Cain's banishment, one may also think of a cultic ritual of purification. It was supposed to clean impurity by using either curse, destruction, or ban (see Milgrom, *Leviticus 1–16*, 1071–79, and already Ewald, "Erklärung der biblischen Urgeschichte," also cited by Westermann, *Genesis 1–11*, 310).

he describes falls in parallel with the one meted out to Adam and Eve: it is a condition of their own devising. God does not need to get angry, Abel's blood is angry, the soil is angry . . . the whole of nature reacts angrily to human monstrosity. If we had to attribute a sentiment to God in this story, it would rather be sadness and disappointment.[116] Cain's errantry is in direct consequence to his becoming inhuman, a beast, a lone wolf kept at bay by "anyone" (4:14).[117] He emigrates to the city of Nod, says the text (4:16), that is, a land which, originary and essentially, is one of vagabondage. The irony is that Abel was the one who used to be constantly moving with his flock from land to land. Cain, the killer of his brother, becomes more Abel-like than Abel ever was!

More than anyone else, Cain is prey to anger and shame (4:5), two of the most powerful human sentiments. Their combination is dangerous on the extreme. It is what drives terrorists and delinquents all over the twenty-first century world. In most cases, as with Cain, their ineptitude is projected upon others, who are seen as unjustly successful. Cain would rather eradicate innocence than personally accede to it on the invitation of Yhwh (4:7). If everybody was regressing to his level, Cain thinks, perhaps his anger and shame would disappear[118]—conveniently forgetting that he is not judged by his brother but by God, and not for evermore but provisionally until he decides to "do well."

Now, Cain could indeed "do well" if he ceased for a while to think exclusively of himself and to speculate about what the whole world owes him.[119] Then he would treat his brother, *who epitomizes the world out there*, as a *Thou*, that is, as his unique chance to be himself an "I." Kass writes, "Cain's display of anger reveals retrospectively his state of soul in making the sacrifice . . . it shows how presumptuous and hubristic were his expectations."[120] "Doing well" is up to Cain to choose. J's message here is the same as in Genesis 2–3: God has created humanity with a free will.

---

116. See above the section "Violence" on the divine pathos.

117. "One who has killed a member of the community is expelled to live with the wild animals . . . He becomes a 'wolf'"; Westermann, *Genesis 1–11*, 316, with reference to Gruppe, "Kain."

118. Above, I said, "all criterion to innocence has disappeared [with Abel as personification of the law]."

119. Nelson-Pallmeyer, *Is Religion Killing Us?* xv, speaks of the "'dysfunctional deflective violence' that shifts anger onto others" and is cause of the "high incidence of murder and crime, etc."

120. Kass, *The Beginning of Wisdom*, 138.

On this score, J and D are in full agreement (see Deuteronomy 30:15, 19). Cain is not unforgivable, although his crime sharply contrasts with the "eating of a fruit" in Genesis 3. While the latter is not by itself an action earning punishment but only a manifestation of disobedience, Cain's deed is "wrong by its very nature."[121] As we saw, it is the first time that the term *sin*, a word avoided in Genesis 2–3, is used. Adam and Eve did disobey; Cain sinned.

True, the situation that transpired in the affair of the sacrifices (in 4:3–5) did not demand "apathy" on the part of Cain. This would amount to indifference. But, as Aristotle insists in his *Nichomachean Ethics*, anger should be with the right people and in the right fashion.[122] On both of these scores, Cain's irascibility is uncalled for. He is from the outset confronted, not by his brother, but by his God (4:6–7), at least in his imagination, and the nature of his anger is redirected in the process. But Cain ignores the warning. He shuns the real or imaginary protagonist and chooses a scapegoat. He refuses to proceed with an examination of his conscience, and he projects his own culpability upon someone else. Further, he allows his wrath to transgress all limits and he kills the innocent. Cain is not just a murderer, he is an assassin.

Cain will be protected against (a judicially justified) vendetta. God promises that "Whoever would kill Cain, he will be avenged sevenfold" (4:15). As it stands in Hebrew, the phrase is highly ambiguous. It seems to say that whoever kills Cain is to be avenged sevenfold. The meaning of the sentence is obviously different (the NRSV has, ". . . will suffer a sevenfold vengeance"). James G. Williams suggests reading this half-verse as addressed to the killer of Cain: sevenfold he [Cain] shall be avenged.[123] Then God's warning makes sense as a dissuasive device to potential avengers of Abel's blood.[124]

---

121. Buber, *Good and Evil*, 81.

122. See *Nichomachean Ethics* IV.5 and VII.6 (on anger).

123. Williams, "Concerning One of the Apodictic Formulas"; "Addenda to 'Concerning One of the Apodictic Formulas.'" Let us add that, although the verb "shall be avenged" (*nqm*) derives from another stem than the "rising up" of Cain in v. 8 (*qum*), there may be here a pun. After all, the context is Cain's plea to not be murdered in retaliation for his murder.

124. When this notion of *deterrence* is brought together with the notion of *retaliation* expressed by Lamech in 4:23–24, it is striking how relevant J's picture is to our twenty-first century.

Cain Builds the First City

As Kenneth Gros Louis says ironically, "God had planted a garden, Cain now constructs a city."[125] Irony aside, interestingly enough J combines the building of cities with the springing of the hallmark of civilization. This is historically correct. The archaeologists call the birth of cities (some as old as 6,000 BCE), the "Urban Revolution" and compare it with the much later Industrial Revolution.

We should, however, bracket in the Ewald-Wellhausen-Gunkel-Mowinckel "archaeological" reading of Cain as representing the Kenites.[126] Such a theory is overblown by those scholars. The only concession to it must be made within the context of the change in Cain's condition. For, the very moment Cain becomes a fugitive "nomad," his name and position *may* allude to the ethnological context of the nomadic smiths called the Qenites (a gentilic associated with the name Cain [the same as here?] in Num 24:21–22). They roamed the Sinai wilderness (they are mentioned in Judg 5:24; 1 Sam 15:6). In Gen 4:22, Tubal-Cain is a smith.

The myth conveyed by J's story—as Hermann Gunkel also saw (with Otto Procksch, Walter Zimmerli, Gerhard von Rad, and Claus Westermann)—is rather offering "great primeval truths about the human race."[127] For, to the question: Is there also a collective dimension to the myth of Cain and Abel? Cain's cry "anyone . . . will kill me" (4:14) stresses the societal dimension of his fratricide. What occurred in the remote place called "the field" in 4:8[128] has an unexpected collective resonance. The whole society feels threatened and reacts with wrath against the troublemaker. Why it is so is explained by Carl Jung in his reflections at the end of World War II.

---

125. Gros Louis, *Literary Interpretations of Biblical Narratives*, 2:44.

126. See above 112 n. 103 and the ginger phraseology there. Westermann, *Genesis 1–11*, 287 says: "There is no sign of anything that could be taken as referring to an incident between two tribes." Cain as a name occurs in Num 24:22 and Judg 4:11, 17 (ancestor of the Kenites); in Josh 15:57 it is the name of a place; in 2 Sam 21:16, it means a "spear." These multiple usages show that we cannot infer from the use of Cain in Gen 4 anything that the narrative does not say about him. Westermann states that the primeval story's object "is not peoples and their divisions but humankind" (317).

127. See Gunkel, *Genesis*, ad loc. Buber forcefully writes, "We are dealing here, as Plato already knew, with truths such as can be communicated adequately to the generality of mankind only in the form of myths"; *Good and Evil*, 66.

128. See the laws on rape that takes place in the field: Deut 22:25–27. In order to indicate the remoteness of a place, the French say, "en pleine campagne."

The murder has been suffered by everyone, and everyone has committed it; lured by the irresistible fascination of evil, we have all made this collective psychic murder possible; and the closer we were to it and the better we could see, the greater our guilt. In this way we are unavoidably drawn to the uncleanness of evil, no matter what our conscious attitude may be. No one can escape this.[129]

Furthermore, the collective dimension of Cain's crime is inherent in its very perpetration. For, even though Cain lures his brother in the remoteness of "the field," the slaying is witnessed at least by God as well as by the personified ground. So, the privacy of the scene is broken. "The eye was in the tomb and stared at Cain."[130]

True, there is not much emphasis on the part of J on this public dimension of the tale, because he wanted to stress other aspects, such as, for instance, Cain's will to eliminate all competition around him in the person of one, his younger brother. But J was conscious of the fact that "microevil, the murder of an individual . . . becomes part of the macroorganism: all the evils breathe the same air, they have the same circulatory system."[131]

Yet, Cain's suppression of competitors has created a tremendous vacuum all around. His eyes are now open (cf. Gen 3:7) and he sees that the new world without Abel is nothing but a desert, an ingrate soil, a desolate space that he roams in his quest for a new company. Eventually Cain realizes that he must himself build a companionship: he founds a city.

The Jewish tradition did not see 4:16 as contradicting v. 14. By way of illustration, Redaq (in concert with *b. Sanh.* 37a) reads the text of v. 16 as saying that Cain settled in the land *as* a vagrant, because he found no rest.[132] According to *Targum Onqelos* on 4:16, Cain did stay on the land he had cultivated before, but there he became a vagrant. And indeed, v. 16 displays a stark verbal contrast: Cain *wanders* from the *face* of God, and he *settles* in the *land* of Nod. It is hard to avoid thinking that Cain actually leaves the spiritual for the sake of the material. In other words, Cain falls back childishly on the body against the symbolic world of the

---

129. Jung, "After the Catastrophe" in *Jung on Evil*, 184–85; also cited by Ortiz-Hill, *The Roots and Flowers*, 81.

130. Victor Hugo, "La conscience," in *La Légende des siècles.*

131. Morrow, "Evil," 50.

132. See Prov 28:1a: "The wicked flee [even] when no one pursues;" v. 17 reads, "If someone is burdened with the blood of another, let that killer be a fugitive until death; let no one offer assistance" [NRSV].

mature person.[133] Killing Abel, Cain kills the idea, he kills poetry. True, at his birth, Yhwh was very present, indeed his presence was performative, as if fathering him. Then we witness "Cain's loss of the presence . . . The land of Nod . . . is thus a place without the Lord."[134]

We must, nonetheless, keep open the possibility of a concomitance of two contradictory aspects to the construction of a city and its outcome. There is an evident ambiguity in having Cain the vagabond build a nest for himself by his labor. At this point, a reminder by Kahn is thought provoking. He calls attention to the human space "after the fall" as a world formed by labor. Without human work, "the world would produce nothing. It remains 'dust' . . . We place ourselves within a geography of cultural and emotional space."[135] It means that, as long as he wanders, Cain moves in a space that is no-space, only dust, only death. It is not the space of the humans but the space of the serpent (the eater of dust, see Gen 3:14), a space without referents, without coordinates. A detail of the biblical text often shortchanged by readers is the preposition in Gen 4:11, "you shall be cursed *from* the ground." Cain is cursed by being estranged from the 'adamah, that is, from the humanized soil. Cain has not his feet on the ground any more; he has lost his footage; he is groundless, like an empty prattle. Now, does this not recall ironically the (alleged) "vanity" of Abel, the brother of Cain?

But, if Cain is indeed a tragic figure, as we saw, biblical tragedy is no Greek tragedy. If Cain's wandering is no nomadism or pilgrimage (the pilgrims have a destination point, their Santiago de Compostela), there is a certain kinship between the one and the others; there is a hidden dimension to Cain's vagrancy. His penalty is not self-contained. Its purpose is purification. His wandering is aimless only when considered short-term; but there is to it a long-term efficacy. Arrives a time when Cain settles. His "penalty is paid" (Isa 40:2). However, here again—as

133. Cain, like all human beings, must face an uncomfortable mixture in our nature. As Cooper reminds us, "[Ernest] Becker [after luminaries like Kierkegaard, Reinhold Niebuhr, Tillich, and others] argues that we human beings are a unique combination of nature and spirit [see Gen 2:7] a condition that creates enormous anxiety" (*Dimensions of Evil*, 129). The human being, says Reinhold Niebuhr is ontologically anxious because she is both contingent and capable of reflecting upon her contingence. Such anxiety, he diagnoses as precondition of sin (*The Nature and Destiny of Man*, 1:182–83, cited by Cooper, *Dimensions*, 223). Cain projects his anxiety upon his brother's "success."

134. Coats, *Genesis*, 64. In a quaint expression, Benno Jacob said (about v. 14), "The roof protects only the person who places himself under it" (*The First Book*, 36).

135. *Out of Eden*, 184.

when Cain concluded that God had no regard for his offering—who says so? Did Cain sense that he was at the benefit of God's pardon? Or did he himself judge that his chastisement's duration was over? As usual, J does not lift the ambiguity. Declaring at this point that Cain was displaying arrogance would render his penalty useless and condemn him without appeal. On the other hand, making God intervene at this juncture with lifting the sentence would prospectively condone the building of Cain's city, something that J was not ready to do.

So, Cain stops wandering and settles down to build a city, arguably for his own dwelling in the first place. The problematic of Cain has changed: from Cain as vagabond to Cain as creator of social agglomerate. The reversal of issues could not be more radical. But this does not mean that the shift is necessarily from negative to positive. The city raises as much problem as the roaming. Cain's wandering publicized a past of delinquency; Cain's building raises doubt about the future orientation of humanity. As, with the ingathering of people in one place, there is now a task to be accomplished, the question is which task and by which means.

When Cain rediscovers love, he also rediscovers work. He builds a city; he creates a human space. For work by itself is no punishment. It pre-exists the "fall" and is essential to the human co-creation with God. The punishment is in the labor's vanity, when it ceases to be also worship.[136] In the case of Cain the builder, we may see a hopeful indication in the name given to the city, namely, Enoch, which means "inauguration" (like the name of the late festival of Hanukkah) and has a definite religious connotation. It may be that Enoch-city is the point of convergence of love and work, a work of love. Cain building a city institutes, to recall, what Freud sees as a social control, "which he now regarded as necessary to save people from themselves . . . [a] theory of the human condition [that] looked quite Hobbesian."[137] In this case, we may understand Cain's move as a voluntary curbing of his impulses.

The final note is not without hope. Cain's love for God had turned to rage and murder, and he had entered a loveless world from which God was absent. But Cain rediscovers love. He "knew his wife" and begot a son (4:17) who, obviously, was dear to him for he named the city he founded

136. See LaCocque, *The Trial of Innocence*, esp. 86–90, 272–75.

137. Cooper, *Dimensions*, 102. To recall, according to Hobbes, Cain's construction of as city would mark the passage from a "bellum omnium contra omnes," through a "salutary submission," to a "social contract of individuals."

by his name. Because of this rediscovery, Cain's death is not reported—as it would be in a Greek tragedy or, for that matter, in a Shakespearian one—and there is no literary closure to his groping in the dark.

In fact, it is often said that throughout Genesis 2–11 J uses a literary pattern that is typically judicial: sin—punishment—forgiveness. The truth is that, at least as regards the third term of the equation, J is particularly nuanced. In Genesis 3, Adam and Eve transgress and are punished, but are they really forgiven? There is on their part no expressed repentance, although there is to be sure a divine reprieve. In Genesis 4, Cain sins and is punished. Here again any move of repentance seems absent. There is still a divine reprieve but no express declaration of forgiveness: Cain might have endlessly remained a fugitive were it not, as we just saw, for J's indirection, which strikes a hopeful note. In Genesis 6, the "sons of God" fornicate with human girls. There is punishment but no forgiveness that I can detect. In Genesis 9, Canaan sins and wrongs his father Noah. Canaan is cursed and enslaved, he is certainly not forgiven. In Genesis 11, the Tower of Babel generation sins, their punishment is to be scattered all over the expanse of the world. There is no divine forgiveness but a divine respite is granted. In fact, J delays the real and decisive forgiveness of humankind until the election of Abraham. Then at last, after all the suspense carefully maintained by the storyteller, Abraham (and his act of faith) is occasion for "all the families of the earth to be blessed" (Gen 12:3).

Cain is the founder of the first city, called Enoch like his son (4:17). Literally, the text seems to indicate a continued activity, something like, "Cain was a builder of cities" (*wayehy boneh*); we rather expected a construction like *wayiben ʿir*. The most elegant rendering of the text, in my opinion, is Redaq's.[138] He says that Cain was in the process of building a city when his son Enoch was born; then Cain named the city in honor of the babe.

Besides, a reading initiated by Karl Budde (and favored by Westermann) sees Enoch as the city builder, not Cain.[139] This requires a text alteration from "in the name of his son" (*kešem beno*) into "according to his [Enoch's] name" (*kišemo*). But this intervention in the text

---

138. See 52 n. 115 above on Redaq (R. David Qimchi).
139. Budde, *Die biblische Urgeschichte (Gen 1–12:5) untersucht.*

is, in my opinion, unnecessary. True, people are wont to call cities by their own names (Tiberias; Alexandria; Antioch; see Deut 3:14 [Jair]; 2 Sam 5:9 [David]; 12:28 [David; it is a seal of ownership]). But, as building a city is put on par with begetting children and thus insuring one's immortality, calling one's construction by the name of a child makes sense. Here, Cain begets a son and builds a city by the latter's name. The two activities are associated because building a city is construed as an act of (pro)creation.[140] Adeptly, Isaac Abravanel (fifteenth century),[141] says that the ostracized Cain fathered children with whom to associate. He was unable anymore to trust anyone else—or perhaps even to find anyone else in his peregrinations.

Indeed, until then, Cain was like the uncouth Enkidu of the Mesopotamian myth.[142] Like him also Cain discovers civilization and the city. At this point, Cain left behind not only his wandering but also his original and natural fare of agriculturist. Whether this is for better or for worse, the fact is that an entirely new chapter in human history has started. From the familial, J's scope is now embracing the political. Cain, deprived of moorings, builds new ones, artificial. The similarity in the name of his son and his city (Enoch) is striking. In Hebrew, the words *son* or *daughter* come from an identical verbal root meaning "to build." Cain builds a son and he builds a city, and behold, both are one in his eyes. He gave death to Abel, his brother, he now gives life to Enoch, his son; he alienated himself from the ground, he now "fathers" a city. But in both cases, his acts remain ambiguous. Enoch-the-son is only a palliative as he will not replace the face to face with God; and Enoch-the-city will not neutralize Cain's curse from the ground. In reality, Cain is now substituting an urban organization for the original lines of kinship, a *Gesellschaft* (association) for a *Gemeinschaft* (community), as we said. The human cannot live outside of kinship, so Enoch-son-and-city is a substitute for the breach of the

140. See above 31 n. 48.

141. *On the Pentateuch.*

142. J pictures Cain and his offspring as uncouth "savages," as Ralph Waldo Emerson would say. That is, he adds, people whose primary instinct of "self-help" remains at its "childish" level without any "other image of [hu]manly activity and virtue . . . a sedative and mature spirit . . . ties that make war look like fratricide, as it is." Emerson concludes, "it is now time that it ["the cultivated soul"] should pass out of the state of beast into the state of [hu]man [being]; it is to hear the voice of God, which bids the devils, that have rended [sic] and torn him, come out of him, and let him now be clothed and walk forth in his right mind" (Ralph Waldo Emerson, "War" delivered in March 1838 in Boston. See on the internet "RWE.org. <The Works of Ralph Waldo Emerson>").

line with Abel's death—and also perhaps an attempt at "teaching a lesson" to God.[143] In Mesopotamia, for instance, where urbanism was pervasive, the law on homicide adjudicates the punishment of murder to a central government—Cain was a pervert but he was not stupid.

The sequel of Genesis 4 within J's narrative is consistent with this broadened perspective. The literary structure in AB/AB is remarkable: from the one (Adam) to the many, and back to the one (Abraham), before a new expansion with Abraham's "descendants." In such a context, the "city" may just be a hiccup, i.e., a wrong turn of history, or an anticipatory parody of Abraham's people.

Cain builds a city of refuge and, because it is the construction of a murderer for the purpose of harboring an outlaw, "Enochville" is highly ambiguous. As its founder cannot blot away the divine sign set upon him, not any more than the leopards can change their spots (Jer 13:23), so the town (any town) can never forget its origin nor to what purpose it exists. It is the originary place where death, shame, and guilt are nested. There, the past is heavy, and the future is dubious.[144]

In the Mesopotamian myths, city building was the prerogative of the gods (and thus the local cities are shielded from the ambiguity inherent in the biblical ones).[145] Within the context of the wanderer Cain and the constant impending threat of disintegration, it is important to remember that the city was "[t]he institutionalization of the desire for continuity in Mesopotamia."[146] As regards J's interest in cities, let us also refer to Gen 10:10–12 and especially to Genesis 11.

143. The persistence of hubris!

144. According to texts, there were in Israel six cities of refuge for accidental manslayers. In case of the discovery that there had been premeditation on the part of the killer, however, he was sent back to his home town for execution. This would apply to Cain were it not for the sign that God set on him. In the absence of cities in the primeval time, Cain's refuge was actually an exile. See Num 35:6, 11–34; Deut 4:41–43; 19:1–13; Josh 20:1–9.

145. "Civilization was a gift from the gods who vouchsafed it to mankind as a full-grown product"; Speiser "Ancient Mesopotamia," 50. Down to the time of Hellenized Asia, "the founder of a city . . . was in Greek eyes something more than human"; Welles, "The Hellenistic Orient," 157.

146. Oppenheim, *Ancient Mesopotamia*, 79. Tsumura, for instance, notes the biblical parallels afforded by the Sumerian *Harab Myth*. The first city (Irad = Eridu, which we may perhaps associate with the name of Cain's grandson Irad) is here also built between two poles, the creation and the flood; Tsumura, "Genesis and Ancient Near Eastern Stories of Creation and Flood," 39.

The city, I said, owes its existence historically to the first murderer and the first pariah! It thus appears as both a nest of brigands and a haven for the lonely. A little further in the text, the original human settlement (after Eden!) becomes also the cradle of art and industry (4:22–23). In short, the town is a medley, almost a hybrid, in the image of Cain himself. From such an alloy anything can be expected; the city can become Jerusalem or Nineveh. Even Jerusalem as a matter of fact can be at times a "den of robbers" that Jesus feels called to cleanse; and conversely, Nineveh may repent (after Jonah's prophecy) and worship Yhwh, along with Egypt, Assyria, and Israel (see Isa 19:23–25).

Whether or not we agree with Jacques Ellul that the city from a psychological point of view is the result of angst,[147] it is at any rate an attempt to substitute for the loss of history and kinship. That is why the Bible is generally critical of city building. But J's interest is not confined in a frozen negativity. Life is not wholesale light or darkness. Time and again, J's art reaches its fullness in a careful exercise in ambiguity. Enochville is indeed susceptible of contradictory appraisals, all legitimate. The city is a new beginning, an "inauguration," and, as such, pregnant with the best and the worst. Its founder is himself ambiguous. To the extent that the city is retrenchment from community the succession of generations that follow the foundation of the city of Enoch (4:18–22) is a return to kinship and also to history. The first city envisaged by J is clannish; it is inhabited by Cain's progeny. In this sense, "Enochville" is no anonymous melting pot. But all the same, among its people there are truly frightening figures that do not augur well for the future. The genealogies in the Bible are historiographic condensations. Cain the violent has spawned descendants still more violent than he (4:23–24).[148] Moreover, a point often overlooked is that Cain's building of a city is by nature "reductionist." Until then, the humans are "citizens of the world," as Philo says.[149] With Cain, there occurs a shrinkage of sorts of the world to the proportions of a human built universe and, consequently, an impressive concentration of power. The city is a powerhouse. Genesis 11 (the building of the city and Tower of Babel) comes to mind. In both cases, of Enoch and Babel, the

147. See Ellul, *The Meaning of the City*. See now the analysis of the biblical negativity regarding the city in Schneidau, *Sacred Discontent*, 5–7.

148. Perceptively, Fishbane writes, "Civilization is built and destroyed by discontent"; *Text and Texture*, 27. And Schneidau states, ". . . civilization and violent change feed on each other"; *Sacred Discontent*, 101.

149. Philo *De Opificio Mundi*, 49.142.

matter is one of power. The parallel with Genesis 3 also is striking. There is indeed in J's narratives on the primeval era a remarkable consistency, the leitmotif of becoming like God (see Gen 3:5).

By building a city, Cain goes through a sublimation of his instincts. Freud writes that it is an "especially conspicuous feature of cultural evolution; it is this that makes it possible for the higher mental operations, scientific, artistic, ideological activities to play such an important part in civilized life."[150] To this, Géza Róheim adds that, while neurosis isolates, sublimation unites. Róheim's main thesis is that culture is the outcome of mankind's fear "of object loss, of being left alone in the dark."[151] And, in his conclusion, Róheim states, "Civilization originates in delayed infancy and its function is security . . . the colossal efforts made by a baby who is afraid of being left alone in the dark."[152]

From the moment Cain kills his brother, he carries death on his shoulders as an indelible mark (that only the divine sign granted to him can counterbalance). Human death had never occurred before in God's creation.[153] As a death-dealer, Cain is also a death-addict. He says that anyone will kill him on sight, either because he has become paranoid and now sees death everywhere, or because indeed anybody seeing Cain will want to get rid of this hellish ghost. Hence Cain, now that there is almost literally a skeleton in the closet, is strongly driven not to undergo the same fate as Abel's. Understandably, Cain builds a city to insure for himself "the spurious immortality of the collective," as Terry Eagleton says.[154] The accent is definitely on the equivocal nature of Cain's enterprise. All the more in that building Enoch is one more act of violence on Cain's part, for culture is an "organized violence" that forces "the chaos of Nature" into cosmos, and "[t]he enterprise of constructing civilization is infiltrated from the outset by death" (see the sequels of city-foundation here in vv. 20–22).[155] To recall, "Freud derives civilization from a primal murder, just as the Bible derives it from Cain."[156]

150. Freud, *Civilization and Its Discontents*, 63.
151. Róheim, *The Origin and Function of Culture*, 100.
152. Ibid., 131.
153. Animal death? Yes, perhaps, see Gen 3:21.
154. Eagleton, *Holy Terror*, 14.
155. Ibid., 11, 12. One remembers that for Freud there is no culture without desire or rather there is no culture unless the desire is channeled (see *Civilization*). That is why, with Lamech's song, there is regression to the point of absence of culture because violence is uncontrolled.
156. Schneidau, *Sacred Discontent*, 48. Westermann concurs. He states that, according

Such wariness on the part of J regarding the city is probably more historically and sociologically motivated than philosophically grounded. The "scientific" and technological evolution up to the time J wrote the primeval stories apparently left him with a feeling of frustration and disappointment. What is more certain is that his judgment on civilization is taking exception to the ancient Near-Eastern conception of its divine origins.[157] Precisely because civilization is not divine but human, its nature is impure.[158]

Ernest Becker, speaking in general terms of "the human condition," says that "It is man's ingenuity, rather than his animal nature, that has given his fellow creatures such a bitter earthly fate."[159] Of this, our tale is an illustration. It had started with the cultic offering of sacrifices; it ends with the development of technology. This evolution should not be seen as merely chronological. Techniques have replaced sacrifice as means of controlling nature. For J, this substitution is no sign of progress. The promoters of "civilization" belong to the line of Cain; the technological manipulation of the cosmos retrospectively reflects upon the rationale behind Cain's sacrifice.

To the extent that J considered the human work of "tilling and keeping" the land as ideal (Gen 2:15), the building of a city is a further distancing from Eden. Then the human work becomes vastly different from what it used to be (4:17ff.), and so also are the working tools. In addition to the refined musical artifacts (4:21; see Ps 150:4; Job 21:12; 30:31), iron and bronze instruments are also mentioned—of which metal weapons are made. To this, Lamech's saying in 4:23–24 testifies (see 1 Sam 13:19–22; Isa 2:4 = Mic 4:3). After all, the city is the principal seedbed of violence. True, "pastoral tranquility" is an illusion, but the surge of violence in the countryside is obviously within narrower limits and is not exacerbated by the overcrowded condition prevailing in slums.

The fact is that, starting with the narrative on Cain and Abel, J is steadily accumulating evidences of unfettered violence in the world. Fratricide, preceded and followed by the human will to power, plus the explosion of hatred and arrogance, lead to universal destruction by the

---

to J, the human achievements are ambiguous and "are often interwoven with the accounts of crime and punishment, for instance, in Genesis 3 and 11. . ." (*Genesis 1–11*, 57).

157. See ibid., 60. See also above 2 n. 4 and 46 n. 97.

158. Psalm 8:7 and Job 28 are more optimistic about human achievements.

159. Becker, *Escape from Evil*, 5.

Flood (Genesis 6–9).[160] In Genesis 3, the original sin is hubris; in Genesis 4 it is violence. As we saw above, this sequential series is intentional. Violence is the by-product of a more fundamental human perversion. Before resorting to fratricide, Cain first developed, with the complicity of his mother, a high opinion of himself and the illusion of being above the laws of common folks. Cain's violence is wrought against someone first demeaned as unsubstantial, a zombie, a vapor. The process of elimination is already an "ethnic cleansing" of sorts. The *Übermensch* grants to the self the right to get rid of "parasites."

Retrospectively, Cain's silence in the field finds here one of its roots. To recall, he first opened his mouth to say something to Abel but then relented. To a *minus habens,* what can you say that he could understand? The only "word" he is susceptible to receive from Big Brother is a blow.[161] Cain's pride has fully asserted itself. He remains the only one standing, and it is well known that "a living dog is better than a dead lion" (Qoh 9:4). Cain behaves truly as if there was no justice in the world. According to Jewish tradition, it is precisely what Cain said to Abel before killing him.[162]

Now, when Enochville is built, the text is uncannily silent about to whom or to what the city is dedicated, although its name is "dedication." The marker remains empty of content, like a previous name, Nod, designated by oxymoron as a settling in vagabondage. "Enoch-dedication" is begging for completion, as if followed by a series of suspension points. Cain, it seems, had reached the edge of a decision making (there may be justice in the world, after all), but felt incapable of going any further (there is no justice in the world).

Cain is wrong. Abel's blood spilled on the ground has "power of attorney." It demands justice, and it is heard on high. How God requites Abel's death is "another story," as Dostoevsky would say. As it stands, the biblical narrative focuses on the fate of the culprit with the purpose to show that crime (eventually) does not pay. If indeed, by the grace of God, Cain escapes the ultimate forensic justice—that would require the death

---

160. As Pagels writes, "[Cain] murdered his brother, exemplifying the lust for power that now dominates and distorts the whole structure of human relationships"; *Adam, Eve, and the Serpent,* 114. Cain as the builder of a city duplicates the feat of gods or kings in the ancient Near Eastern power games celebrated in myths.

161. "When an individual represses certain things, they reassert themselves later with extreme violence"; Wiesel, *Evil and Exile,* 132.

162. See *Tg. Ps.-J.* on Gen 4:8, cited above, and in 69 n. 7.

penalty against him—he does not escape "poetic justice" that makes the guilty one pay in kind for his/her crime.[163]

"Poetic justice" to which Cain is exposed and which makes of him a fugitive for life can at any moment kill him. God need not "descend" from heaven (see Gen 11:5) to mete out Cain's punishment. The latter meets his cursed fate in his daily life, like Raskolnikov in *Crime and Punishment*.[164] His building of a city is the erection of a wall around himself. To the paranoid isolation of wandering has succeeded the isolation of the staying-at-home (a house-arrest?). Noticeably, the societal and the forensic are tied together. God being the Judge, the pattern, to recall, is typically: discovery of the crime, interrogation, defense, verdict, punishment/reprieve.[165] Chances are that Enochville is still a part of the latter.

Enoch-the-son *may* be in the process of *dedicating* a substitute sanctuary for God's presence—here again there is no determinism to do evil. For, in spite of Ellul's negative analysis, Enochville is not (yet) Babel, which comes only in chapter 11 of Genesis.[166] Furthermore, the J narrative on Cain and Abel ends on a high note: then the humans "began to call on the Name of Yhwh" (4:26).

It means that even in the case of Cain the murderer, there is no irremediable "fall" as traditional Christianity understood Genesis 3. In Genesis 4, there is an onslaught against innocence in the person of Abel, but not an erasure of innocence. Abel's blood continues to cry out, and Cain's crime does not crash against a wall of the irredeemable. Cain the lonely wolf rebuilds a family cell with his wife and Enoch, and he builds a city that is no Nod-of-No-Place anymore. To Cain there is a future, to which the J genealogy that follows testifies (4:17–26).

163. See Patrick D. Miller, *Sin and Judgment in the Prophets.*

164. The ʿ*awon* Cain speaks about in 4:13 means both sin and punishment; see Gen 15:16; 1 Sam 28:10; Ibn Ezra on Gen 4:13 also refers to these texts.

165. See Westermann, *Elements of Old Testament Theology*, 118–20. Clines would rather underscore the "reprieve" part. He comes with the pattern: sin—speech—mitigation—punishment (see in the third chapter of Gen: 3:6/ 3:14–19/ 3:21/ 3:22–24; in the fourth chapter: 4:8/ 4:11–12/ 4:15/ 4:16; etc.) *I Studied Inscriptions*, 290.

166. Ellul is free-associating on the homonyms ʿ*ir* as city, and ʿ*ir* as Watching Angel, from which he draws unfounded conclusions; *The Meaning of the City*, 9; see also 164. The tally of these homonyms would rather emphasize the ambivalence of the city.

CHAPTER FIVE

Genealogy and Culture

Cain's Genealogy in Genesis 4 (and 5)

G EORGE A. BARTON, IN his article "A Sumerian Source of the Fourth and Fifth Chapters of Genesis,"[1] argues that we can trace the list of names in Genesis 4–5 to a Sumerian tablet of Nippur, held at the University Museum in Philadelphia. Barton's lists, set in parallel, of the documents from Akkad and the Bible are particularly interesting.[2] They would show the derivation of the name "Abel" from Etana the shepherd, who went to heaven, and of the name "Cain" from Pilikam, which means "with intelligence to build."[3]

But even if Barton were right, the "Sumerian source" appears rather remote and tangential. More interesting for our inquiry here is another article by Richard H. Moye mentioned earlier.[4] Moye speaks of "the interweaving of myth and genealogy in Genesis" and of "the interrelation and mutual transformation of myth and genealogy."[5] He cites Hesiod's *Theogony* and the Akkadian myth of creation, *Enuma elish*, as well as "numerous other Near Eastern parallels" that "indicate [that] genealogy plays a significant role in myth itself." Let us also note his remark that "genealogies are informed by the mythical narratives they surround."[6] In a following section below ("The Song of Lamech") I shall call attention to the song's allusion to the myth of Cain and Abel.

1. Barton, "A Sumerian Source."
2. Ibid., 5, 8.
3. Ibid., 8–9.
4. Moye, "In the Beginning."
5. Ibid., 580.
6. Ibid., 582.

Another striking point made by Moye is the evolutionary pattern of the Genesis genealogies that goes from inclusivity to exclusivity in their formulation. So, there is contrast between "the genealogies of the excluded sons" that "are explicitly or implicitly inclusive in their listings" and "the genealogical lists of the chosen sons" that "follow a precise and exclusive pattern" (compare Gen 4:20–22, for instance, and Gen 5:3–31; 11:10–26). "[T]he direct line leading to the crucial son is carried down."[7]

Moye's remarkable study speaks in favor of Genesis 4 as a literary unit, a conclusion that we have defended all along here. Besides, an element in the J genealogy confirms this even further, namely, "fratriarchy," a theme well illustrated throughout the Hebrew Bible, but its frequency in Genesis 4 is striking. Not only is Abel constantly called the brother of Cain, but Seth is the brother of Abel (4:25, this in contradistinction with Cain, a point to be stressed in what follows); Jubal is the brother of Jabal (4:21); Naamah is the sister of Tubal-Cain (4:22). These references and several others in the rest of the Bible are highlighted by Cyrus H. Gordon.[8] He writes, "[I]f one of the sons, such as the first-born, is to succeed his father as patriarch, he will, as a matter of course, assume some degree of authority over his brothers" (see Gen 36:22; 1 Chron 2:32, 42; 24:25).[9] Of great importance is that in each case the primogeniture of the older brother is emphasized and that there is a frequent substitution of the brother or brothers for the father (see Gen 24:29ff.; 34:11). We have insisted above upon the egregious textual passing over Adam in the narrative. The designation of Abel as Cain's brother is to be seen as another move at eliminating Adam. Abel in other words is less the son of his father than the brother of Cain. In another substitutive stroke, Cain—as the holder of primogeniture—is replaced by no one else but the murdered Abel in Gen 4:25 (about the birth of Seth, brother of *Abel*), as was probably the case already with Abel sacrificing after his brother Cain.[10] God has indeed heard the voice of the victim's blood.[11]

---

7. Ibid., 591.

8. Gordon, "Fratriarchy in the Old Testament."

9. Ibid., 224.

10. See above, chapter 2, section "In the Field."

11. Vawter expresses surprise to find "'God' rather than 'Yhwh' [in v. 25] in these lines that unmistakably come from the Yahwist" (*On Genesis*, 100). But such a shift in the name of the divinity finds its justification in the following verse (v. 26) whose effect would have been spoiled.

Gordon comes to the unwarranted conclusion that "fratriarchal organization was more widespread in a very remote antiquity, pictured as before the Flood, than it was in later historic times."[12] Gordon's own discussion of the late Chronicles texts in particular does not confirm such a suggestion. I believe rather that J's point was to set Abel within the shadow of Cain and Seth within the shadow of Abel, and that the other cases of fratriarchy in Genesis 4 strike echoes of this paradigm. Besides, there is no way to turn J into a paleontologist!

The Genesis 4 genealogy comports with the inserted narrative on Cain and Abel. As usual the sequence is patrilineal. It is also linear with seven generations including Lamech in the seventh position; then it becomes segmented with four children of Lamech.[13]

A closer look into the list of Lamech's children shows that three out of four of them are credited with some cultural achievement (Jabal with husbandry; Jubal with music instruments; Tubal-Cain with metallurgy). Victor Hamilton is right to stress that the fourth child, a girl named Naamah, is the only one "with no designated archetypal role."[14] That she is at all mentioned by name is already a remarkable phenomenon (but P tells us that Adam sired also [anonymous] daughters, see 5:4). Perhaps her fame is in her name: Naamah means "pleasant, nice-looking," for, as is well known, *nomen est omen* ("name is omen"). Besides, "[t]here is an excitement about each" of her brothers' names, as says Hamilton on the basis of their common Hebrew root *yabal* = "to bring in procession"[15]—and a stark contrast is created with the savage song of Lamech that follows (4:23–24). The dissimilarity in fact starts with the twinning of the two names Tubal-Cain and Naamah, for Tubal is the man of "brass and iron," a Vulcan of sorts, while his sister is all sweetness and pleasantness. The variance between the two is stark: "war and peace," "Mars and Venus," the male as death-carrier and the female as life-carrier.[16] Note that, according to P's genealogy in Genesis 5, Lamech sired a son, Noah, as carrier of appeasement, saying, "Out of the ground that the Lord has

12. Gordon, "Fratriarchy in the Old Testament," 231.

13. See Wilson, *Genealogy and History in the Biblical World*, 158.

14. Hamilton, *Genesis*, 239.

15. The *Bible de la Pléiade* prefers to retain the meaning of "to shepherd." Then, if, as some suggest, "Abel" is also a derivative of the root *yabal* in this sense, there is a philological wordplay with Abel/Jabal/Jubal/Tubal in the genealogy that vv. 3–16 interrupt.

16. It is not the first time that J pays reverence to the one sex he calls *ḥawah*, life, Eve (see 3:20).

cursed this one shall bring us relief from our work and from the toil of our hands" (5:29). Neither here nor in 4:20–22, 25–26 [J] is there any trace of transgenerational curse (see Exod 20:5).

The Yahwist and the Origin of Culture and Civilization

Clearly, J's general inclination is to look with suspicion at the technological evolution. Already in the Garden of Eden, the human invention of loincloth to hide their nakedness is an outcome of the "fall." In the story that follows, about Cain and Abel, J presents civilization as inaugurated by the sinister descendants of Cain. Eventually, the generation of the Babel tower is critically described as fabricating bricks so that "they had bricks for stones and clay they had for mortar" (Gen 11:3).

Why this mistrust on the part of J? The question finds a beginning of resolution when, in agreement with Otto Rank's discernment of the universal basic human motivation, we see as fundamental to the human condition "the principle of immortality striving" or "dominant immortality-ideology."[17] Within this perspective, all cultural forms seek to grant immortality to the individual and to the group.

This now needs to be seen against the background of the murder of Abel. With his slaughter, death for the first time has made its awesome irruption on the human stage. What earlier had appeared as a doomsday theory has become reality. And it is at this very juncture that humanity starts to summon up its energies into gaining immortality. To that effect, Cain eventually builds himself a city, named after his son Enoch. The city is the panacea. "Together, we stand." Guilt then can be shared, and instruments can be invented to fabricate a "tower whose top be in heaven" (Gen 11:4). The city is the technological center of immortality. It is the concentrated space where all are speaking the same language, that is, all are sharing the same and unique referent: the denial of death. The Tower is meant to be their survival forever, a pyramid defeating time, defeating motion, defeating finitude. For death is perceived as the upshot of movement. Hence, the monument will be as static as death itself and, therefore, will transcend death by deriding it, so to speak.[18]

---

17. See Rank, *Psychology and the Soul*, 87; see Becker, *Escape*, 64.

18. ". . . the dead things which alone endure," says Norman O. Brown, *Life Against Death*, 286.

With the genealogy into which the tale dovetails, Cain acquires a double representation. He is prototype of humanity as murderous, even fratricidal, *and* of humanity as frantically seeking immortality. On this score, the previous J myth of Adam and Eve provides the indispensable introductory background to the Cain and Abel story. It is in the latter that the human condition "after Eden" reaches its supreme expression.

The striving for immortality falls neatly in parallel with the Mesopotamian epos of Gilgamesh, for instance. In both the Babylonian and the biblical myths, we find the recognition of the fundamental human desire for transcending death. But while Gilgamesh's quest is for a magical *pharmakon*, J's diagnosis concludes that such quest is morbid and vain.[19] It paradoxically leads to granting more power to death. The latter can adopt various forms, murder/fratricide (as in Genesis 4), collective suicide (as in Genesis 6–9), or the fragmentation of humanity into a disconnected archipelago (as in Genesis 11).

In the Epic of Gilgamesh, the city (Babylon) is the *axis mundi* whose "head is in heaven" (Gen 11:4). It is the earthly dwelling of the gods and the channel par excellence of the communication with the divine. J tears this conception apart. Babel is in reality a powerhouse of human hubris. Moreover, as the first city built by Cain shows, the place is empty of the gods and is a haven for people addicted to murder and haughtiness.

The city as cemetery! Instead of being overcome, death is everywhere. In fact it is merely denied, covered-up, disguised. And strikingly enough, at this point, we encounter anew the Oedipus complex. As Brown writes, "The adult flight from death . . . perpetuates the oedipal project of becoming father of oneself."[20] It is really ironic to see Cain building a city as a monument to his "denial of death" as well as denying his father in order to become his own father. Calling the city by the name of his son Enoch becomes a transparent symbol.

Cain, from being the odd man out expelled from the human club of immortality-seekers—they would kill him on sight because he represents the negation of death-immunity—must at all cost start a "counter-club" of his own. The basic rule of the renegades is a classic one among rebels: revenge. Cain's demise would be avenged by a sevenfold massacre; Lamech's by a seventy-sevenfold one. And so it goes assumedly, with an exponent progression from generation to generation. (In the wars of the

19. Today's pharmacopia are gold, power, sex, and drugs.
20. Norman O. Brown, *Life Against Death*, 127.

twentieth century [derisively "A.D."], tens of millions of human beings have been annihilated.)

Among the city-dwellers' ingenious discoverers, J mentions Jubal as the inventor of musical instruments. The apparition of these marvelous artistic implements could be thought of as tempering the Yahwist's ostensible critique of the city and its culture. But, as Becker reminds us, "[M]usical instruments were built in astrological proportions so as to make the most divinely harmonious sounds."[21] As it is true of any secularized object we today take for "neutral," the "harp and pipe" (Gen 4:21) used to be sacred and belong to magic, suffice it to turn to 1 Sam 16:23.[22]

The Song of Lamech

"One thing which is important I know well: how to return with interest the evil which others have done me."[23] Lamech comes as the seventh generation of humankind and his mention closes a literary section of the text. The genealogy splits the history of civilization into two categories: the sedentary farmer and founder of the city, and the nomadic inventors of arts and crafts. Incidentally, it is to be noted with Westermann that J sees his people Israel as "an heir to the common patrimony of humankind."[24]

Lamech's song serves as a transition to J's following narrative in Genesis 6: the impure confusion of categories and the explosion of societal violence. First, J showed the deterioration of the human couple's relationship; then of the intra-familial kinship; with Genesis 6 and the following chapters, he deals with societal violence. The end-result is the Flood and the dispersion of the new humanity.

Lamech has two wives, Adah and Zillah. There may be here no criticism of polygamy, as Westermann insists,[25] but it is the first time that a man is said to have two wives, and Lamech is certainly not generally

21. Becker, *Escape*, 78. Furthermore, one remembers Amos's complaint against the upper class people, who, among other things, "pluck the lute's strings and invent musical instruments" (6:4–6).

22. Not so long ago, Niccolo Paganini's violin was considered as demonic!

23. Archilochus [seventh century BCE] 66, quoted by Snell, *The Discovery of the Mind*, 54.

24. Westermann, *Genesis 1–11*, 325; see 326; see Deut 6:10–11.

25. Ibid., 330–31.

presented as a paragon of virtues. Invoking the polygamy of the patriarchs with Westermann is not decisive. Benno Jacob calls attention to
the similarity of expression "he took wives for himself" here and in 6:2
(an act perpetrated by the "sons of God"), "thus," he says, "it includes a
disapproval of polygamy which Lamech introduced."[26] Indeed, there is
polygamy and there is polygamy, for one must distinguish between styles
of sexuality that one single term may classify together. Rashi here, on the
basis of the Midrash, says that the generation of the Flood adopted the
sinful practice of having two wives, one for childbearing, and the other
for pleasure. Adah was the genetrix and Zillah the "mistress." Note that
when, unexpectedly perhaps, Zillah gives birth to children, the text seems
to express surprise by saying, "she also" (*gam he*', v. 22, a construction that
sounds very much like the *gam hu*', "he also" about Abel's offering in v. 4).
This kind of demeaning polygamy is condemned by Jewish tradition.

Whatever may be the ostensible reason for Lamech to boast before
his wives, it ultimately covers up a deep anxiety about his own insignificance, that is, the ultimate insignificance of leaving no existential imprint
in the world.[27] In this sense, the song of Lamech is not just repulsive, it is
also pitiful. As is characteristic of this type of self-assertion, it is made at
the expense of others. Self-feeling creates a desert around with the illusion
that "*l'enfer, c'est les autres*" (hell is other people). That is why the figures of
Cain and Lamech are so similar and complementary. It is not just because
the one and the other are killers, but also because the motivation for killing and for boasting is so much the same in both: self-aggrandizement
and outshining of others.[28]

Lamech's martial poetry could figure in the *Iliad*. Kass speaks of a
"combination of Achilles and Homer." While Cain, Lamech's ancestor,
would be avenged seven times over *by God*, Lamech takes it into his own
hands to satisfy his desire for vengeance through a seventy-sevenfold retaliation.[29] At this point, the principle of retributive justice is pushed to the

---

26. Benno Jacob, *The First Book*, 38.

27. To recall, also Haman in the Book of Esther boasts in front of his wife (Esth
5:11–12; see also Prov 28:11).

28. Canetti writes, "It is the *first* death which infects everyone with the feeling of
being threatened. It is impossible to overrate the part played by the first dead man in the
kindling of wars"; *Crowds and Power*, 138.

29. Note that the root *nqm* is used here in a pejorative sense as "malicious retaliation
for inflicted wrongs," as Pitard says (*ABD* 6:786 *s. v.* "vengeance"); see Ezek 25:12, 15; Ps
8:3; and Lam 3:60. The song of Lamech finds a parallel in the story of Samson, who says

point of becoming the caricature of itself. Moreover, there is a profound irony in Lamech's effrontery to refer to the divine protection of his ancestor Cain. As Lamech's "immunity," by contrast, is at the cost of unlimited violence, he has turned the divine grace into its ugly counterfeit.

Like everything else in the genealogy reworked by J, the components of Lamech's discourse are highly ambiguous and ominous. The "song" is the last spasm, so to speak, of the Cain's murder story. As such, it neatly combines narrative and genealogy, and brings the horror of the fratricide to its apex. Any trivial inconvenience is occasion for Lamech to yield to violence. What he demands is not an eye for an eye, but a life for a wound, even the life of a child for a slight hurt.

The two wives of Lamech are the audience chosen by him to boast about his low tolerance of inconvenience. It is to be wondered why Lamech's terrible boasting is addressed to women. We, readers of the *Iliad* in particular, rather expected his discourse to be a threat to his enemies. The oft invoked parallel text of Isa 32:9 must be taken with caution.[30] Formally, it is true, the two texts are equally addressed to women, but the discrete intentions are very different. While Lamech calls upon his wives as witnesses to his "prowess," the prophet's call is a diatribe against "women who are at ease/complacent" (see also Amos 4:1; Ps 123:4). Isaiah 32's ideological parallel is rather found in the numerous prophetic confrontations of individual or collective culprits.

Have Lamech's wives become his foes that he must repress? Or, as a milder alternative, is Lamech here showing off before the females so as to merit their admiration? An admiration for his capacities of destructiveness, not of co-creativity as Eve's paean was in v. 1.[31] At any rate, we get the feeling that, ever since Cain, everyone has become an enemy to everyone else. As Hobbes says, "The condition of man [*sic*] . . . is a condition of war of everyone against everyone."[32] At the horizon the clouds are gathering that will soon bring about the Flood (Genesis 6–9).

---

about killing three thousand Philistines, "that I may be avenged for one of my two eyes" (Judg 16:28).

30. "Women of complacency, arise, hear ye my voice. Girls of carelessness, give ear to my speech."

31. As Westermann says, "One will have to distinguish then between the meaning which the song once had in its original life-setting as the braggart song of a man of might in the presence of his wives, and the meaning it has acquired in the intent of J as the conclusion of a genealogy which describes the origin of civilization" (*Genesis 1–11*, 336).

32. Hobbes, *Leviathan*, pt. 1, ch. 4.

Lamech magnifies and glorifies violence (he is boasting like a peacock before a receptive audience). As Hedges writes (about Achilles' cry of victory over the corpse of Hector),[33] "Here is the instant creation of heroic myth, out of murder" (to recall, Hector was unarmed).[34] Lamech introduces *war* in the world and extols its excitement and seduction. His song is the only thing J deems we should know about him. War, it is intimated, is Lamech's only reason for living, "the chance to exist for an intense and overpowering moment."[35] The primeval murderous act of envy has spawned the state of war that permeates the entire human history and will some time explode the universe. The man of Nazareth shared the same vision with J when he warned that even a verbal slighting of someone else is already an act of slaughter (see Matt 5:22).

Note the anonymity of Lamech's enemies, a man, a child, many others.[36] The namelessness of the foes is essential; they must be dehumanized, just ciphers in a statistic: one, seven, seventy-seven . . . . Only Lamech and his wives have names, for, in their own eyes, they are in the right while the others are by definition in the wrong. But the very paean Lamech sings is itself so savage that it is to be wondered who the barbarians really are.

Hope Has the Last Word

There is, however, a kind of clearing up with Eve giving birth to Seth, a more promising son. As noted above, Eve's tone changes in celebrating this newborn "in replacement of Abel whom Cain killed" (v. 26). Seth himself, we are told, had a son whom *he* called Enosh. This shift from the naming mother is one more token of the newness of times.[37] With Enosh, whose name is the equivalent of Adam (that is, "Human being"), there is a rebound of history with a much greater optimistic expectation attached to it. Like its correspondent "Adam," Enosh is fundamentally a collective noun, and the situation obtained with its appearance points in the direc-

33. See Shakespeare, *Troilus and Cressida*, Act V, sc. 8 (Hector: "I am unarm'd; forego this vantage, Greek"). In Homer's *Iliad*, the scene (somewhat different) can be found in book 22.

34. Hedges, *War Is a Force*, 30; see the preceding note.

35. Ibid., 5.

36. Krašovec suggests to see here a merism: man, boy, in the sense of "each, anyone"; *Reward, Punishment, and Forgiveness*, 34 n. 2.

37. See von Rad, *Genesis*, on 4:26. Enosh appears also in the P genealogy of Gen 5:6. Note, however, the absence there of Cain and Abel. See also the parallels of Gen 5:6–31 (P) and J's Gen 4:17–19. In P, Lamech is the father of Noah.

tion of a substitution. For, once more in this chapter of Genesis, Adam is sidetracked. Nothing redemptive is expected from him apart from insuring humanity's survival through procreation.[38]

Enosh is "human" like Adam, but with a definite accent upon weakness. Enosh is "only human." Nahum Sarna stresses this sense of frailty, hence of "utter dependence upon God."[39] And now, strikingly, Enosh as it were binds up Adam, like him a fully human being, and Abel, like him vulnerable, a "breath," a "vanity." Both men are anodynes to human hubris in which J saw the root of all sins. With Enosh, hope reenters history.

The clearing up of the clouds is confirmed by the last and majestic statement that closes up the story of Cain and Abel: "Then people began to call on the Name of Yhwh" (4:26b). Westermann rightly understands the statement as saying that the cult to Yhwh began in the primeval time. With the birth of Seth, the child of the promise, people started to invoke Him. Beforehand, Yhwh to be sure had intervened in the course of history, that is, in the events involving "Adam and Eve," and later "Cain and Abel." But, properly speaking, no one had called on the Name of God, that is, until the end of Genesis 4 there is *no prayer*. The Name is used all along by the narrator J, as the "singer of tale" is endowed with omniscience, but his knowledge is not a common one. Until Seth, it is here intimated, the humans had taken the intercourse with the deity for granted. They felt no need to call on God by name, and in this sense one may speak of "religion." Religion permeated time and space. God and the human spoke to one another freely and naturally. With the advent of Seth, however, something has changed in their relationship. Even when the free intercourse is rare, the Name of God can be called on for help and succor.

At this point, a historic shift occurs from "religion" in general to communion with God in particular (4:25–26). With these verses, J is far from closing his work but he is clearly closing the cycle inaugurated by the words "at the end of an era" in v. 3. Verses 25–26 are a return to calm after the storm provoked by Cain and Lamech. That is why Enosh—rather than Enoch, another case of unfulfilled promise—named by a father (rather than by a mother)[40] is the one who inaugurates a new beginning: "Then began the calling up of the Name of Yhwh."

38. The eclipse of Adam in the tale retrospectively demonstrates that J's alleged singling Eve in Genesis 3 as responsible for the "fall" is groundless.

39. Sarna, *Understanding Genesis*, 40.

40. Why this J's marker of newness? Because Eve's discernment as regards her chil-

True, J pursues his description of the human regression to chaos, that is, to the Flood that will efface almost all traces of cosmos. But, as usual, J does not lose sight of "the last of the Just."[41] Noah, he says, "finds favor in Yhwh's eyes" (6:8); he replaces the altar of Cain with another that he "built to Yhwh," taking "of every clean animal and every clean bird, and offered burnt offerings on the altar" (8:20 [NRSV]).

Noah is only a reprieve, however, a kind of "John the Baptist" pointing—like in the famous painting of Matthias Grünewald—to someone else who "must increase," namely, Abraham. For the J's narrative is oriented toward that particular advent, which is presented as occurring in the midst of an utterly corrupt humanity (Gen 6:5, 11–13; 8:21; 11:3–4).

With Abraham, it is not yet the beginning of Israel's history, although Gen 4:26 announces its birth—relayed by Noah's righteousness and by Abraham's faith. What is of primordial import here is that, according to J, the invocation of Yhwh did precede the advent of the people of Israel. Whether this stance of J can or cannot be historically substantiated has no real relevance.[42] J's statement is not archaeological but theological: Yhwh is God of the whole of humanity.

It is, therefore, paradoxical when scholars like Delitzsch and Gressmann and now Westermann say that J in 4:26b is speaking of religion in general! Nothing is farther from the truth. "Religion" as a term can only be used when the deity is either nameless or a member of a pantheon. When the Name of Yhwh is invoked, the relationship is not any longer simply "religious" but covenantal. Those in Genesis that are said to invoke the Name of Yhwh are Abram in Gen 12:8 and 13:4, or Isaac in Gen 26:25. J does not say that Abram inaugurated the invocation,[43] but he points to the fact that Abram's conversion led him to join a chorus that began with Seth. Abram, of course, is no Israelite and this feature contributes to J's sense of universalism (see Gen 12:3; Exod 19:5).

Thus, J's conception of God is not of one religious phenomenon among many theological conceptualizations. Israel's Scriptures emphasize "in time and out of time" this very conviction of incomparability. Other

---

dren has raised grave doubts and concerns. She still names Seth in a move of confession that rehabilitates Abel in her own eyes. Then she makes way, as it were, to males calling the names of males.

41. After the title of an impressive book by André Schwarz-Bart.

42. *Pace* Gunkel, *Genesis*.

43. Although the Jewish tradition wishes to accord the priority to Abraham and thus struggles with the text of Gen 4:26b.

peoples may have religious rapports with the deity, but only "Israel," understood in its broadest sense, calls upon the Name of Yhwh.

Conclusion

Concluding this literary study of the tale about Cain and Abel, a reflection on J's rhetorical devices is appropriate. Analyzing these devices shows to what a large extent the author's selected vehicles are to be taken seriously in any interpretation of the text. To be sure, divorcing the story from its author does open up some unused tracks. It becomes possible, for instance, to accuse the divine character of manipulating Cain into despair and eventually into murder. God's subsequent accusation of the killer is then fraught with hypocrisy and cruelty.

This way, J's story is blown to pieces. The modern analyst reconstructs another story, which she presents as being more psychologically accurate than the original one. But the slope is slippery. The transformation of Israel's God into a sadistic manipulator in disguise is not particularly difficult to do. In fact it is suspiciously easy. Besides, any interpersonal relationship can always be regarded as hiding a dubious agenda. Genesis 3:1 elicits a perfect example: "Did God really say . . . ? On the contrary you shall not die!" (3:4). The result of such disfiguration is highly questionable. At the end of the process, is there still a story of fratricide and of onslaught against innocence? Is such a God still the God of Abraham, Isaac, and Jacob? Or is he the "god of the philosophers [and the critics]" (Pascal)?[44]

True, the biblical text is not beyond ethical criticism. A towering figure in the Hebrew Bible as is Abraham shows us the way in disputing with God the impending destruction of Sodom and Gomorrah in Genesis 18, for instance. For, if it is true, as Pascal says, that "the heart has its reasons which reason does not know,"[45] it is even more true that God is moved by reasons that our reason cannot comprehend—and must, notwithstanding, probe for an explanation. Why did God favor Abel's sacrifice but not Cain's? Why did God test the faith of Abraham by requiring from him a quasi infanticide? Why did Abraham accept such a terrible challenge in the first place? Why imagine such an outrageous wager between God

---

44. When God is replaced by some kind of "psychological correctness," the resulting anthropology is so horizontal as to be flat; it is devoid of all poetic power.

45. Pascal, *Pensées* 4: "le coeur a ses raisons que la raison ne connaît pas."

and the Satan in Job's prologue, and the eventual submission of Job at the end? Questions are endless and the text often becomes a theological and anthropological confrontation of its readers.

Accepting to be confronted entails to accept being disoriented and reoriented. With Genesis 4, the *disorientation* consists in recognizing ourselves in paradigmatic Cain, the envious one, plagued by a terrible complex of inferiority that readily assumes that God favors others more than they deserve and shuns him who notwithstanding is the worthy one. It is also to confess that in our eyes the weak ones are always wrong. The *reorientation* consists in existentially choosing to be the slain Abel rather than the slaughterer Cain. Abel "was despised and rejected of all; he was afflicted, yet he did not open his mouth; he was brought as a lamb to the slaughter; he was cut off from the land of the living . . . ." in the words of Isaiah 53:7. But, when siding with him, "by his wound we are healed" (53:5), because with him we have chosen innocence.

The choice is costly; it may be paid with our life. But, siding with Abel is also siding with J's God. All the Cains of the earth, unable to kill God, turn to the "next of kin," that is, the innocent and the just. Cain endlessly continues to kill Abel, and Abel's blood spilled on the ground continues to cry for justice and redress.[46]

Such is the power of Cain and Abel story. The seemingly generous attempt after that at blanching Cain is at the very least suspect of being a *pro domo* kind of defense, as we said above.[47] If anyone wants to forward an apology of Cain, the inescapable way, I think, is to adopt a Nietzschean category of "master morality" and apply it to Abel's brother. In the words of Nietzsche,

> For solitude is a virtue for us, as a sublime bent and urge for cleanliness which guesses how all contact between man and man—"in society"—involves inevitable uncleanliness. All community makes men—somehow, somewhere, sometime "common."[48]

A Nietzschean hero or superman, however, is foreign to J's anthropology.

46. According to the media, there are presently nine million children refugees. They are among the innumerable Abels gagged to muteness by the innumerable Cains.

47. Note that there is a positive side to such a critique, as ungrounded as it may be. As Ricoeur says, "God [is] the source of everything good in creation, including our indignation against evil" ("Evil as Challenge," 647); here it would be running—even though unwisely—to the defense of Cain as allegedly accused unjustly.

48. *Beyond Good and Evil*, par. 284, 226.

There is nothing redeeming in Cain's character. The only redemption comes, not from a hidden innocence of his, but from the ungrounded grace of God. Cain lives, alas, for if it is indeed true that "the poor will always be with you" (Matt 26:11 and parallels). This is because of the continuous presence of those who impoverish others. The weeds grow with the wheat. Cain is far from closing a parenthesis after him. In his wake come worse than he, a Lamech, and then the corrupted and corrupting people before the Flood, and after them the megalomaniac builders of the Tower of Arrogance.

Truly, "the inclination of the human heart is evil from youth" (Gen 8:21), and the universal crushing-under of innocence is so appalling that all the waters of the Deluge are unable to cleanse the world of its violence. But the truth is that there *is* innocence to be crushed. There are still Abels in the midst of humanity. Sometimes the just are so numerous as to be counted by the millions, as in the Nazi and Stalinist concentration camps, or the killing fields of Cambodia and Darfur. This is a part, indeed a crucial part, of J's kerygma: there are Abels, there are Seths and Noahs, and, "at the time of the Visitation," there are Abrahams.

Abraham in Genesis 12 is more than a silver lining in the clouds. With him, according to J, a new humanity emerges from East of Eden. A movement of return. Abraham inaugurates the odyssey of a people whose history will atone for the blood of all the Abels and proclaim the victory of the defeated and the filling of the hungry for justice. Abraham's people will be the resurrection of the dead Abel.

In the tale of Cain and Abel, J has shown that, after Eden, the human being is psychologically, that is, fundamentally, sick. True, he/she is also always physically impaired, but while the physical impairment finds some relief in natural herbs, the psychological neurosis must be treated from the inside. "If you do well" (Gen 4:7) is *ad extra*. It ultimately means, "If you love." Cain is the antipodal demonstration of this basic truth. Love is the individual and social cure, because "God is love" (1 John 4:8).

J's string of primeval cameos (Genesis 2–11) is like a movie about "not doing well." Because the humans are capable of love, they are also capable of hatred and violence. Because love encounters a *Thou* and *ipso facto* establishes an *I*, lovelessness is murderous of the other and deconstructs the hater into a zombie. Cain becomes a ghost; he is like a punctured balloon flying in all directions propelled by the escaping air. Just retaliation for destroying someone else whose name was "Breath." Indeed for the killer, the victim always appears as no more concrete than a breath in winter. But the killer himself disintegrates in his crime; he becomes a deflated airbag.

Now, in contrast, "Breath" is heard by God and so, after all, the martyr was not an insubstantial epigone of his brother. He was a "living being" in whose "nostrils" God had "insufflated a living breath" (Gen 2:7). Abel, breath of God. He was so before Cain killed him, and so will he ever be until comes the one who is more Abel than Abel ever was (Heb 11:4, 40). His cry sounds from one end of human history to the other end: "he still speaks out." Thanks to him and to all the Abels of the world, innocence has a voice and triumphs over death.

As for the creator of the myth of Cain and Abel, his song modulates the cry of Abel's blood.[49]

---

49. Since J "speaks in primordial images," he also "speaks with a thousand voices," as Jung says (*CW* 20:par. 129).

Bibliography

Abravanel, Isaac. *On the Pentateuch*. Warsaw, 1862.

Ackerman, J., and K. R. R. Gros Louis, editors. *Literary Interpretation of Biblical Narrative*. Nashville: Abingdon, 1982.

Adler, Alfred. "Der Aggressionstrieb im Leben und in der Neurose." *Fortschritte der Medizin* 26 (1908) 577–84.

Alonso-Schökel, Luis. *Donde esta tu hermano? Textos de fraternidad en el libro del Genesis*. Valencia: Artes Graphicas Soler, 1985.

Alter, Robert. *The Art of Biblical Narrative*. New York: Basic, 1981.

Anderson, Gary A. *The Genesis of Perfection, Adam and Eve in Jewish and Christian Imagination*. Louisville: Westminster John Knox, 2001.

Ansbacher, Heinz L., and Rowena R. Ansbacher, editors. *The Individual Psychology of Alfred Adler: A Systematic Presentation in Selections from His Writings*. New York: Basic, 1956.

Arendt, Hannah. *Eichmann in Jerusalem: A Report on the Banality of Evil*. New York: Penguin, 1963.

————. *The Origins of Totalitarianism*. San Diego: Harcourt, Brace & World, 1968.

Arenhoevel, D. "Kain und Abel." *Wort und Antwort* 8/6 (1967) 172–77.

Aristotle. *The Nichomachean Ethics*. Translated by Harris Rackham. Introduction by Stephen Watt. Ware, Hertfordshire: Wordsworth, 1996.

————. *Poetics*. In *The Complete Works of Aristotle. The Revised Oxford Translation*. 2 vols. Edited by Jonathan Barnes. Bollingen Series LXXI-2. Princeton: Princeton University Press, 1971.

————. *Rhetoric*. In *The Complete Works of Aristotle. The Revised Oxford Translation*. 2 vols. Edited by Jonathan Barnes. Bollingen Series LXXI-2. Princeton: Princeton University Press, 1971.

Atkinson, David. *The Message of Genesis 1–11: The Dawn of Creation*. The Bible Speaks Today. Downers Grove, IL: InterVarsity, 1990.

Audet, Jean-Paul, "La Revanche de Prométhée." *Revue biblique* 73 (1967) 5–29.

Auerbach, Erich, *Mimesis: The Representation of Reality in Western Literature*. Translated by W. A. Trask. Princeton: Princeton University Press, 1974.

————. *Wüste und gelobtes Land: Geschichte Israels von den Anfangen zum Tode Salmos*. Berlin: Schocken, 1932.

Augustine, *Concerning the City of God: Against the Pagans*. Translated by Henry Bettenson. Middlesex: Penguin, 1984.

——. *Confessions*. Translation and notes by Henry Chadwick. Oxford World's Classics. Oxford University Press, 1991.

Badiou, Alain. *Ethics: An Essay on the Understanding of Evil*. Translated by Peter Halward. London: Verso, 2001.

Bakan, David. *Disease, Pain, and Sacrifice: Toward a Psychology of Suffering*. Chicago: University of Chicago Press, 1968.

Bakhtin, Mikhail. *Art and Answerability: Early Philosophical Essays by M. M. Bakhtin*. Edited by Vladimir Liapunov and Michael Holquist. Austin: University of Texas Press, 1990.

——. "Author and Hero in Aesthetic Activity." In *Art and Answerability: Early Philosophical Essays by M. M. Bakhtin*, edited by Michael Holquist and Vadim Liapunov, 4–256. Austin: University of Texas Press, 1990.

——. *The Dialogic Imagination: Four Essays by M. M. Bakhtin*. Translated by Caryl Emerson and Michael Holquist. Austin: University of Texas Press, 1981.

Bar-Efrat, Shimon. *Narrative Art in the Bible*. Bible and Literature Series 17. Sheffield: Sheffield Academic, 1989.

Barton, George A. "A Sumerian Source of the Fourth and Fifth Chapters of Genesis." *JBL* 34 (1915) 1–9.

Baudelaire, Charles. "Abel and Cain." In *Flowers of Evil: A New Translation with Parallel French Text*, 266–68. Translated with notes by James McGowan. Oxford World's Classics. Oxford : Oxford University Press, 1998.

——. "Abel et Cain." In *Les Fleurs du mal, Baudelaire, Oeuvres Complètes*. Edited by Y. G. Le Dantec and C. Pichois. Paris: La Pléiade, 1964.

——. "La Destruction." In *Les Fleurs du mal, Baudelaire, Oeuvres Complètes*. Edited by Y. G. Le Dantec and C. Pichois. Paris: La Pléiade, 1964.

Bauer, J. B. "Kain und Abel." *Theologisch-praktische Quartalschrift* 103 (1955) 126–33.

Baumgartner, Walter et al., editors. *Festschrift, Alfred Bertholet zum 80. Geburtstag*. Tübingen: Mohr/Siebeck, 1950.

Becker, Ernest. *The Birth and Death of Meaning: An Interdisciplinary Perspective on the Problem of Man*. New York: Free Press, 1962.

——. *Denial of Death*. New York: Free Press, 1973.

——. *Escape from Evil*. New York: Free Press, 1975.

Berger, Peter L. *Questions of Faith: A Skeptical Affirmation of Christianity*. Malden, MA: Blackwell, 2004.

Bernanos, Georges. *Journal d'un curé de campagne*. Paris: Plon, 1974.

Bernstein, Michael André. "The Poetics of *Ressentiment*." In *Rethinking Bakhtin: Extensions and Challenges*, edited by Gary S. Morson and Caryl Emerson, 197–223. Evanston, IL: Northwestern University Press, 1989.

Bespaloff, Rachel. "On the Iliad." In *War and the Iliad*. Simone Weil and Rachel Bespaloff. Translated by Mary McCarthy. New York: New York Review Books, 2005.

Blenkinsopp, Joseph. "Theme and Motif in the Succession History (2 Sam xi 2ff) and the Yahwist Corpus." In *Volume du Congrès: Geneva*, 1965. VTSup 15. Leiden: Brill, 1966.

Bloch, Ernst. *Atheism in Christianity: The Religion of the Exodus and the Kingdom*. Translated by J. T. Swann. New York: Herder and Herder, 1972.

Blocher, Henri. *In the Beginning: The Opening Chapters of Genesis.* Translated by David Preston. Downers Grove, IL: InterVarsity, 1984.

Bloom, Harold. *The Book of J.* New York: Vintage, 1991.

Blumenthal, David. *Facing the Abusing God: A Theology of Protest.* Louisville: Westminster John Knox, 1993.

Bollas, Christopher. "The Structure of Evil." In *Cracking Up: The Work of Unconscious Experience,* 180–220. New York: Hill and Wang, 1995.

Branham, R. Bracht, editor. *Bakhtin and the Classics.* Rethinking Theory. Evanston, IL: Northwestern University Press, 2002.

Brecht, Bertolt. *Mother Courage and Her Children: A Chronicle of the Thirty Years' War.* Translated and edited by Eric Bentley. New York: Grove Weidenfeld, 1991.

Brenner, Athalya, editor. *A Feminist Companion to Genesis.* Feminist Companions to the Bible 2. Sheffield: Sheffield Academic, 1993.

Brichto, H. C. "Cain and Abel." In *Interpreter's Dictionary of the Bible, Supplementary Volume,* 121–22. Edited by Keith Crim. Nashville: Abingdon, 1976.

Brown, Norman O. *Life against Death: The Psychoanalytical Meaning of History.* 2nd ed. New York: Viking, 1959.

Brown, Robert McAfee. *Theology in a New Key: Responding to Liberation Themes.* Philadelphia: Westminster, 1978.

Brown, William P. *The Ethos of the Cosmos: The Genesis of Moral Imagination in the Bible.* Grand Rapids: Eerdmans, 1999.

Brueggemann, Walter. *Genesis.* Interpretation. Louisville: Westminster John Knox, 1982.

Bryan, D. T. "A Reevaluation of Gen 4 and 5 in the Light of Recent Studies in Genealogical Fluidity." *ZAW* 99 (1987) 180–88.

Buber, Martin. *Good and Evil: Two Interpretations.* Upper Saddle River, NJ: Prentice Hall, 1977.

———. *The Tales of the Hasidim: The Early Masters.* Translated by Olga Marx. New York: Schocken, 1947.

———, and Franz Rosenzweig. *Die Schrift.* Vol. 1. Berlin: Schocken, 1925.

Budde, Karl. *Die biblische Urgeschichte (Gen 1–12:5) untersucht.* Giessen: Ricker, 1883.

Bühler, Pierre. *Le problème du mal et la doctrine du péché.* Nouvelle série théologique. Geneva: Labor et Fides, 1976.

Burrows, Millar. "Ancient Israel." In *The Idea of History,* edited by Robert C. Dentan, 99–131. American Oriental Series 38. New Haven: Yale University Press, 1955.

Callender, Dexter E. Jr. *Adam in Myth and History: Ancient Israelite Perspective on the Primal Human.* Harvard Semitic Studies 48. Winona Lake, IN: Eisenbrauns, 2000.

Canetti, Elias. *Crowds and Power.* Translated by Carol Stewart. New York: Viking, 1962.

Castellino, G. R. "Genesis IV 7." *VT* 10 (1960) 442–45.

———. "The Origins of Civilization According to Biblical and Cuneiform Texts." *I Studied Inscriptions from before the Flood: Ancient Near Eastern, Literary, and Linguistic Approaches to Genesis 1–11,* edited by Richard S. Hess and David Toshio Tsumura, 75–95. Sources for Biblical and Theological Study 4. Winona Lake, IN: Eisenbrauns, 1994.

Cassuto, Umberto. *Commentary on the Book of Genesis, Part I: From Adam to Noah.* Translated by Israel Abrahams. Jerusalem: Magnes, 1961–1964.

Céline, Louis-Ferdinand. *D'un château l'autre.* Paris: Gallimard, 1957.

———. *Nord.* Paris: Gallimard, 1960.

———. *Rigodon,* Paris: Gallimard, 1969.

Chabrol, Claude. "L'Enfer." (movie).

Chavel, Charles B. *Ramban*. New York: Shilo, 1971.

Clark, Katerina, and Michael Holquist. *Mikhail Bakhtin*. Cambridge: Harvard University Press, 1984.

Clines, David J. A. "Theme in Genesis 1–11." In *I Studied Inscriptions from before the Flood: Ancient Near Eastern, Literary, and Linguistic Approaches to Genesis 1–11*, edited by Richard S. Hess and David Toshio Tsumura, 285–309. Sources for Biblical and Theological Study 4. Winona Lake, IN: Eisenbrauns, 1994.

Coats, George W. *Genesis with an Introduction to Narrative Literature*. Forms of the Old Testament Literature 1. Grand Rapids: Eerdmans, 1983.

Colombo, J. A. "Christian Theodicy and the Genuineness of Evil." *Journal of Pastoral Counseling* 25 (1990).

Cooley, Mason. *City Aphorisms*. Fifth selection. New York, 1988.

Cooper, Terry D. *Dimensions of Evil: Contemporary Perspectives*. Minneapolis: Fortress, 2007.

Cover, Robin C. "Sin, Sinner in the Old Testament." In *ABD* 6:31–40.

Crenshaw, James L. *Defending God: Biblical Responses to the Problem of Evil*. Oxford: Oxford University Press, 2005.

Culbertson, P. "De-Demonizing Cain . . . and Wondering Why." A paper presented to the "Psychology and the Bible" section at the Society of Biblical Literature annual meeting in Philadelphia, November 19, 2005.

Damrosch, David. *The Narrative Covenant: Transformations of Genre in the Growth of Biblical Literature*. Ithaca, NY: Cornell University, 1987.

Davidson, Robert. *Genesis 1–11*. Cambridge Bible Commentary. London: Cambridge University Press, 1973.

Davis, Stephen T., editor. *Encountering Evil: Live Options in Theology*. New edition. Louisville: Westminster John Knox, 2001.

Dentan, Robert C., editor. *The Idea of History in the Ancient Near East*. American Oriental Series 38. New Haven: Yale University Press, 1955.

Des Pres, Terrence. *The Survivor: An Anatomy of Life in the Death Camps*. New York: Oxford University Press, 1976.

Deurloo, K.A. *Kain en Abel: Onderzoek naar exegetische methode inzake een 'kleine literaire eenheid' in de Tenakh*. Amsterdam: W. ten Have, 1967.

———. "*tŝuqh*, 'dependency,' Gen 4, 7." *ZAW* 99 (1987) 405–6.

Dostoevsky, Fyodor, *The Adolescent*. Translated by Podrostok. Edited by Andrew R. MacAndrew. New York: Norton, 1971.

———. *The Brothers Karamazov*. Edited by Richard Pevear and Larissa Volokhonsky. New York: Farrar, Straus and Giroux, 1990.

———. *Crime and Punishment*. Edited by Richard Pevear and Larissa Volokhonsky. New York: Knopf, 1992.

Eagleton, Terry. *Holy Terror*. Oxford: Oxford University Press, 2005.

Edgerton, W. Dow. *Speak to Me That I May Speak: A Spirituality of Preaching*. Cleveland: Pilgrim, 2006.

Eigen, Michael. *Rage*. Disseminations. Middletown, CN: Wesleyan University Press, 2002.

Ellington, J. "Man and Adam in Gen 1–5." *Bible Translator* 30 (1979) 201–5.

Ellis, Peter F. *The Yahwist: The Bible's First Theologian*. Notre Dame: Fides, 1968.

Ellison, Ralph. *Invisible Man*. New York: Random, 1947.

Ellul, Jacques. *The Meaning of the City*. Translated by Dennis Pardee. Grand Rapids: Eerdmans, 1993.

Emerson, Ralph Waldo. "War." A speech delivered in March 1838 in Boston. www.RWE. org. <The Works of Ralph Waldo Emerson>.

Enslin, Morton S., "Cain and Prometheus." *JBL* 86 (1967) 88–90.

Ephrem, Saint. *Commentary on the Diatessaron*. Translated by C. McCarthy. Oxford: Oxford University Press, 1993.

Euripides. *Medea and Other Plays*. Penguin Classics. Translated by John Davie. Edited by Richard Rutherford. New York: Penguin, 1996.

Ewald, Heinrich. "Erklärung der biblischen Urgeschichte. I, 4. Die Geschlechter des ersten Weltalters." *Jahrbücher der biblischen Wissenschaft* 6 (1853–54) 1–19.

Faulkner, William. *As I Lay Dying*. New York: Random House, 1957.

Finkelstein, Israel, and Neil Asher Silberman. *The Bible Unearthed: Archaeology's New Vision of Ancient Israel and the Origin of Its Sacred Texts*. New York: Free Press, 2001.

Fishbane, Michael. *Text and Texture: Close Readings of Selected Texts*. New York: Schocken, 1979.

Fisher, Loren R. "Creation at Ugarit and in the Old Testament." *VT* 15 (1965) 313–24.

Fokkelman, J. P. *Narrative Art in Genesis: Specimens of Stylistic and Structural Analysis*. Amsterdam: Van Gorcum, 1975.

Fretheim, Terrence E. *God and World in the Old Testament: A Relational Theology of Creation*. Nashville: Abingdon, 2005.

————. *The Suffering of God: An Old Testament Perspective*. Overtures to Biblical Theology. Philadelphia: Fortress, 1984.

Freud, Sigmund. *Beyond the Pleasure Principle*. [*SE* xviii]. Translated by James Strachey. New York: Liveright, 1950.

————. *Civilization and Its Discontents*. Translated by James Strachey. New York: Norton, 1961.

————. *Collected Papers*. Edited by J. Riviere and J. Strachey. 5 vols., New York: International Psycho-Analytical Press, 1924–1950.

————. *The Ego and the Id*, 1923 [= *SE* xix]. Translated by J. Strachey. New York: Norton, 1960.

————. "The Future of an Illusion." [1927] In *Civilization, Society and Religion, Group Psychology, Civilization and Its Discontents and Other Works*. Translated by James Strachey. London: Penguin, 1985.

————. *The Interpretation of Dreams* [= *SE* iv–v] Translated by J. A. Underwood. Penguin Modern Classics. New York: Penguin, 2006.

————. "Instincts and their Vicissitudes." 1915 (= *SE* 14).

————. "Negation." [1925] (= *SE* xix) in *Revue Française de Psychanalyse*, vol. 7/2, 174–77.

————. *New Introductory Lectures on Psycho-Analysis*, 1933 (= *SE* xxii).

————. "Notes upon a case of obsessional neurosis." [= "Rat Man." 1909] (= *SE* x). *Three Case Histories*. Edited by Philip Rieff, New York: Macmillan, 1963.

Frick, Frank S. *The City in Ancient Israel*. Society of Biblical Literature Dissertation Series 36. Missoula, MT: Scholars, 1977.

Friedman, Maurice. "The Human Dimension of Evil." *Journal of Pastoral Counseling* 25 (1990) 26–36.

Friedman, Richard Elliott. *The Hidden Book in the Bible*. San Francisco: HarperSanFrancisco, 1998.

Fromm, Erich. *The Heart of Man: Its Genius for Good and Evil*. New York: Harper and Row, 1964.

Frymer-Kensky, Tikva, "The Atrahasis Epic and Its Significance for Our Understanding of Genesis 1–9." *Biblical Archaeologist* 40 (1977) 147–55.

Gabriel, Johannes. "Die Kainitengenealogie, Genesis 4, 17–24." *Biblica* 40 (1959).

Gandhi, Mahatma. *Essential Writings*. Edited by John Dear. Maryknoll, NY: Orbis, 2002.

Gardner, Anne. "Genesis 2.4b–3: A Mythological Paradigm of Sexuality or of the Religious History of Pre-exilic Israel." *Scottish Journal of Theology* 43 (1990) 1–18.

Gaylin, Willard. *Hatred: The Psychological Descent into Violence*. New York: Public Affairs, 2003.

Gesenius, Wilhelm, Emil Kautzsch, and A. E. Cowley. *Gesenius' Hebrew Grammar*. 2nd ed. Oxford: Oxford University Press, 1910.

Gevirtz, Stanley. "Lamech's Song to His Wives." In *I Studied Inscriptions from before the Flood: Ancient Near Eastern, Literary, and Linguistic Approaches to Genesis 1–11*, edited by Richard S. Hess and David Toshio Tsumura, 405–15. Sources for Biblical and Theological Study 4. Winona Lake, IN: Eisenbrauns, 1994.

Ginzberg, Louis. *The Legends of the Jews*. Vol. 1. Philadelphia: Jewish Publication Society, 1954.

Girard, René. Foreword to James Williams, *The Bible, Violence, and the Sacred: Liberation from the Myth of the Sanctioned Violence*. San Francisco: Harper, 1991.

———. *Violence and the Sacred*. Translated by Patrick Gregory. Baltimore: Johns Hopkins University Press, 1979.

Gordon, Cyrus H. "Fratriarchy in the Old Testament." *JBL* 54 (1935) 223–31.

Gore, Charles. "A Kenotic Theory of the Incarnation." In *The Power of God: Readings on Omnipotence and Evil*, edited by Linwood Urban and Douglas N. Walton. New York: Oxford University Press. 1978.

Grawe, Paul H. *Comedy in Space, Time, and the Imagination*. Chicago: Nelson-Hall, 1983.

Griffin, David Ray. "Creation out of Nothing, Creation out of Chaos, and the Problem of Evil." In *Encountering Evil: Live Options in Theology*, edited by Stephen T. Davis. Louisville: Westminster John Knox, 2001.

Gros Louis, K. R. R. et al., editors. *Literary Interpretation of Biblical Narratives*. Nashville: Abingdon, 1982.

Gruber, Mayer I. "The Tragedy of Cain and Abel: A Case of Depression." *Jewish Quarterly Review* 69 (1978) 89–97.

———. "Was Cain Angry or Depressed?" *Biblical Archaeology Review* 6/6 (1980) 35–36.

Gruppe, O. "Kain." *ZAW* 39 (1921) 67–76.

Gunkel, Hermann. *Creation and Chaos in the Primeval Era and the Eschaton: A Religio-Historical Study of Genesis 1 and Revelation 12*. Translated by K. William Whitney Jr. Grand Rapids: Eerdmans, 2006.

———. *Genesis*. Handkommentar zum Alten Testament 1. 3rd ed. Göttingen: Vandenhoeck & Ruprecht, 1910.

———. *Genesis*. Translated by Mark E. Biddle. Mercer Library of Biblical Studies. Macon, GA: Mercer University Press, 1997.

———. *The Stories of Genesis*. Edited by William R. Scott. Translated by John J. Scullion. Berkeley: Bibal, 1994.

Halpertal, Moshe. *People of the Book: Canon, Meaning, Authority.* Cambridge: Harvard University Press, 1997.

Hamilton, Victor. *The Book of Genesis, Chapters 1–17.* Grand Rapids: Eerdmans, 1990.

Hansen, Ron. "The Story of Cain." In *Genesis as It Was Written: Contemporary Writers on Our First Stories,* edited by David Rosenberg, 51–58. San Francisco: HarperSanFrancisco, 1996.

Harris, William V. *Restraining Rage: The Ideology of Anger Control in Classical Antiquity.* Cambridge: Harvard University Press, 2001.

Hauser, Alan J. "Linguistic and Thematic Links between Genesis 4:1–16 and Genesis 2–3." *Journal of the Evangelical Theological Society* 23 (1980) 297–305.

Hedges, Chris. *War Is a Force That Gives Us Meaning.* New York: PublicAffairs, 2002.

Herion, G. A. "Why God Rejected Cain's Offering: The Obvious Answer." In *Fortunate the Eyes That See: Essays in Honor of David Noel Freedman,* edited by Astrid B. Beck et al., 52–65. Grand Rapids: Eerdmans, 1995.

Heschel, Abraham. *Man Is not Alone: A Philosophy of Religion.* New York: Harper and Row, 1951.

Hesiod. *Theogony, Works and Days.* Translated by M. L. West. Oxford World's Classics. Oxford: Oxford University Press, 1999.

Hess, Richard S. "Abel." In *ABD* 1:9–10.

———. "The Genealogies of Genesis 1–11 and Comparative Literature." In *I Studied Inscriptions from before the Flood: Ancient Near Eastern, Literary, and Linguistic Approaches to Genesis 1–11,* edited by Richard S. Hess and David Toshio Tsumura, 58–72. Sources for Biblical and Theological Study 4. Winona Lake, IN: Eisenbrauns, 1994.

Hick, John. "An Irenaean Theodicy." In *Encountering Evil,* edited by Stephen T. Davis, 45–52. Louisville: Westminster John Knox, 2001.

Hicks, R. Lansing, "Abel." In *Interpreter's Dictionary of the Bible,* edited by George Arthur Buttrick, 1:4. Nashville: Abingdon, 1962.

———. "Cain." In *Interpreter's Dictionary of the Bible,* edited by George Arthur Buttrick, 1:482. Nashville: Abingdon, 1962.

Higgins, J. M. "The Myth of Eve: The Temptress." *Journal of the American Academy of Religion* 44 (1976) 639–47.

Hirsch, Samson R. *The Pentateuch.* Vol. 1: *Genesis.* Translated by Isaac Levy. London: Judaica, 1932.

Hobbes, Thomas. *Leviathan.* Edited by Michael Oakeshott. New York: Simon and Schuster, 1997.

Holland, R. F. "On the Form of 'The Problem of Evil.'" In *Against Empiricism,* 237–38. Oxford: Blackwell, 1980.

Holquist, Michael, and Caryl Emerson. *The Dialogic Imagination: Four Essays by M. M. Bakhtin.* Austin: University of Texas Press, 1981.

Horowitz, J. and N. Rosenblatt. *Wrestling with Angels.* New York: Delta, 1995.

Huffmon, Herbert B. "Cain the Arrogant Sufferer." In *Biblical and Related Studies Presented to Samuel Iwry,* edited by A. Kort and S. Morschauer, 109–13. Winona Lake, IN: Eisenbrauns, 1985.

Hughes, Richard A. *Cain's Lament: A Christian Moral Psychology.* Studies in Biblical Literature 35. New York: Lang, 2001.

———. *Theology and the Cain Complex.* Washington DC: University Press of America, 1982.

Hugo, Victor. "La conscience." In *La Légende des siècles*. Edited by Jacques Truchet. Bibliothèque de la Pléiade 82. Paris: Gallimard, 1950.

Humbert, Paul. "Démesure et chute dans l'Ancien Testament." In *Maqqél Shâqédh: Hommage à Wilhelm Vischer*, 63–82. Montpellier: Causse Graille Castelnau, 1960.

―――. "*Qânâ'* en hébreu biblique." In *Festschrift, Alfred Bertholet zum 80. Geburtstag*, edited by Walter Baumgartner et al., 251–66. Tübingen: Mohr/Siebeck, 1950.

Hume, David. *Dialogues Concerning Natural Religion*. 2nd ed. Edited by Norman Kemp Smith. New York: Bobbs-Merrill, 1947.

Humphreys, W. Lee. *The Character of God in the Book of Genesis: A Narrative Appraisal*. Louisville: Westminster John Knox, 2001.

Ibn Ezra's Commentary on the Pentateuch: Genesis (Bereshit). Translated by H. Norman Stickman and Arthur M. Silver. New York: Menorah, 1988.

Jacob, Benno. *The First Book of the Bible interpreted by B. Jacob: His Commentary, Abridged, Edited, and Translated by Ernest I. Jacob and Walter Jacob*. New York: Ktav, 1974.

Jacob, Edmond. *Les Thèmes essentiels d'une théologie de l'Ancien Testament*. Geneva: Delachaux et Niestlé, 1955.

Jason, Heda. "The Narrative Structure of the Swindler Tales." *ARV: Journal of Scandinavian Folklore* 27 (1971) 141–60.

Jonas, Hans. "Immortality and the Modern Temper." In *Mortality and Morality: A Search for the Good After Auschwitz*. Edited by Lawrence Vogel. Evanston: Northwestern University Press, 1996.

Jung, Carl. "After the Catastrophe." In *Jung and Evil*.

―――. *Answer to Job*. Translated by R. F. C. Hull. New York: Meridian, 1960.

―――. *The Collected Works of C. G. Jung*. Vol. 9, Pt. 1: *Archetypes and the Collective Unconscious*. Bollingen Series 20. Princeton: Princeton University Press, 1953–78.

―――. *Jung and Evil*. Edited by Murray Stein. London: Routledge, 1995.

Kafka, Franz. *The Diaries of Franz Kafka*. New York: Schocken, 1988.

Kahn, Paul W. *Out of Eden: Adam and Eve and the Problem of Evil*. Princeton: Princeton University Press, 2007.

Kant, Immanuel. *Religion within the Limits of Reason Alone, and Other Writings*. Cambridge Texts in the History of Philosophy. Edited by Allen Wood, George Di Giovanni, Robert M. Adams. Cambridge University Press, 1998.

Kapelrud, Arvid. *The Violent Goddess: Anat in the Ras Shamra Texts*. Oslo: Universitets-forlaget, 1969.

Kass, Leon R. *The Beginning of Wisdom: Reading Genesis*. New York: Free Press, 2003.

Kaufmann, Walter. *The Portable Nietzsche*. New York: Viking, 1954.

Keller, Catherine. *Face of the Deep: A Theology of Becoming*. New York: Routledge, 2004.

Kierkegaard, Søren. *The Concept of Anxiety*. Edited by Reidar Thomte. Princeton: Princeton University Press, 1980.

―――. *The Concept of Dread*. Translated by Walter Lowrie. Princeton: Princeton University Press, 1946.

―――. *The Sickness Unto Death*. Translated by Howard V. Hong and Edna H. Hong. Princeton: Princeton University Press, 1980.

King, Martin Luther Jr. "Where Do We Go from Here." In *I Have a Dream: Writings and Speeches That Changed the World*. Edited by James Melvin. San Francisco: HarperSanFrancisco, 1992.

Kline, Meredith G. *Kingdom Prologue: Genesis Foundations for a Covenantal Worldview*. Overland Park, KS: Two Age, 2000.

Koch, Klaus. "Der Spruch 'Sein Blut bleibe auf seinem Haupt' und die israelitische Auffassung vom vergossenen Blut." *VT* 12 (1962) 396–416.

Krašovec, Jože. *Reward, Punishment, and Forgiveness: The Thinking and Beliefs of Ancient Israel in the Light of Greek and Modern Views.* VTSup 78. Leiden: Brill, 1999.

Kugel, James L., *The Bible As It Was.* Cambridge: Belknap, 1997.

LaCocque, André. "About the 'Aqedah' in Genesis 22, A Response to Laurence A. Kant." *Lexington Theological Quarterly* 40 (2005) 191–201.

———. *The Trial of Innocence: Adam, Eve, and the Yahwist.* Eugene, OR: Cascade Books, 2006.

———, and Paul Ricoeur. *Thinking Biblically: Exegetical and Hermeneutical Studies.* Translated by David Pellauer. Chicago: Chicago University Press, 1998.

La Fontaine, Jean de. *Fables.* Translated by Walter Thornbury. Turnhout, Belgium: Brepols, 1982.

LeFevre, Perry, editor. *The Meaning of Health.* Chicago: Exploration, 1984.

Levenson, Jon. *Creation and the Persistence of Evil: The Jewish Drama of Divine Omnipotence.* San Francisco: Harper & Row, 1988.

Levi, Carlo. *Of Fear and Freedom.* New York: Farrar Straus, 1950

Levin, Christoph. "The Yahwist: The Earliest Editor in the Pentateuch." *JBL* 126 (1997) 209–30.

Levin, Saul. "The More Savory Offering: A Key to the Problem of Gen 4:3–5." *JBL* 98 (1979) 85.

Levinas, Emmanuel. *Difficult Freedom: Essays on Judaism.* Baltimore: Johns Hopkins University Press, 1995.

———. *Totality and Infinity: An Essay on Exteriority.* Translated by Alphonso Lingis. The Hague: Nijhoff, 1969.

L'Heureux, Conrad. *In and Out of Paradise: The Book of Genesis from Adam and Eve to the Tower of Babel.* New York: Paulist, 1983.

Lipinski, Edward. "Ancient Types of Wisdom Literature." In *Isac Leo Seeligman Volume,* edited by Alexander Rofé and Yair Zakovitch, 39–55. Jerusalem: Rubenstein, 1983.

Luther, Martin. *Lectures on Genesis.* Vol. 1. Luther's Works 6. Saint Louis: Concordia, 1958.

Madaule, Jacques. *Amour et Violence.* Etudes Carmélitaines. Bruges, Belgium: Desclée de Brouwer, 1948.

Malbim (R. Meir Leibush ben Yehiel Michael). *Genesis: Otsar Midrashim Perushim.* Jerusalem: Feldheim, 1999.

Matuštik, M. Beck. "Violence and Secularization, Evil and Redemption." In *Modernity and the Problem of Evil,* edited by Alan D. Schrift, 39–50. Bloomington: Indiana University Press, 2005.

May, Gerhard. *Creatio ex Nihilo: The Doctrine of 'Creation out of Nothing' in Early Christian Thought.* Translated by A. S. Worrall. Edinburgh: T. & T. Clark, 1994.

McEntire, Mark R. *The Blood of Abel: The Violent Plot in the Hebrew Bible.* Macon, GA: Mercer University Press, 1999.

Melville, Herman. "The Indian Hater." In *The Confidence Man: His Masquerade.* Evanston: Northwestern University Press, 1984.

———. *Moby Dick or, The Whale.* Kila, MT: Kessinger, 2004.

Miles, Jack. *God: A Biography.* New York: Simon and Schuster, 1996.

Milgrom, Jacob. *Leviticus 1–16*. Anchor Bible 3. New York: Doubleday, 1991.

————. *Leviticus: A Book of Ritual and Ethics*. Continental Commentary. Minneapolis: Fortress Press, 2004.

Miller, J. Maxwell. "The Descendants of Cain: Notes on Gen 4." *ZAW* 86 (1974) 164–74.

Miller, Patrick D. "Eridu, Dunnu, and Babel: A Study in Comparative Mythology." In *I Studied Inscriptions from before the Flood: Ancient Near Eastern, Literary, and Linguistic Approaches to Genesis 1–11*, edited by Richard S. Hess and David Toshio Tsumura, 143–68. Sources for Biblical and Theological Study 4. Winona Lake, IN: Eisenbrauns, 1994.

————. *Genesis 1–11: Studies in Structure and Theme*. Journal for the Study of the Old Testament Supplements 8. Sheffield: University of Sheffield Press, 1978.

————. *Sin and Judgment in the Prophets*. Society of Biblical Literature Monograph Series 27. Chico, CA: Scholars, 1982.

————. "*Yeled* in the Song of Lamech." *JBL* 85 (1966) 477–78.

Milne, Pamela J. *Vladimir Propp and the Study of Structure in Hebrew Biblical Narrative*. Sheffield: Sheffield Academic Press, 1988.

Milton, John, *Paradise Lost*, I. Edited by William Zunder. New York: St. Martin's, 1999.

Miscall, Peter D. *The Workings of Old Testament Narrative*. Philadelphia: Fortress, 1983.

Montaigne, Michel de. "Apology for Raymond Sebond." In *Essays of Montaigne*. New York: Modern Library, 1946.

Moore, Stephen. *God's Gym: Divine Male Bodies of the Bible*. New York: Routledge, 1996.

Morrow, Lance. "Evil." *Time* [magazine] 137/23 (June 10, 1991).

Morson, Gary Saul. "Contingency and the Literature of Process." In *Bakhtin and the Classics*. Edited by Branham R. Bracht. Evanston: Northwestern University Press, 2002.

————, and C. Emerson. *Mikhail Bakhtin: Creation of a Prosaics*. Stanford: Stanford University Press, 1990.

Du Moulin, Pierre. *Regii Sanguinis Clamor*. The Hague: Viac, 1652.

Mowinckel, Sigmund. *The Two Sources of the Predeuteronomic Primeval History (JE) in Genesis 1–11*. ANVAO II. Oslo: Dybwad, 1937.

Moye, Richard H. "In the Beginning: Myth and History in Genesis and Exodus." *JBL* 109 (1990) 577–98.

Munch, Edvard. "The Cry." 1893. (painting).

Murray, Henry A., *Explorations in Personality*. New York: Oxford University Press, 1938.

————. "What Should Psychologists Do about Psychoanalysis." *Journal of Abnormal and Social Psychology* 35 (1940) 150–75.

Musil, Robert. *Tagebücher*. Edited by Adolf Frisé. Vol. 2. Reibeck bei Hamburg: Ronwohlt, 1983.

Mystère d'Adam, Ordo Representacionis Ade. Edited by Paul Aebischer. New York: French and European, 1965.

Nagy, Gregory. "Reading Bakhtin Reading the Classics: An Epic Fate for Conveyors of the Heroic Past." In *Bakhtin and the Classics*. Edited by Branham R. Bracht. Evanston: Northwestern University Press, 2002.

Neher, André. Lectures at the University of Strasbourg, 1956.

Neiman, Susan. *Evil in Modern Thought: An Alternative History of Philosophy*. Princeton: Princeton University Press, 2002.

Nelson-Pallmer, Jack. *Is Religion Killing Us? Violence in the Bible and the Quran*. Harrisburg: Trinity, 2003.

Niebuhr, H. Richard. *The Meaning of Revelation.* New York: Macmillan, 1941.

Nietzsche, Friedrich. *Beyond Good and Evil, Prelude to a Philosophy of the Future.* Translated with commentary by Walter Kaufmann. New York: Vintage, 1989 [1966].

———. *The Birth of Tragedy.* In *The Portable Nietzsche.* Edited by Walter Kaufmann. New York: Viking, 1977 [1959]).

———. *Daybreak.* In *The Portable Nietzsche.* Edited by Walter Kaufmann. New York: Viking, 1977 (1959).

Olrik, Axel. "Epic Laws of Folk Narratives." In *The Study of Folklore.* Edited by Alan Dundes. Engelwood Cliffs: Prentice Hall, 1965.

Oppenheim, A. Leo. *Ancient Mesopotamia.* Chicago: Chicago University Press, 1964.

Ortiz-Hill, Claire. *The Roots and Flowers of Evil in Baudelaire, Nietzsche, and Hitler.* Chicago: Open Court, 2006.

Oz, Amos. *Under This Blazing Light.* Translated by N. de Lange. Cambridge: Cambridge University Press, 1979.

Pagels, Elaine. *Adam, Eve, and the Serpent.* New York: Vintage, 1988.

Pardes, Ilana. "Beyond Genesis 3: The Politics of Maternal Naming." In *A Feminist Companion to Genesis.* Edited by Athalya Brenner. Feminist Companions to the Bible 2. Sheffield: JSOT Press, 1993.

Peck, M. Scott. *People of the Lie: The Hope for Healing Human Evil.* New York: Simon & Schuster, 1983.

———. "Reflections on the Psychology of Evil." In *The Journal of Pastoral Counseling* 25 (1990) 8–14.

Pedersen, Johannes. *Israel: Its Life and Culture.* Vol. 1. London: Oxford University Press, 1926.

Peters, H. F. *My Sister, My Spouse: A Biography of Lou Andreas-Salomé.* New York: Norton, 1962.

Phillips, D. Z. *The Problem of Evil and the Problem of God.* Minneapolis: Fortress, 2005.

Pitard, Wayne T. "Vengeance." In *ABD* 6:786–87.

Pritchard, James B., editor. *Ancient Near Eastern Texts Relating to the Old Testament.* 3rd ed. Princeton: Princeton University Press, 1969.

Procksch, Otto. *Die Genesis.* KZAT. Leipzig: Dreichertsche, 1913/1924.

Propp, Vladimir, *Morphology of the Folktale.* 2nd ed. Edited by L. A. Wagner. Austin: University of Texas Press, 1968.

Rad, Gerhard von. *Das erste Buch Mose.* Das Alte Testament Deutsch. Göttingen: Vandenhoeck & Ruprecht, 1949.

———. *Genesis.* 2nd ed. Translated by John H. Marks. Old Testament Library. Philadelphia: Westminster.

———. *The Problem of the Hexateuch and Other Essays.* Edinburgh: Oliver and Boyd, 1966.

Radin, Paul. *The World of Primitive Man.* New York: Grove, 1960.

Ramban [Moses ben Nachman]. *Ramban (Nachmanides) Commentary in the Pentateuch.* Translated by Israel Abrahams. In *Chapters on Jewish Literature.* Philadelphia: The Jewish Publication Society of America, 1899.

Rank, Otto. *The Incest Theme in Literature and Legend: Fundamentals of a Psychology of Literary Creation* [1912]. Translated by Gregory C. Richter. Baltimore: Johns Hopkins University Press, 1992.

———. *Psychology and the Soul* [1931]. New York: Perpetua, 1961.

————. *The Myth of the Birth of the Hero: A Psychological Exploration of Myth* [1909]. Translated by Gregory C. Richter and E. James Lieberman. New York: Vintage, 1959.

————. "Völkerpsychologische Parallelen zu den infantilen Sexual-theorien." in *Psychoanalytische Beiträge zur Mythenforschung* [1913]. Leipzig: Internationaler Psychoanalistischer Verlag, 1922.

Rendtorff, Rolf. *Das überlieferungsgeschichtliche Problem des Pentateuch.* Beihefte zur Zeitschrift für die alttestamentliche Wissenschaft 147. Berlin: de Gruyter, 1977.

Resnais, Alain, director. "Nuit et brouillard." Written by Jean Cayrol. 1960.

Rhees, Rush. *On Religion and Philosophy.* Edited by D. Z. Phillips. Cambridge: Cambridge University Press 1997.

Ricoeur, Paul. "Evil, a Challenge to Philosophy and Theology." *Journal of the American Academy of Religion* 53 (1985) 635–48.

————. *Figuring the Sacred: Religion, Narrative, and Imagination.* Translated by David Pellauer. Edited by Mark I. Wallace. Minneapolis: Fortress 1995.

————. *History and Truth.* Translated by Charles Kelbley. Evanston: Northwestern University Press, 1965.

————. "L'identité narrative." In *La Narration: Quand le récit devient communication,* edited by P. Bühler and J.-F. Habermacher, 287–300. Lieux théologiques 12. Geneva: Labor et Fides, 1988.

————. *Temps et Récit.* Vol. 3. Paris: Le Seuil, 1985.

————. *Time and Narrative.* 3 vols. Translated by Kathleen McLaughlin and David Pellauer. Chicago: University of Chicago Press, 1988.

————. *Vivant jusqu'à la mort.* La Couleur des Idées. Paris: Le Seuil, 2007.

Riemann, Paula. "Am I My Brother's Keeper?" *Interpretation* 24 (1970) 482–91.

Rilke, Rainer-Maria, Letter to Lou Andreas-Salomé of September 1914, and Letters to E. Cassirer in *Letters.* Translated by Jane B. Greene. Gloucester, MA: Peter Smith, 1979.

————. *Tagebücher aus der Frühzeit.* Leipzig: Insel, 1942.

Róheim, Géza. *The Origin and Function of Culture.* Garden City, NY: Doubleday, 1971 (1943).

Rollins, Wayne G., and D. Andrew Kille, editor. *Psychological Insight into the Bible: Texts and Readings.* Grand Rapids: Eerdmans, 2007.

Rosenberg, David, editor. *Genesis as It Was Written: Contemporary Writers on Our First Stories.* San Francisco: HarperSanFrancisco, 1996.

Rosenblatt, Naomi H., and Joshua Horowitz. *Wrestling with Angels: What the First Family of Genesis Teaches Us about Our Spiritual Identity, Sexuality, and Personal Relationships.* New York: Delacorte, 1995.

Rousseau, Jean-Jacques. *The First and Second Discourses* [1755]. New York: St. Martin's, 1964.

Rudnytsky, Peter L. *Reading Psychoanalysis: Freud, Rank, Ferenczi, Groddeck.* Ithaca: Cornell University Press, 2002.

Saba, Abraham (Rabbi). *Tseror ha-Mor.* Tel Aviv: Brody, 1975.

Sacks, Robert. "The Lion and the Ass: A Commentary on the Book of Genesis [Chapters 1–10])." *Interpretation: A Journal of Political Philosophy* 8/2–3 (1980).

Saint-Cheron, Philippe de, and Elie Wiesel. *Evil and Exile.* Notre Dame: University of Notre Dame Press, 1990.

Sandmel, Samuel. "Genesis 4:26b." *HUCA* 32 (1961) 19–29.

Sarna, Nahum. *Understanding Genesis: The World of the Bible in the Light of History.* New York: Schocken, 1966.

Sartre, Jean-Paul. *La Nausée.* Paris: Gallimard, 1970.

Scheler, Max. *Ressentiment.* Milwaukee: Marquette University Press, 1998.

Schneidau, Herbert N. *Sacred Discontent: The Bible and Western Tradition.* Berkeley: University of California Press, 1977.

Schottroff, Willy. "Soziologie und Altes Testament." *Verkündigung und Forschung* 19 (1974) 46–66.

Schrift, Alan D. *Modernity and the Problem of Evil.* Bloomington: Indiana University Press, 2005.

Schulte, Hannelis. *Die Entstehung der Geschichteschreibung im alten Israel.* Beihefte zur Zeitschrift für die alttestamentliche Wissenschaft 128. Berlin: de Gruyter, 1972.

Schwarz-Bart, André. *The Last of the Just.* Woodstock, NY: Overlook, 2000.

Schwarz, Regina M. *The Curse of Cain: The Violent Legacy of Monotheism.* Chicago: University of Chicago Press, 1997.

Shafranske, Edward P. "Evil: A Discourse on the Boundaries of Humanity, an Introduction." In *The Journal of Pastoral Counseling* 25 (1990) 1–7.

Shakespeare, William. *Sixteen Plays of Shakespeare.* Edited by George L. Kittteredge. Boston: Ginn, 1946.

Shapiro, Moshe, editor. *The Gaon of Vilna's Adereth Eliahu.* Artscroll Judaica Classics. New York: Mesorah, 1997.

Snell, Bruno, *The Discovery of the Mind: The Greek Origins of European Thought.* Translated by T. G. Rosenmeyer. New York: Harper, 1960.

Sommet, Jacques. *L'honneur de la liberté.* Paris: Centurion, 1987.

Speiser, Ephraim A. "Ancient Mesopotamia." In *The Idea of History in the Ancient Near East*, edited by Robert C. Dentan, 35–76. American Oriental Series 38. New Haven: Yale University Press, 1955.

———. *Genesis.* Anchor Bible 1. New York: Doubleday, 1964.

Spina, Frank A. "The 'Ground' for Cain's Rejection (Gen 4): '*Adamah* in the Context of Gen 1–11." *ZAW* 104 (1992) 319–32.

Stade, Bernhard. *Ausgewählte akademische Reden und Abhandlungen.* 2nd ed. Giessen: Ricker, 1907.

Steinbeck, John. *East of Eden.* New York: Bantam, 1952, 1976.

Steiner, George. *The Death of Tragedy.* New York: Oxford University Press, 1980.

Steinmetz, Devora. *From Father to Son: Kinship, Conflict, and Continuity in Genesis.* Literary Currents in Biblical Interpretation. Louisville: Westminster John Knox, 1991.

Stratton, Beverly. *Out of Eden: Reading, Rhetoric, and Ideology in Genesis 2–3.* Journal for the Study of the Old Testament Supplements 208. Sheffield: Sheffield Academic, 1995.

Suares, Carlo. *The Cipher Of Genesis: Using the Qabalistic Code to Interpret the First Book of the Bible and the Teachings of Jesus.* York Beach, ME: Weiser, 2005.

Tillich, Paul. "The Theological Significance of Existentialism and Psychoanalysis." In *The Meaning of Health: Essays in Existentialism, Psychoanalysis, and Religion,* edited by Perry LeFevre. Chicago: Exploration Press, 1984.

Tsumura, David Toshio. "Genesis and Ancient Near Eastern Stories of Creation and Flood." In *I Studied Inscriptions from before the Flood: Ancient Near Eastern, Literary, and Linguistic Approaches to Genesis 1-11*, edited by Richard S. Hess and David Toshio Tsumura, 27–57. Sources for Biblical and Theological Study 4. Winona Lake, IN: Eisenbrauns, 1994.

Twain, Mark. *The Adventures of Huckleberry Finn.* Buffalo, NY: First World, 2004.

Uffenheimer, Benjamin. "Cain and Abel." In *In Memory of Gedaliahu Alon: Essays in Jewish History and Philosophy,* edited by Menahem Dorman. Tel Aviv: Hakibbutz Hameuchad, 1970.

Urban, Linwood, and Walton Douglas N., editors. *The Power of God: Readings on Omnipotence and Evil.* New York: Oxford University Press, 1978.

Van Seters, John, *Abraham in History and Tradition.* New Haven: Yale University Press, 1975.

———. *Prologue to History: The Yahwist as Historian in Genesis.* Louisville: Westminster John Knox, 1992.

———. "The Yahwist as Theologian? A Response." *Journal for the Study of the Old Testament* 1 (1976) 15–19.

Vaux, Roland de. *Ancient Israel.* Vol. 2: *Religious Institutions.* New York: McGraw-Hill, 1965.

Vawter, Bruce. *On Genesis: A New Reading.* Garden City, NY: Doubleday, 1977.

Vischer, Wilhelm. *Jahwe: Der Gott Kains.* Munich: Kaiser, 1929.

Voegelin, Eric. *Israel and Revelation.* Vol. 1 in *Order and History.* Baton Rouge: Louisiana University Press, 1956.

Waltke, Bruce K. *Genesis: A Commentary.* Grand Rapids: Zondervan, 2001.

———. "Cain and his Offering." *Westminster Theological Journal* 48 (1986) 363–72.

Waschke, Ernst-Joachim. "*rabas.*" In *Theological Dictionary of the Old Testament*, edited by Johannes Botterweck et al., 13:298–303. Grand Rapids: Eerdmans, 2004.

Weil, Simone. "Are We Struggling for Justice?" Translated by Marina Barabas. *Philosophical Investigations* 10 (1987) 1–10.

———, and Rachel Bespaloff. *War and the Iliad.* Translated by Mary McCarthy. New York: New York Review Books, 2005.

Welles, C. Bradford. "The Hellenistic Orient." In *The Idea of History*, edited by Robert C. Dentan, 135–67. American Oriental Series 38. New Haven: Yale University Press, 1955.

Wenham, Gordon. *Genesis 1–15.* Word Biblical Commentary 1. Dallas: Word, 1987.

Westermann, Claus. *Elements of Old Testament Theology.* Translated by Douglas Stott. Atlanta: John Knox, 1982.

———. *Genesis 1–11; A Commentary.* Translated by John J. Scullion. Minneapolis: Augsburg, 1984.

White, Hugh C. "Where is your brother? Genesis 4." In *Narration and Discourse in the Book of Genesis*, 146–47. Cambridge: Cambridge University Press, 1991.

Wiesel, Elie. "Cain and Abel: The First Genocide." In *Messengers of God: Biblical Portraits and Legends*, 37–68. New York: Simon and Schuster, 1976.

———. *Night.* Translated by Stella Rodway. New York: Hill and Wang, 1960.

Wilder, Thornton. *The Skin of Our Teeth.* New York: Harper, 1942.

Williams, James. "Addenda to 'Concerning One of the Apodictic Formulas.'" *VT* 15 (1965) 113–15.

———. *The Bible, Violence, and the Sacred: Liberation from the Myth of the Sanctioned Violence*. San Francisco: Harper, 1991.

———. "Concerning One of the Apodictic Formulas." *VT* 14 (1964) 484–89.

Williams, Patricia A. *Doing without Adam and Eve*. Minneapolis: Fortress, 2001.

Wilson, Robert R. *Genealogy and History in the Biblical World*. Yale Near Eastern Researches 7. New Haven: Yale University Press, 1977.

Wolde, Ellen van. *Words Become Worlds: Semantic Studies of Genesis 1–11*. Biblical Interpretation Series 6. Leiden: Brill, 1994.

———. "The Story of Cain and Abel: A Narrative Study." *Journal for the Study of the Old Testament* 52 (1991) 25–41.

Wolff, Hans W. "The Kerygma of the Yahwist." *Interpretation* 20 (1966) 129–58.

Zimmerli, Walther. "Zur Exegese von Genesis 4:1–16." *Der Evangelische Erzieher* 20 (1968) 200–203.

Index of Ancient Sources

New Testament

Rabbinic Sources

Islamic Sources

Author Index

Lightning Source UK Ltd.
Milton Keynes UK
UKOW02f1427170416

272350UK00002B/48/P